PRENTICE HALL

Language Teaching Methodology Series

Teacher Education
General Editor: Christopher N. Candlin

Understanding Language Classrooms

Other titles in this series include

Understanding Language Classrooms

A guide for teacher-initiated action

DAVID NUNAN

National Centre for English Language Teaching and Research
Macquarie University, Sydney

ENGLISH LANGUAGE TEACHING

Prentice Hall

New York   London   Toronto   Sydney   Tokyo   Singapore

First published 1989 by
Prentice Hall International (UK) Ltd
66 Wood Lane End, Hemel Hempstead
Hertfordshire HP2 4RG
A division of
Simon & Schuster International Group

Printed and bound in Great Britain at the
University Press, Cambridge

Library of Congress Cataloging-in-Publication Data

Nunan, David.
    Understanding language classrooms: a guide for teacher
    initiated action / David Nunan.
    p. cm. – (Prentice Hall international language teaching
methodology series. Teacher education)
Includes bibliographies and index.
ISBN 0–13–935935–4 : $12.60
1. Language and languages – Study and teaching. I. Title. II.
Series
P51.N86   1989
418′.007 – dc20   89–3984

British Library Cataloguing in Publication Data

Nunan, David
    Understanding language classrooms: a guide for teacher
    initiated action. – (Language teaching methodology series;
    teacher education).
    1. Schools. Curriculum subjects: Languages. Teaching
    methods
    I. Title   II. Series
    407′.1

    ISBN 0–13–935935–4

---

3   4   5   93   92   91

Contents

Chapter Four Collecting Data

Chapter Five Classroom Observation

Chapter Six Teacher-research and Professional Development

Chapter Seven Implementing Teacher-research

Acknowledgements

The author and publisher would like to acknowledge, with grateful thanks, the following sources for the use of copyright material:

Kemmis, S. and McTaggart, R. (eds) (1988) *The Action Research Planner*, Geelong: Deakin University Press.

Pica, T. and Doughty, C. (1986) 'Information gap tasks: Do they really facilitate second language acquisition?', *TESOL Quarterly*, 20, 2 June 1986.

Hopkins, D. (1985) *A Teacher's Guide to Classroom Research*, Milton Keynes: Open University Press.

Nerenz, A. and Knop, C. (1982) 'A time-based approach to the study of teacher effectiveness', *Modern Language Journal*, 66, autumn 1982, University of Wisconsin Press.

Good, T. and Brophy, J. (1973) *Looking into Classrooms*, New York: Harper and Row.

Pak, J. (1986) *Find Out How You Teach*, Adelaide: National Curriculum Resource Centre.

Ullman, R. and Geva, R. (1984) 'Approaches to observation in second language classes', in C. Brumfit (ed.) *ELT Documents: Language Issues and Education Policies*, Oxford: Pergamon Press.

Allen, J. P. B., Frohlich, M. and Spada, N. (1984) 'The communicative orientation of language teaching', in J. Handscombe, R. Orem and B. Taylor (eds) *On TESOL '83*.

Every attempt has been made to trace and acknowledge ownership of copyright. The publisher will be glad to make suitable arrangements with any copyright holders whom it has not been possible to contact.

General Editor's Preface

There is always, I suspect, a problem with coordinating philosophy with classroom action in teacher education. Ideas circulate and are impressively publicised in all manner of media, they fail to take hold and are then recycled, as if novel, in a repetitive and thoroughly unsatisfactory manner. They lack an anchorage in practice. In a similar way, teachers embark upon curricula whose relevance and effects they are only dimly aware of, not having been party to their formulation, their underpinning ideas or to their often implicit criteria for evaluation. Learners, too, suffer from this discontinuity: they are taught but they frequently are ignorant why they learn or, more often, fail to learn.

In short, we need to connect. To do so, however, requires an altered stance. We need to tune the demands of the ideas themselves to the conditions for their realisation. We need to encourage a reflexive attitude to our activity. In short, we have a problem of communication between theory and practice.

Indirectly, this refreshing and eminently practical book of David Nunan's suggests a path out of the dilemma, one that can be taken by teachers and learners. We need first to examine the participants in the educational process, most obviously, teachers and learners, evaluating their characteristics, their purposes and, significantly for this book, what they bring to the activity of teaching and learning. Second, we need to assess the data they generate, the modes of teaching and the modes of learning, the particular 'goings-on' of classrooms. Third, we need an experimental process to relate activity to purpose and transform the results into new and altered practice. We need to learn from teaching and learning in our professional development. Seen like this, of course, understanding language classrooms is itself a research process. We have participants, we have data and we have modes of evaluation. The issue is how we can practice theoretically and make the connections, and for that we need procedures.

It is these procedures that David Nunan's new book provides. It does so not as a collection of unmotivated methodologies for observing classrooms, but as a set of tools for addressing the particular problems of learning and teaching that arise from practice. Like all good examples of applied linguistics research, it begins from the issues and then seeks to describe their nature and explain their relevance in terms of the participants and their objectives, informed by theory, and in turn contributing to it. As readers we learn to explore and then to explain. The book has a subtitle: A Guide for Teacher-Initiated Action — the words are significant. They guarantee what the book delivers. In particular, through its tasks and illustrative examples, teachers can discover how to address their data, how to evaluate their practice how to understand when they succeed and when they fail.

Seen from the standpoint of professional development, the book guides the reflection that ought to underpin action and offers the means whereby such action can be achieved.

The Language Teaching Methodology Series has as its characteristic objective what this latest book also intends: offering the means whereby language teachers and learners can alter their modes of practice from transmission to interpretation, from training to education, and to make the link between philosophy and action.

Christopher N. Candlin
General Editor,
Macquarie University, Sydney

Preface

The general aim of this book is to introduce teachers, teacher trainees, teacher trainers and in-service coordinators to classroom observation and research, with a particular focus on ways and means whereby teachers might investigate their own classrooms. The intention is to provide a serious introduction to classroom research to language professionals who do not have specialist training in research methods in an accessible, yet non-trivial manner, and to give readers opportunities for developing knowledge and skills in conducting their own classroom-oriented research. While the book should be of interest to students of applied linguistics generally, it is aimed specifically at the classroom teacher and teachers in preparation.

Having read the book and worked through the questions and tasks set out at the conclusion of each chapter, readers should understand the key concepts and issues involved in classroom-oriented research. They should also appreciate the relevance and applications of these concepts and issues to second- and foreign-language learning. In particular, they should be able to identify problems and issues in the language area, and be able to formulate these as questions amenable to investigation by teachers in their own classrooms.

Readers are introduced to a wide range of research methods and techniques including case studies, questionnaires, observation schedules, field notes, diaries, interviews, protocol analysis, think-aloud techniques, seating charts, movement plans, sociograms and simulations. There is also an appendix which introduces readers to the experimental method.

The book also aims to provide readers with the knowledge and skills to work through, either collaboratively or individually, the various steps involved in planning, conducting, evaluating and reporting a research project. They should also come to appreciate the relevance of the issues raised in this book for professional development.

The book is, I believe, in line with the prevailing trend in language teaching away from a preoccupation with methods which are imported in their various guises into the language classroom, away from a reliance on luminaries who appear from time to time with their applied-linguistic commandments engraved on tablets of stone, and away from the notion that the classroom itself is an unfashionable place to be.

Interest in what actually goes on between teachers and learners, and learners and learners, (in contrast with what people think goes on, or say ought to go on) is underlined by the spate of recent publications which address themselves directly to the classroom itself. This interest is to the good. It is, I believe, a sign of maturity within the profession, and it is to be particularly welcomed in that it enhances the role and importance of the teacher as an autonomously functioning individual, rather than the servant to someone else's curriculum.

The view of research which emerges in this book is a broad one – too broad for some tastes, I suspect. In outlining an agenda for the teacher–researcher, I am not suggesting that teachers should add the cap of academic researcher to the numerous other hats they are required to wear. Rather, I am trying to encourage a particular attitude in which critical reflection on practice leads naturally into classroom investigation. This book will have achieved its purpose if it encourages teachers to change their spectacles rather than their hats.

The book is distinguished from the several other recent publications in the field in that it tries to provide a balanced introduction to both qualitative and quantitative approaches to classroom observation and research. While I believe that interpretative studies of classroom life are likely to be of most value to the teachers wishing to deepen their understanding of their own classrooms and the classrooms of others, I have not ignored quantitative research, and the major quantitative studies which have been published in recent years are fully reported here.

The book also provides a great deal of detail to teachers on how to go about planning, implementing and reporting their own classroom investigations. Potential problem areas and pitfalls are pointed out, and suggestions are made on ways of avoiding these.

Writing a book such as this is both time-consuming and arduous. It would not have been written without the encouragement and support of many individuals. Foremost among these is Chris Candlin who, for the second time, has been generous (or foolhardy) enough to take on the job of editing a book of mine. Only those other writers who have been fortunate enough to have been edited by Professor Candlin will know what a valuable role he performs. I must also thank members of my family who, once again, have had to make enormous sacrifices and yet whose support has never waned.

A book such as this owes a great deal to the other teachers and researchers in this field. Foremost among these are Dick Allwright, who has played a leading role in investigating life in language classrooms for many years. I should also mention Craig Chaudron and Leo van Lier who have very different approaches to classroom research, but who are both leading figures in the field. Thanks also go to Jack Richards who has, for many years, argued the cause of the classroom teacher, and whose extended view of classroom research is, I hope, reflected here.

Finally, I should like to acknowledge the interest and encouragement of past and present colleagues at the National Curriculum Resource Centre in Adelaide and the National Centre for English Language Teaching and Research at Macquarie University in Sydney.

One

Basic Issues and Concerns

1.1 Introduction

In this chapter, we look at some of the central issues and concerns surrounding classroom observation and research. The aim of the chapter is to set the scene for the rest of the book, and so should serve as a map to provide some idea of the terrain to be covered.

I begin by giving an impressionistic account of two concepts which are central to any informed understanding of language classrooms: 'theory' and 'practice'. Discussion of these concepts will provide a backdrop against which we can highlight some of the major methods of finding out about language classrooms.

While some of the initial discussion may, at times, seem rather removed from the language classroom, I hope that the relevance for language teaching of the points made is readily apparent.

A major theme of this book is that the language classroom is part of the wider educational community, and that it has a great deal to gain from trends and directions in general educational theory and practice. In addition, language teachers and researchers have much to gain from a study of the methods and procedures of classroom investigators in other areas of education. It is for this reason that many of the references in this book are taken from general education rather than being restricted to TESOL and applied linguistics.

In their recent book on action research, Carr and Kemmis (1985) refer to a trend to extend the professionalism of teachers by providing them with opportunities to participate in theory and research. They cite as evidence school-based curriculum development, research-based in-service education and professional self evaluation projects, and suggest that the 'teacher as researcher' movement is 'well under way'.

This is a healthy trend, and one which is reflected in language-curriculum development (Nunan 1987, 1988). There are several reasons why teachers might become interested in researching their own classrooms. Carr and Kemmis suggest that for some it is the inevitable consequence of being involved in a period of intellectual and social change. For others, it is a consequence of having to justify involvement in educational innovations of one sort or another. Yet others see the teacher-researcher role as a logical end point of professional self-development. Finally, there are those who have grasped the opportunities offered by the trend towards school-based curriculum development which demands greater autonomy and professional responsibility on the part of teachers.

In the course of this book, you will find that many illustrative studies have been interpolated into the text at various points. These have been taken from various sources. Some are summaries of published studies, while others are unpublished reports by and from teachers themselves. The aim of these studies is to put some flesh onto the bones of the text, to illustrate the major points being made.

1.2 Teachers and research

Within the teaching profession, there often seems to be an insurmountable gap between theory and practice. Carr and Kemmis cite evidence purporting to show that teachers regard theory and research as esoteric activities 'having little to do with their everyday practical concerns' (Carr and Kemmis 1985:8). In a similar vein, Beasley and Riordan report that

> the gulf between research bodies and the teaching profession has ensured that many research programmes are not related to professional concerns and interests of teachers and students. Priorities for research too often reflect the interests of academic researchers or central office administrators not school people. Teachers and students in the classroom are rarely actively engaged in the research. Within the experimental framework the researcher protects his or her independence for the sake of 'objectivity'. The tacit knowledge of teachers is devalued. Many of the findings are recorded in a form and style which is accessible to the trained researcher but fails to communicate to teachers, school administrators, parents or advisory people. The primary audience for research has been the research community not the practising teacher. Not surprisingly, we the practising teachers have come to distrust and reject theoretical research and the researcher who takes but does not give (Beasley and Riordan 1981:60).

While academics and others involved in educational research often complain about the lack of rigour with which teachers formulate and seek answers to the problems and issues which confront them in the course of teaching, seminars, workshops and conferences are frequently punctuated by complaints by teachers of excessive jargon and mystification on the part of researchers and academics.

This mistrust on the part of many teachers is interesting in light of the view expressed by Carr and Kemmis that educational research is essentially practical in nature: its aims are to solve problems, bring about change and get things done. This distinguishes it from many other areas of research which are concerned with discovering 'truth'.

> One extremely important consequence of the practical nature of education is that educational research cannot be defined by reference to the aims appropriate to research activities concerned to resolve theoretical problems ... the problems it seeks to address are always educational problems. Moreover, since education is a practical enterprise, these problems are always practical problems which, unlike theoretical problems, cannot be resolved by the discovery of new knowledge, but only by adopting some course of action (Carr and Kemmis 1985:108).

This, in turn, leads to the notion that effective curriculum research and development cannot be carried out by specialists divorced from the field of action: the classroom. Well over a decade ago, Stenhouse (1975) noted that it was not enough for teachers' work to be researched: they need to research it themselves.

In language teaching, the application of theories of adult learning, the needs-based notions of the Council of Europe (see, for example, Holec 1979; Richterich 1983) and a move away from centralised curricula in favour of localised, learner-centred models, have all thrust the teacher into the limelight. In fact, in some language-teaching systems, it is now the teacher who is the principal agent of curriculum development.

Not surprisingly, this has brought its own problems. If language teachers are to be charged with the responsibility of developing their own curricula, they need more time, greater skills and more support than if they are implementing a curriculum developed by others. While this support might include syllabus outlines and curriculum models of one sort or another, it should also include counsellors, bilingual support personnel, and curriculum advisers. These resources should not be seen in isolation from the more traditional or conventional support. Nor should they be considered luxuries to be dispensed with at times of economic stringency.

The knowledge and skills which teachers need if they are to be centrally involved in curriculum change can be developed if teachers are encouraged to take a critical and experimental approach to their own classrooms. They thus become action researchers, carrying out research in their own classrooms, research which is focused on practical problems and which is more likely to lead to change than research conducted by someone removed from the classroom.

As an extension of this notion, Walker (1985) sees research as a useful way of ensuring the relevance of teacher-education programmes. Involving student teachers in real research is likely to make teacher-education programmes more relevant. It is also a way of redistributing power. Because it is the trainees who formulate and carry out the research, it is they, rather than the tutor, who will have first-hand experience of the problem and its context as well as the difficulties associated with the research. The tutor is thus placed in 'a responsive rather than an instructional role, a pressure that will be increased by the somewhat eclectic way in which problems naturally suggests themselves' (Walker 1985:6).

It has been suggested that teacher-initiated research has the following advantages:

1. It begins with and builds on the knowledge that teachers have already accumulated.
2. It focuses on the immediate interests and concerns of classroom teachers.
3. It matches the subtle, organic process of classroom life.
4. It builds on the 'natural' processes of evaluation and research which teachers carry out daily.
5. It bridges the gap between understanding and action by merging the role of the researcher and practitioner.
6. It sharpens teachers' critical awareness through observation, recording and analysis of classroom events and thus acts as a consciousness-raising exercise.
7. It provides teachers with better information than they already have about what is actually happening in the classroom and why.
8. It helps teachers better articulate teaching and learning processes to their colleagues and interested community members.

9. It bridges the gap between theory and practice (From Beasley and Riordan 1981:36).

Most of the writers cited so far have been writing within a general educational context. One writer who has specifically addressed the issue of the second-language teacher as classroom researcher is Long (1983). He reports on a survey showing that classroom centred research is comparatively neglected in teacher-preparation programmes. The survey revealed that only 18 per cent of MA programmes in Canada and the United States gave it minor attention and that 82 per cent ignored it altogether. In calling for a greater role for classroom-centred research in graduate programmes, Long points to three principal roles for such courses. In the first place, despite its infancy, classroom-centred research can provide a great deal of useful information about how foreign-language instruction is carried out (in contrast with statements about how it should be carried out, or how people imagine it is carried out). Second, classroom-centred research can promote self-monitoring by classroom practitioners. The various observational schemes for classifying classroom interaction can be used by teachers to monitor their own classes or the classes of colleagues. Finally, involvement of teachers in classroom research can, according to Long, help them resist the temptation to jump on to the various bandwagons which seem to roll along from time to time. Descriptive studies of what actually goes on in classrooms can help teachers evaluate the competing claims of different syllabuses, materials and methods.

1.3 Research traditions

Having looked at some of the reasons why teachers should become involved in investigating their own classrooms, I should now like to take a closer look at the field of classroom-centred research as it has emerged over recent years.

In his comprehensive survey of the field, Chaudron (1988) identifies four different research traditions in the language classroom. These are as follows:

1. Psychometric
2. Interaction analysis
3. Discourse analysis
4. Ethnography.

In psychometric studies, the researcher investigates the effectiveness of particular methods, activities and techniques by measuring language gain on proficiency tests. In interaction analysis, researchers use systems and schemes for studying classroom behaviours and interactions. Discourse analysis involves analytical schemes for the linguistic analysis of classroom interactions. Finally, in ethnographic studies, the researcher observes, describes and interprets the classroom in ways similar to those employed by anthropologists when they study unfamiliar cultures and societies.

Each of these research methodologies has a different focus and function, and it is not possible to say that one is necessarily better than another without knowing what it is that the researcher is trying to find out, and what he/she intends to do with the information which is obtained from the investigation (see Table 1.1).

TABLE 1.1 *A comparison between different research traditions, issues and methods in the language classroom (after Chaudron 1988)*

Tradition	Typical issues	Methods
Psychometric	Language gain from different methods, materials and methods	Experimental method – pre- and post-test tests with experimental and control groups
Interaction analysis	Extent to which learner behaviour is a function of teacher-determined interaction	Coding classroom interactions in terms of various observation systems and schedules
Discourse analysis	Analysis of classroom discourse in linguistic terms	Study classroom transcripts and assign utterances to predetermined categories
Ethnographic	Obtain insights into the classroom as a 'cultural' system	Naturalistic 'uncontrolled' observation and description

In fact the typology set out in Table 1.1 is rather misleading, in that interaction and discourse analysis are basically research techniques rather than research traditions. In this book I shall, in the first instance, draw a two-way distinction between the psychometric or quantitative tradition and the interpretive or qualitative tradition. From this perspective, interaction and discourse analysis, as techniques, could feature in either psychometric or interpretive studies. (Later we shall see that this distinction is a rather crude one.)

The psychometric tradition involves the comparison of different methods, materials, teaching techniques and so on, in order to determine whether one or more of these variables results in significantly more or better learning than competing methods, materials, techniques or programmes. Test scores for students using the competing methods, etc., are analysed using a range of inferential statistical tools to determine whether differences are due to the variable in question or are a matter of chance (an introduction to the reasoning behind statistical inference can be found in Appendix C).

Scherer and Wertheimer (1964) is a widely cited psychometric investigation into two different methods of foreign-language instruction (although it is generally cited today as an example of the futility of attempting large-scale methods comparisons). In this study, the researchers set out to investigate whether foreign languages might be learned more effectively in classes employing a grammar-translation approach, or in classes in which the innovative audiolingual approach was employed.

Subjects for the study were two groups of college students learning German as a foreign language. One group was instructed in German using a grammar-translation method in which students were instructed in listening, speaking, reading and writing using translation and grammar studies. The other group received instruction in what at the time was an innovative approach to foreign-language instruction: audio-lingualism. In this approach, the emphasis was on listening and speaking rather than reading and writing, and the use of translation was avoided and grammatical rules were learned inductively. At the end of the two-year experimental period, both groups were tested, and the test scores were analysed in order to determine whether differences were statistically significant.

The study was unable to demonstrate the unequivocal superiority of one method over another. In fact, the experiment showed that students' levels of skill reflected the respective emphases of the different approaches. In other words, students instructed under the grammar-translation method were significantly better at reading and translation, while the students instructed audiolingually were significantly better at listening and speaking.

Many criticisms have been made of this study. However, it is not my purpose to review these here. I have included the study to illustrate the type of language research falling under the 'psychometric' or 'quantitative' rubric. The aim of such research is to identify certain objective 'truths'. In Scherer and Wertheimer, the principle which the researchers hoped to uncover can be formulated as follows: 'Is audiolingualism a more effective method of learning a foreign language for college-level learners than grammar-translation?'

The second research tradition we have identified is the qualitative or interpretive one. The approach developed partly as a reaction to the psychometric tradition. This tradition focuses more on processes of instruction and learning than on the end products or outcomes, and its major thrust is to uncover insights into the complexities of teaching and learning, rather than on obtaining 'proof' that method X works better than method Y, or that coursebook A works better than coursebook B. This approach is therefore centrally concerned with documenting and analysing what actually goes on in the classroom, rather than simply measuring the end point of learning.

In his book on interpretive or ethnographic approachs to the classroom, van Lier (1988) justified his focusing on the subjective, qualitative tradition on five major grounds:

1. Our knowledge of what actually goes on in classrooms is extremely limited.
2. It is relevant and valuable to increase that knowledge.
3. This can only be done by going into the classroom for data.
4. All data must be interpreted in the classroom context, i.e., the context of their occurrence.
5. This context is not only a linguistic or cognitive one, it is also essentially a social context.

He goes on to comment on the many different methods which might be employed in ethnographic research, which has its roots in anthropology.

> In anthropology, the ethnographer observes a little-known or 'exotic' group of people in their natural habitat and takes field notes. In addition, working with one or more informants is often necessary, if only to describe the language. Increasingly, recording is used as a tool for description and analysis, not just as a *mnemonic device*, but more importantly as an *estrangement device*, which enables the ethnographer to look at phenomena (such as conversations, rituals, transactions, etc.) with detachment. The same ways of working are applied in classrooms. However, recording (and subsequent transcription) is of even greater importance here than in anthropological field work, since many more things go on at the

same time and in rapid succession, and since the classroom is not an exotic setting for us but rather a very familiar one, laden with personal meaning (van Lier 1988:37).

The flavour of ethnographic work as a generator of insight rather than 'truth' is captured in the following case study of an ESL teacher reported in Nunan (1987).

Sally Smith worked in an intensive language programme for adult learners of English as a second language. She was an experienced teacher with a post-graduate diploma in TESOL. She had more than ten years' experience in Asia, Europe and Australia. For several years she had worked in a new arrivals programme, which provided low-proficiency immigrants and refugees with survival English-language skills.

However, when she was switched to an intermediate programme with learners who had already had several courses, she experienced difficulties. The class she has been given was a disparate one. The learners had a range of proficiency levels, their aptitude varied, and their age range and literacy levels were quite disparate. In addition, there was no core curriculum. Each teacher was expected to develop her own curriculum in consultation with her learners.

Sally contacted a curriculum consultant, and they decided to use the challenge provided by the difficult class to carry out a study. The purpose of the study was to document and gain insights into the problems confronting and solutions sought by teachers operating within a negotiated curriculum. Teaching sessions were recorded and jointly analysed by the teacher and consultant, and a series of interviews between the teacher and consultant were carried out during the course.

The role of the consultant in this study was that of 'critical friend' rather than 'expert'. In other words, his role was to help the teacher to find her own solutions rather than provide solutions for her.

During the first weeks of the course, the classroom environment was poor. Students seemed apathetic, and were offering passive resistance to Sally's efforts. This was particularly the case whenever students were required to work in pairs and small groups. Her recorded comments at the time underlined her frustration:

'I don't know where to go to cater for all the variables. During the first week, I've also had problems with group cohesion which may have been solved by forcing more contact. Yesterday, I saw them sitting there as a group of isolated individuals.

At last I've got a class who could understand if I gave them a list of objectives, and I can't do it because of the disparate group – it's so frustrating! I don't know what they want, they haven't been able to tell me and I haven't been able to ask them in the right way. They may have ideas later, but in the meantime I have to do something.'

A turning point in the course came when, after a lengthy discussion with the consultant, Sally decided to carry out an extensive survey of the students' attitudes towards the content, methodology, materials and class groupings. This was followed by an intensive counselling session in which Sally followed up on the major points arising out of the survey. In reviewing her students' reaction to the consultative process, Sally stated that:

At first they were a bit stunned and amused at the teacher wanting them to give their opinions on content and methodology. I explained that I'd been worried because of the disparate levels and that some things would be difficult for some learners and that I was very interested to know. They were really pleased to be consulted . . . Explaining and giving the rationale is crucial.

As a result of the consultation process, all learners were quite prepared to continue with pair and small group work. Clarifying the rationale 'made an incredible difference to how they went about their pair work. Before they were really sluggish and reluctant – just going through the motions. Now they really get into it.'

As a result of the study, the teacher and consultant were able to reach a number of conclusions about problems and solutions in a negotiated curriculum. Some of the more significant of these were as follows:

1. The initial grouping of learners into classes is extremely important and, while current proficiency level is one of the most significant variables, other variables such as real-life goals need to be taken into consideration.
2. Learners are quite capable of negotiating content and methodology, and do have views (some quite definite) about the nature of the learning process.
3. Leaners have a right to know *what* they will learn, *how* they will learn it and *why* they will learn.
4. In a negotiated curriculum, not only must curriculum processes change, but supporting administrative and managerial structures must change.
5. It is worth exploring the feasibility of dividing learners into smaller sub-groups for parts of the learning day rather than sticking to the 'one room, one teacher, twenty student' syndrome (adapted from Nunan 1987).

It can be seen from the 'Sally' case study that naturalistic studies are different in many respects from psychometric research. In particular, what is admissible as evidence is very different in the two research traditions.

There is growing interest in the use of ethnographic techniques in classroom research. This is no doubt partly due to the difficulty of setting up psychometric studies. Two practical difficulties are controlling all the variables which might affect the experiment, and identifying suitable subjects who can be randomly assigned to control and experimental groups. There are other reasons for the popularity of ethnography, and interest in ethnographic techniques has not developed simply as a reaction to the difficulty of setting up psychometric experiments. In fact, ethnography brings its own problems, some of which are every bit as difficult to solve as those confronting the psychometrician. In addition, as Chaudron (1988) points out, the procedures for carrying out such research require 'considerable training, continuous record keeping, extensive participatory involvement of the researcher in the classroom, and careful interpretation of the usually multifaceted data'.

As already indicated, many researchers feel that ethnographic approaches speak more readily to the concerns of the classroom practitioner, who is likely to be more interested in gaining insights into his/her own classroom processes than establishing generalisable truths. In addition, as Sanday (1982) has pointed out, the well-written ethnography is capable of reaching a wider audience than reports of psychometric studies and is therefore more likely to lead to a change in classroom practices. Certainly the language of many research reports can be offputting to those classroom teachers who are unused to reading such material.

The gap between the two research traditions we have been discussing at times seems impossible to breach and, indeed, the proponents of the different approaches often seem to be speaking different languages. It is important, therefore, to bear in mind that we are talking about the ends of a continuum, rather than two mutually exclusive research domains. In fact, pscyhometric studies need to have an ethnographic dimension, as Swaffar *et al.* (1982) demonstrate.

Swaffar *et al.* set out to investigate which of two methods, audiolingualism or cognitive code learning, was more effective in the teaching of German as a foreign language. This study had several similarities to the Scherer and Wertheimer investigation, in that both were attempting to adjudicate between two different methods. As we saw, the earlier study was inconclusive. However, in that study, the researchers never actually entered the classrooms where the methods they were investigating were being used. Nor did they collect information on the teachers' understanding of the methods under investigation.

The rationale for the study by Swaffar *et al.* shows that they were alive to the need for assessing what actually happens in the classroom as opposed to assumptions about what happens on the part of both researchers and teachers. The study was initiated by a questionnaire which

> was administered in conjunction with a performance study designed to contrast the classroom implementation of rationalist and empiricist approaches to foreign language instruction. The questionnaire under discussion produced an admixture of distinctive and non-distinctive responses. When we attempted to identify the features which led us to the relative success or failure of our items, we uncovered as well the criteria which distinguished the two approaches. In seeking to quantify attitudes about these two approaches to language teaching we identified fundamental task hierarchies which distinguished them. Therefore, in the analysis of our data, we identify the problems presented by inconclusive items in order to illustrate the essential differences in the two teaching philosophies which contrasting items revealed. We underscore the importance of the assessment of actual curricular practices in any methodological comparison.

The questionnaire required participating teachers to rate a series of statements according to the extent to which the statements reflected their teaching practices. The key for the questionnaire was as follows:

1. Virtual non-use. This principle or activity forms little or no part of my curriculum. If possible I reject it for things more consistent with my goals.
2. Trivial incidental use. This principle or activity forms a limited part of my curriculum, but I tend to reject its use more than I favour its use.
3. Uncertain. Uncertain as to what role this principle or activity plays in my curriculum.
4. Important supplemental use. This principle or activity forms a supplemental part of my curriculum. I favour its use more than I reject its use.
5. Essential use. This is essential to my curriculum. I use it either throughout first year – or extensively during appropriate limited periods.

Sample statements from the questionnaire are as follows:

1. The use of English sentences by the teacher or students is encouraged in the classroom, to make explanations, explain difficulties or translate.
2. The teacher discussed a point of grammar in English with the class.
3. Students take dictation in German: they either write down entire sentences or fill in blanks with words, phrases or sentences omitted from the text they are listening to.
4. When students summarise what they have read or heard, they write short summaries using mostly complete German sentences, either in free composition format or controlled format.
5. Students show comprehension by drawing pictures to represent what they have read.

As a result of their research, Swaffar *et al.* concluded that teachers cannot be seen to belong to strictly separable methodological camps, and that the methodological labels often attached to classroom tasks and activities do not reflect what teachers actually do.

> Methodological labels assigned to teaching activities are, in themselves, not informative, because they refer to a pool of classroom practices which are universally used. The differences among major methodologies are to be found in the ordered hierarchy, the priorities assigned to the tasks. Not *what* classroom activity is used, but *when* and *how* form the crux of the matter in distinguishing methodological practice....
>
> Our conclusions, then, suggest a fundamental rethinking of one of the most vexing problems of our profession: the issue of methodological differences. Our study indicates that for teachers working in two different methodologies, defining method solely in terms of activities proved inadequate. We feel it is reasonable to generalise from our experience that defining methodologies in terms of characteristic activities has led to distinctions which are ostensible, not real – i.e. not confirmable by classroom practice. Unless an activity, be it translation, grammar explication, drill, or comprehension exercises, is analyzed in terms of its position in a learning sequence, teachers cannot locate its functions as it delimits a methodology. It is not the characteristic activities per se that discriminate between methodologies, but the ways in which those characteristic activities reinforce each other in the foreign language learning process.

Despite the apparent advantages of incorporating process and product into research studies, the long-standing debate between those who favour psychometric, or quantitative studies, and those who favour more qualitative approaches such as those employed by ethnographers, has continued to be quite heated. This is as true of language teaching as it is of other areas of education. While there have been attempts at reaching an accommodation – for instance, van Lier (1988), points out the advantage of research projects which include both a quantitative and qualitative dimension; Chaudron (1987) also attempts to demonstrate the mutual dependence of the two research traditions – the debate has continued to be as vigorous as ever, and there is little evidence that an accommodation will be reached in the foreseeable future. The wisest course at the present time is perhaps to acknowledge that different projects will have different purposes and audiences, and that it is these purposes and audiences which should determine the research methodology and design.

While I shall, for convenience, adhere to the basic distinction between psychometric and interpretive research, I should, in concluding this section, point out that they represent rather gross categories. Grotjahn (1987) has pointed out that the quantitative/qualitative distinction can refer to three different aspects of research. These are the design (whether the researcher has set up a classical experimental design with pre- and post-tests, and control and experimental groups); the form of data collected (whether qualitative or quantitative) and the type of analysis (whether interpretive or statistical). Mixing and matching these variables gives us eight research paradigms as follows:

PURE FORMS

Paradigm 1: exploratory–interpretative
   (a) non-experimental design
   (b) qualitative data
   (c) interpretative analysis
Paradigm 2: analytical-nomological
   (a) experimental or quasi-experimental design
   (b) quantitative data
   (c) statistical analysis

MIXED FORMS
Paradigm 3: experimental-qualitative-interpretative
   (a) experimental or quasi-experimental design
   (b) qualitative data
   (c) interpretative analysis
Paradigm 4: experimental-qualitative-statistical
   (a) experimental or quasi-experimental design
   (b) qualitative data
   (c) statistical analysis
Paradigm 5: exploratory-qualitative-statistical
   (a) non-experimental design
   (b) qualitative data
   (c) statistical analysis
Paradigm 6: exploratory-quantitative-statistical
   (a) non-experimental design
   (b) quantitative data
   (c) statistical analysis
Paradigm 7: exploratory-quantitative-interpretative
   (a) non-experimental design
   (b) quantitative data
   (c) interpretative analysis
Paradigm 8: experimental-quantitative-interpretative
   (a) experimental or quasi-experimental design
   (b) quantitative data
   (c) interpretative analysis
(Grotjahn 1987:59–60)

1.4 The concept of 'action research'

There has been increasing interest in the use of 'action research', both as a way of increasing our knowledge of classrooms and as a tool in teacher education, although the term itself is not always explicitly defined by the user. Carr and Kemmis offer the following definition:

> a form of self-reflective enquiry undertaken by participants in social situations in order to improve the rationality and justice of their own practices, their understanding of these practices, and the situations in which these practices are carried out (Carr and Kemmis 1985:220–1).

Cohen and Manion, in their comprehensive introduction to research methods in education, suggest that action research consists of small-scale interventions 'in the functioning of the real world'. Such research is closely related to the context in which it takes place, involves the collaboration of researchers as well as teachers, and is self-evaluative. Cohen and Manion outline eight stages in the action-research process:

1. Identify the problem.
2. Develop a draft proposal based on discussion and negotiation between interested parties, i.e., teachers, advisors, researchers and sponsors.
3. Review what has already been written about the issue in question.
4. Restate the problem or formulate hypotheses; discuss the assumptions underlying the project.
5. Select research procedures, resources, materials, methods, etc.
6. Choose evaluation procedures.
7. Collect the data, analyse it and provide feedback.
8. Interpret the data, draw out inferences and evaluate the project (adapted from Cohen and Manion 1985: 220–1).

In an excellent little booklet designed to introduce teachers to action research, Kemmis and McTaggart suggest that the growing interest in action research is a result of a move towards school-based curriculum development and a growing professional awareness among teachers. These trends have given classroom teachers much greater responsibility for curriculum planning, implementation and evaluation, and action research affords a way of experimenting with and evaluating the intervention into curriculum processes.

Kemmis and McTaggart's procedure for carrying out action research consists of four developmental phases. These are as follows:

Phase I   Develop a plan of action to improve what is already happening.
Phase II   Act to implement the plan.
Phase III Observe the effects of action in the context in which it occurs.
Phase IV   Reflect on these effects.

These four phases are meant to form part of an ongoing cycle. Thus, the critical reflection which occurs during phase IV provides a basis for further planning and reflection. Figure

Figure 1.1

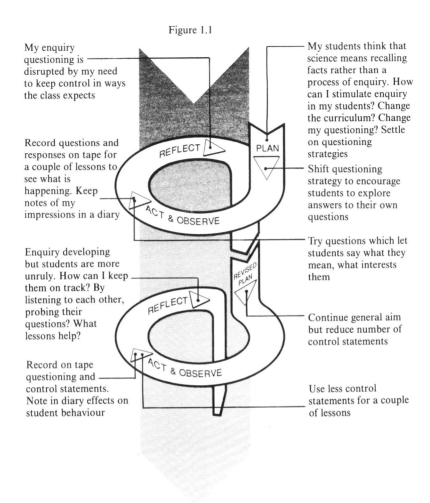

My enquiry questioning is disrupted by my need to keep control in ways the class expects

My students think that science means recalling facts rather than a process of enquiry. How can I stimulate enquiry in my students? Change the curriculum? Change my questioning? Settle on questioning strategies

Record questions and responses on tape for a couple of lessons to see what is happening. Keep notes of my impressions in a diary

Shift questioning strategy to encourage students to explore answers to their own questions

Try questions which let students say what they mean, what interests them

Enquiry developing but students are more unruly. How can I keep them on track? By listening to each other, probing their questions? What lessons help?

Continue general aim but reduce number of control statements

Record on tape questioning and control statements. Note in diary effects on student behaviour

Use less control statements for a couple of lessons

REFLECT — PLAN — ACT & OBSERVE — REVISED PLAN — REFLECT — ACT & OBSERVE

FIGURE 1.1 *The individual aspect in action research (Kemmis and McTaggart 1985:14).*

1.1 illustrates the way these four phases recycle to form an action-research spiral.

One important feature of action research is that it is carried out principally by those who are best placed to change and, hopefully, to improve, what goes on in the classroom, that is, by classroom teachers themselves. This is not to say that studies carried out by non-classroom-based teachers are not intended to lead to change, nor that professional researchers might not collaborate with teachers in research projects of various sorts. However, such studies are more often motivated by a desire to uncover regularities and generalisations which go beyond the particular classroom or classrooms in which the research has taken place. The primary motivation for action research, on the other hand, is the more immediate one of bringing about change and, hopefully, to improve the state of affairs in the classroom in which it has taken place. It is thus problem focused. The

TABLE 1.2 *Key questions in exploring language classrooms*

Questions		Examples
What	Curriculum processes	Planning Implementing Assessing Evaluating
	Curriculum components	Teachers Learners Materials Interactions Roles Management Administration Support (e.g. counselling)
How	Controlled	True experiment Standardised test Observation schedules
	Naturalistic	Case study Observation Diary Journal Interview Field notes
Why	Generalised	'Truth'
	Localised	Insight Self-development
Who	Bureaucrats	Government officials Programme manager
	Professional	Head teacher Teacher Academics
	Support	Counsellors Interpreters Bilingual aides
	Learners	

main concern is to come up with solutions to a given problem, and any given research project is usually concerned with a single case in a specific situation.

1.5 The structure of the rest of the book

In the rest of the book, we shall explore the central questions of *what, how, why* and, *who* in our efforts to deepen our understanding of language classrooms. Table 1.2 illustrates the range of elements and issues which can be investigated in relation to these key questions.

In the next two chapters, we shall look at some of the studies which have been carried out in language classrooms. Chapter Two looks at research on teachers, while Chapter Three looks at studies which focus predominantly on learners. The aim of these chapters is to provide the reader with insights into some of the findings of classroom research, and to act as a stimulus, suggesting topics and issues for teachers to explore in their own classrooms.

Chapters Four and Five are devoted to research methods. In Chapter Four we look at methods which have a broad focus, and which are intended to capture the maximum amount of information about the life of the classroom. The methods in Chapter Five are focused more narrowly on specific aspects of classroom interaction and behaviour. Here we look at systems, schemes and schedules designed to identify specific features and regularities of classroom life.

In Chapter Six, we look at ways in which classroom observation and investigation can provide a framework for professional development. The chapter also contains a detailed outline of a workshop programme designed to introduce teachers to the principles of observation and classroom-research and to provide them with basic skills and knowledge to establish their own investigations.

Chapter Seven looks at ways of establishing, supporting and maintaining teacher-research. A particular focus of this chapter is the notion of collaborative research. We look at collaboration, not only between teachers and those with expertise in conducting research, but also at collaboration between teachers and learners. We also look at ways in which investigations by teachers might be documented and disseminated.

The book concludes with three appendixes. These are an integral part of the work as a whole and are intended as such. Appendix A consists of transcribed extracts from two language lessons. They have been included as a resource for those readers who do not have ready access to their own classroom data and who want to undertake some of the tasks set out at the end of each chapter. Appendix B contains sample schedules and instruments for coding classroom interactions.

Appendix C is an introduction to basic concepts in statistics as these relate to language learning and teaching. While I believe that for the most part teachers will be more usefully served by interpretive methods, I should not like to preclude or preempt consideration of quantitative approaches. In any case, it is important for teachers who are seriously interested in understanding research to be familiar with the logic and rationale of quantitative research methods so that they can read and understand published research studies and reports. As a result of considering the issues presented in this appendix, readers should be better able to appreciate the scope and complexity, as well as the shortcomings, of the experimental method.

1.6 Conclusion

In this chapter, I have mapped out the terrain for the rest of the book. I have suggested that in order for language teachers to understand the classrooms in which they work, they need to systematically observe and investigate these classrooms. I have suggested that in the first instance such investigations should be related to issues or problems in a specific classroom (rather than trying to come up with findings which might be generalised to the language learning and teaching world at large). This type of teacher-research is distinguished from other forms of research by its practical focus. Teacher-research should grow out of the problems and issues which confront teachers in their daily work. The outcome of such research is intended to be fed back into the classroom, rather than becoming part of the pool of knowledge on a particular aspect of language learning and teaching. This is not to suggest that theoretical concerns have no place in teacher-research. On the contrary, the exploration of classroom issues and problems should lead teachers from practice to theory and back to practice again as a sort of on-going professional growth spiral (see, for example, Candlin's 1987 conceptions of strategic principles and tactical action).

In the next two chapters, we shall explore some of the issues which teachers might focus on as they attempt to deepen their understanding of their own classrooms and the classrooms of others. These lead us naturally to the next pair of chapters which introduce techniques and methods for investigating classrooms in a systematic way.

1.7 Questions and tasks

1. Consider your own attitude towards the notion of the 'teacher as researcher'. What sort of mental image does it evoke? What are some of the skills which might be required by a teacher who is interested in carrying out research projects?
2. What is your view on the theory/practice issue? How regularly, if at all, do you consult journals on teaching or applied linguistics? If you do read such articles from time to time, what type of article do you look for? What sort of return do you expect on the investment of time and effort required to find and read professional literature?
3. Which of the reasons advanced by Beasley and Riordan in 1.2 do you think provide the most compelling arguments in favour of the notion of teacher-as-researcher?
4. Long suggests that teacher involvement in CCR can:
   (a) provide teachers with useful information about what actually happens in classrooms;
   (b) give teachers techniques for monitoring and evaluating their own teaching and the teaching of peers, and
   (c) help teachers resist bandwagons.
   Given your own teaching situation, what do you see as the advantages of teacher involvement in CCR?
5. What major differences (e.g., in terms of method, nature and type of evidence, etc.) can you discern between the different studies described in the chapter? What lessons or insights, if any, did you obtain from reading the case study on Sally Smith?
6. Carr and Kemmis suggest that action research is a form of self-reflective enquiry. To what extent are you encouraged or stimulated to reflect critically on your own teaching practice? Have you ever tried to formalise this by, for example, keeping a log or a diary?
7. What are the similarities and differences between the action-research procedures of Cohen and Manion and Kemmis and McTaggart? How realistic are these suggestions, given the demands they would make on the time, expertise, etc. of classroom teachers?
8. Find examples in the literature of two or three of Grotjahn's 'mixed' research paradigms.

Chapter Two

Looking at Teachers

2.1 Introduction

This is the first of two chapters which set out some of the things we might look at in our efforts to understand language classrooms. In the last chapter, we saw that any element or aspect of teaching can form the basis for investigation. In this chapter, we look at teacher behaviour and, in the next, learner behaviour. I realise that this division is, to a certain extent, an arbitrary one, in that teacher behaviour needs to be studied in relation to learner behaviour and vice versa, and that the division between the chapters is mainly one of convenience. Following these issue-oriented chapters, we look at methods for finding out about classrooms.

Deciding to deal with issues for investigation first, and methods of investigation second is, in a sense, also arbitrary. It does not mean that issues have a logical or necessary priority over methods, although some researchers argue that they should, and that the issues, i.e. what it is we wish to investigate, should determine how we go about our investigation.

Others adopt a different approach in their efforts to understand language classrooms. Van Lier (1988) argues very strongly against the identification of issues as an initial step in investigating the classroom. His argument is based on the belief that if we enter into an investigation with certain issues, problems or research questions firmly in mind, then this will create a particular mind set, a pair of mental blinkers which may blind us to other perhaps potentially more interesting aspects of the classroom.

> it is often difficult, and probably largely counterproductive, from an ethnographic point of view, to select certain specific facts or details beforehand while at the same time aiming to be true to the participants' perspective and to the interactive and wider social context (van Lier 1988: 88).

I believe that the desirability of letting issues determine the method, and the ethnographer's desire not to be blinkered by the issues can be accommodated if we adopt a five-stage procedure as follows:

Stage 1   Collect data, e.g. samples of classroom language for transcription, analysis and study;

Stage 2   study the data and see what issues emerge;

Stage 3 identify an issue and formulate it as a question or problem;
Stage 4 identify the methods and techniques most likely to give you the answers you
    are seeking;
Stage 5 carry out the investigation.

I should point out here, in fairness to van Lier, that he would not, I believe, object to this five-stage procedure. His basic objection is to the identification of an issue or issues as one's initial point of departure. Against this, however, we must ask to what extent observation of any kind can ever be 'objective' or 'neutral', given the fact that we bring to any observation all the conscious and subconscious baggage bequeathed to us by our education and experience as teachers.

Table 2.1 presents the results of a survey in which a group of classroom language teachers nominated those areas and issues they would like to investigate in their own classroom. I have included them here to illustrate the range of issues which might be

TABLE 2.1 *Areas and issues nominated by teachers as worth investigating*

Area	Issues
Methodology	Task analysis and the different demands that tasks create What materials/methods learners do/do not respond to The learning and teaching of vocabulary
Classroom management and interaction	The occurrence of digressions within a lesson by teachers and students and the extent to which these lead to useful learning outcomes or simply distract, confuse or mislead students The management of classroom interactions Effective and ineffective instruction giving How to increase student talking time. Do students think this is valuable? Does it enhance learning?
Professional development and self-evaluation	How do teachers perceive peer analysis? In what ways is it helpful, threatening, inhibiting? How action research can improve cohesion/sense of progression from the students' perspective Peer teaching/learning for teachers Promoting personal responsibility for professional development Using classroom analysis with new teachers to assist them develop their own practices more effectively
Applying skills	Encouraging and monitoring students' use of English outside the classroom Encouraging the use of English outside the classroom
Affective factors	Students' attitudes towards games and drama activities Student perceptions of language learning
Assessment and evaluation	Evaluating the effectiveness of teaching Methods of post-learning arrangement assessment How to develop classroom tests for end-of-course assessment
Acquisition	Whether plateaux in language learning really exist

investigated and to show the sorts of things which at least one group of teachers thought worthy of investigation. They are of interest because they were nominated at the end of a workshop in which teachers analysed data from their own classrooms, and therefore give some idea of the deficiencies or problems teachers noted in their own classrooms.

2.2 Researching teachers

Table 2.1 shows the range of issues which teachers identified as worthy of exploration. When we look specifically at teachers, we find a similar range of issues. Table 2.2 sets out some of the investigative questions which might be posed in relation to teachers' planning and implementation practices, their classroom management and talk. We can see from Table 2.2 the varied ways in which the issues can be formulated, and that they do not need to be dressed up in abstract or academic jargon.

One way of finding issues to investigate is to look through books and journals on teaching and consider the investigations reported in these in relation to one's own classroom. You can consider the extent to which findings relate to your own situation, and can even replicate some studies. Some of the illustrative studies in this book should also provide insights and examples.

TABLE 2.2 *Issues and sample investigative questions on teachers*

Issue	Investigative questions
Planning	What are the bases on which I select my goals and objectives?
	What are the major factors I take into consideration when selecting content?
Implementation	What is the relationship between the lesson plans I draw up before class and what actually happens in class?
	To what extent does my teaching reflect a systematic procedure of specifying objectives, selecting content and learning tasks and evaluating the effectiveness of instruction, and to what extent is it *ad hoc*?
	What events in the classroom cause me to deviate from my planned lessons?
Classroom management	Some of my learners are disruptive. Is there anything in my behaviour towards them which might account for this behaviour?
	What effect will modified behaviour on my part have on them?
	What aspects of learner behaviour do I respond to?
	How efficient/effective am I at setting up group work?
Talk	How much talking do I do in class? Is this too little, or too much?
	What happens when I vary the amount of talking I do?
	How clear and/or useful are the explanations I give to students?
	What sort of questions do I ask?
	How and when do I correct errors? With what effect?
	What typical patterns of interaction are there between myself and my learners?

Teacher cognitive processes
Information selection and integration
• Attributions
• Heuristics
  Availability
  Representativeness
  Anchoring
  Saliency
  Conflict/stress

Teacher characteristics
• Beliefs
• Conceptions of subject
  matter
• Cognitive complexity

Antecedent conditions
Information about students
• Ability
• Participation
• Behaviour problems

Nature of instructional task
• Goals
• Subject Matter
• Students
• Activities

Inferences
• Judgments
• Expectations
• Hypotheses
• Decisions

Classroom/school environment
• Groupness
• Evaluative climate
• Extra-class pressures

Consequences for teachers planning instruction
• Selection of content
• Grouping of students
• Selection of activities
• Interaction with students
• Teaching routines
• Behaviour problems
• Tutoring

Teacher evaluation   **Consequences for students**
• of judgments
• of decisions
• of teaching routines

FIGURE 2.1 *The domain of research on teachers' judgments, decisions and behaiour (after Shavelson and Stern 1981).*

2.3 Teachers as planners

There has been a great deal of research on teachers as programme planners, although comparatively little of this work has been on language teachers. In their major review of research into teachers' pedagogical thoughts, judgments, decisions and behaviours, Shavelson and Stern (1981) develop the schema illustrated in Figure 2.1. This schema summarises issues covered by the research.

Figure 2.1 shows the scope of research which focuses on the thinking and decision-making processes of teachers as they plan, implement and reflect on their programmes. The research, as Shavelson and Stern point out, is based on two fundamental assumptions. The first of these is that teachers are rational beings whose work requires them to make decisions in complex environments. The second is that what teachers actually do in class is guided by their thoughts, judgments and decisions which in turn will be influenced by their training, personal characteristics, etc. The research reminds us that in order to understand classrooms we may sometimes need to go beyond the actual classroom situation itself.

Antecedent conditions

Under the heading of 'antecedent conditions' Shavelson and Stern summarise research which looks at the effect of learner, task and environmental factors on teachers' decision-making. This research suggests that the learner factors most likely to influence teachers are student ability, sex, participation in class, self-concept, social competence, independence, classroom behaviour and work habits. 'Task' seems to be a central concept for teachers, and one which is more likely than, say, performance objectives, to be the point of departure in programme planning (for a detailed examination of 'task' as a planning tool in language education, see Nunan 1989a). In terms of classroom and school environment, the establishment of a sense of community or 'groupness' is a high priority for teachers. Development and use of reward structures is also extremely important.

Teacher characteristics

There is a rich seam of literature on teacher characteristics likely to influence their judgments, decisions and behaviour. Ideological factors (e.g. whether one believes in traditional or communicative approaches to instruction), and the location of the teacher on a continuum from traditional to progressive beliefs, are particularly important. Of relevance to language teachers is research on methods of reading.

> Pearson and Kamil (1978) describe three informal models of reading: (1) bottom-up models, which assume that the reading process begins with the printed word and goes to meaning, (2) top-down models which assume that the reading process begins in the mind of the reader with an hypothesis about the meaning of the printed word and (3) interactive models, which assume that these two types of information-processing model work simultaneously to mutually facilitate reading.
>
> These models suggest different instructional methods and strategies (e.g. a decoding emphasis for the bottom-up model versus a meaning emphasis for the top-down model). Further, they suggest that teachers make different instructional decisions based on the particular instructional model to which they adhere. For example, the teacher who holds the bottom-up model would decide to remediate a reading problem by teaching the student basic decoding skills on which he is weak. In contrast, a teacher who adheres to the top-down conception would teach a child to generate meaningful hypotheses by capitalizing on the components of the reading process in which the child showed strength (Shavelson and Stern 1981: 468).

Cognitive style and planning style

Other teacher characteristics which have been investigated include cognitive style and planning style. In terms of planning style, teachers can be grouped into those who tend to plan on a day-to-day basis, focusing on classroom activities as their basic unit of planning, and those who develop long-term, comprehensive plans, and proceed from these to a consideration of day-to-day and lesson-to-lesson plans.

Cognitive processes

Another group of studies include those which examine teachers' cognitive processes. Here, one interesting line of research has looked at the (often implicit) rules and operating procedures teachers utilise in making decisions. These enable teachers to make decisions in the face of enormous quantities of information (relating, for instance, to learners' ability, progress, test scores, individual differences, nature of instructional task, etc.) which might otherwise overwhelm them.

Consequences for teaching

A great deal of research has been carried out under the rubric 'consequences for teaching'. Shavelson and Stern subcategorise these into studies which focus on planning for instruction on the one hand and interaction with students on the other. Planning looks at the grouping of students and the selection of content and learning activities, while interaction is concerned with teaching routines, dealing with behaviour problems and tutoring.

Planning

In the area of planning, we have already seen that there is evidence to suggest that many teachers focus on classroom tasks and activities rather than following a logical sequence of needs analysis/entry behaviour specification, objective setting, task design and evaluation. Shavelson and Stern suggest that

> there is a mismatch between the demands of classroom instruction and the prescriptive planning model. This mismatch arises because teachers must maintain the flow of activity during a lesson or face behavioural management problems. Hence they are faced first and foremost with deciding what activities will engage students during the lessons or, to put it another way, the teacher must decide how to entertain his or her audience while attending to the curriculum. Activities, then, and not the prescriptive model are the focus of teacher planning (Shavelson and Stern 1981: 477).

While there is sense in what Shavelson and Stern suggest, it needs to be pointed out that deriving appropriate objectives and maintaining lesson flow are not mutually exclusive. It may well be that one solution to the problem of misbehaviour might be to spend more time developing a rational link between goals, objectives and tasks.

Teaching routines

Research on decision-making during instruction suggests that teachers follow habitual routines until something goes wrong. It is only then that the teacher must decide whether to persist with the routine, adapt it in some way or abandon it altogether. In fact, apparently established routines are resistant to change, and teachers generally change their routines only in extreme circumstances.

> ... teachers' main concern during interactive teaching is to maintain the flow of the activity. To interrupt this flow to reflect on an alternative and consider the possibility of changing a routine drastically increased the information-processing demands on the teacher and increases the probability of classroom management problems (Shavelson and Stern 1981: 484).

Self-evaluation

The final area dealt with by Shavelson and Stern is teacher self-evaluation. The major findings in this area are as follows:

1. In the area of language arts, teachers do not take into consideration their teaching style.
2. When reviewing their teaching (e.g. through video or transcript analysis) teachers are surprised at the behaviours and events they did not pick up when actually teaching.
3. Teachers are not accurate in identifying cues they used to judge students.

In Chapter Four we shall look at techniques for finding out about teachers' planning, judgment and decision-making behaviour. These techniques include such things as self-report inventories, analysis of verbal protocols and stimulated recall. In the educational mainstream, researchers have looked at the influence of learner characteristics on teachers' judgments and decision-making. Teachers are provided with biographical information about a given group of learners and are then asked to make professional judgments about the learners. The data provided can vary from things such as IQ scores and father's occupation. Judgmental questions can include such things as:

1. Do you expect this student to get an A or a B grade at the end of term?
2. What kinds of reading materials would you select for this student?
3. If you asked a question and this student hesitated, would you:
   (a) rephrase the same question?
   (b) ask a similar though easier question?
   (c) give a further explanation and then repeat the question?
   (d) ask another student?
   (e) answer the question yourself?

Information provided through techniques such as these can be used to make generalisations about specific teachers and specific teaching practices. If there is

TABLE 2.3

ID	Age	Time in target country (years, months)	L1	Ed'n	Occupation	Proficiency	Aptitude	Goal
1	26	1,6	Viet	5	Dressmaker	1–	Average	Mix with parents of children's friends
2	35	2,0	Chin	8	Small business	0+	Slow	Get a better job
3	62	12,0	Russ	6	Home duties	0+	Slow	Mix with Australians
4	31	1,1	Span	5	Bricklayer	0	Average	Get a job
5	59	12,0	Arab	4	Plasterer	1	Average	Talk to g'children, doctor
6	55	3,0	Chin	3	Cook	0	Slow	Read English
7	33	1,0	Chin	6	Factory	0+	Average	Communicate at work
8	26	1,2	Polish	12	Secretary	0+	Fast	Retrain, get better job
9	28	2,0	Span	6	Dressmaker	0+	Average	Talk to employer, clients
10	20	1,6	Arab	12	Student	0+	Fast	Undertake tertiary study
11	46	2,0	Hung	11	Secretary	1–	Average	Get a better job
12	19	1,0	Viet	10	Student	1	Fast	Undertake tertiary study
13	39	8,0	Croat	6	Mechanic	0+	Average	Social, job retraining
14	37	5,0	Korea	8	Policeman	0+	Average	Social, child's school
15	27	1,0	Czech	12	Nurse	0+	V. fast	Retrain as nurse
16	54	3,0	Khmr	Unknown	Home duties	0+	Slow	Make Austn. friends
17	61	7,0	Span	5	Home duties	0+	Slow	More confid in speaking
18	25	1,0	Viet	10	Welder	1–	Average	Retrain for better job
19	32	1,0	Turk	14	Accountant	2	Fast	Further study, better job
20	58	18,0	Russ	12	Librarian	0+	Average	Talk to neighbours
21	44	9,0	Croat	6	Cleaner	0+	Average	Talk to employer, workmates,

audiotaped or videotaped data available, the responses can also be compared with what teachers actually do. (For example, many of us answer our own questions far more frequently than we might imagine.)

You might like to study the above data (Table 2.3) and think about which of the variables you would take into account in making professional decisions and judgments about these learners, e.g. how they might be grouped, what goals and objectives might be suitable for them, what teaching materials would be relevant (for a detailed account of the use of learner data in curriculum design, see Nunan 1988).

In this section, we have looked in a rather general way at the scope of research on teachers. In the next session, we focus more narrowly on the area of teacher talk.

2.4 Teacher talk

There has been much research on teacher talk in recent years. This interest reflects the importance of such talk in language teaching. As it is so important for language teachers, and also because it is an area which readily lends itself to investigation by teachers, I shall spend a little time reviewing some of the published studies in the area. Issues which have been investigated include the amount and type of teacher talk, speech modifications made by teachers, instructions and explanations, type and number of questions asked and error correction.

Modifications to teacher speech

One aspect of teacher talk which has been intensively studied is the speech modifications made by teachers. A number of studies have shown that native speakers (teachers and non-teachers alike) modify their speech to non-native speakers in a number of different ways. It has been suggested that these modifications make the language easier to comprehend and that this, in turn, helps the learner to acquire the target language (based on the premiss that we cannot acquire what we do not understand). Other studies have looked at the types of questions teachers ask, the functions of teacher talk, the nature of teachers' explanations, and the types of corrective feedback (error correction) provided by teachers.

Pica and Long (1986) investigated the linguistic and conversational performance of experienced and inexperienced teachers. The purpose of the research was to determine whether there were any differences in the speech characteristics of experienced and inexperienced teachers in their classroom interactions.

The hypothesis upon which the research was based was that the development of a second language occurs when learners are exposed to language which is comprehensible to them and which contains grammatical features which are one level of complexity beyond their current second-language ability. It has been suggested that certain speech modifications made by native speakers in interactions with second-language learners can make language more comprehensible and thus facilitate the acquisition process.

The two questions addressed by Pica and Long are as follows:

1. In what ways do teachers modify their speech when talking to second-language learners in the classroom?
2. Is the ability to modify one's language appropriately part of any teacher's competence, or must it be developed through experience over time?

For their first study, Pica and Long collected ten-minute recorded samples of speech from ten ESL teachers. These were compared with informal native speaker/non-native speaker recorded conversations made outside the classroom. The researchers found that ESL classroom conversation differed from conversations out of the class in a number of ways. There was much less negotiation for meaning in the classroom (this was measured by the number of times teachers adjusted their speech to check that students had understood them, and that they had correctly understood the learners). Pica and Doughty suggest that the smaller amount of negotiation is due to the fact that teachers tended to ask display questions, i.e. questions to which they already knew the answer, and that the need to negotiate was therefore greatly reduced. (Of the questions teachers asked in class 91 per cent were ones to which they already knew the answer, whereas virtually none of the questions asked out of class were of this type.)

In a second study, Pica and Long looked for differences between the language of experienced and inexperienced teachers. While some differences were found (experienced teachers were more fluent, and used a wider range of question forms), these were not particularly marked. In general, the similarities outweighed the differences.

Pica and Long concluded from their studies that:

> the influence of the classroom context is strong enough to outweigh the effects of teaching experience. Consequently, even those with little or no previous experience immediately exercise the power when given the opportunity.... If one accepts the claims of Krashen and others concerning the importance of comprehensible input in SLA, the two studies reported here are not very encouraging for learners whose primary acquisition environment is the SL classroom ... the lessons examined here were found to provide less opportunity for the negotiation of meaning than is necessary if learners are to obtain comprehensible input than did informal NS-NNS conversations outside the classroom.
>
> The reason for this state of affairs is not hard to appreciate: it is difficult for learners to negotiate if they have nothing to negotiate with. Their most obvious potential bargaining chip – information unknown to the teacher that he, she, or other students need in order to do something – is not available to them so long as teachers structure discourse such that information flows in one direction only, from teacher to students.

One implication of this research for classroom practice is that classroom-learning tasks should be provided which give learners access to unequal quantities of information. In the next chapter, we shall look at information-gap tasks which attempt to do just this.

Quantity of speech

Not surprisingly, classroom observation has revealed that teachers tend to do most of the talking. In content classrooms (e.g. science, mathematics classrooms) it has been found that teachers tend to talk for about two-thirds of the available class time, leaving just a third for learners. In some language classrooms it has been shown that teachers talk for up to 89 per cent of the available time.

Whether this is a good thing or not will depend on what one believes about the role of language input in acquisition. If one believes that learners learn best by actually practising in the target language, one will probably try to structure classroom activities so that the amount of learner talk is increased at the expense of teacher talk. If, on the other hand, one believes that teacher talk is a valuable source of comprehensible input, one will be much less worried by teacher dominance.

Teachers who undertake to record and analyse their classroom interactions are generally disconcerted at the quality and quantity of their talk. In workshops with teachers, I have found that particular areas of concern are the amount of time they talk and the nature of the instructions and explanations they provide.

Explanations

A major pedagogic function of teacher talk is to provide explanations, and it is rather surprising that the area has not been investigated more extensively. Allwright (1986) claims that many teachers' explanations simply do not make sense. He provides some interesting examples in which the explanations are either confusing or simply wrong. He hastens to add that it is probably unreasonable to expect teachers to provide coherent explanations on points of language when put on the spot by learners.

In the following extract, the teacher provides an explanation which at least one student does not find entirely satisfactory. When the student asks for a further explanation, the teacher claims (incorrectly) that there is no explanation for this particular grammatical feature. (The full tapescript of the lesson segment can be found in Appendix A.)

T OK, he's looking for a house with three bedrooms and, what do we say? We don't, in English we don't usually say house with three bedrooms ... What do we usually say?
S Three bedroom house.
T A three bedroom house, a three bedroom house, a three bedroom house. So what's he looking for?
S For three bedroom house.
T What's he looking for?
S [Inaudible]
   [Laughter]
T What's he looking for?
S House
T What's he looking for?
S Three bedroom house.
T All right.
S Why three bed, or three bedroom? Why we don't say three bedrooms?
T Ahh, oh ... I don't know, um.
S Is not right.
T We don't say it. We don't say it. There's no explanation. But we often do that in English. Three bedroom house.
S Don't ask for it.
S Yes.
T Well, do ask why. Ask why, and 99 per cent of the time I know the answer. One per cent of the time, nobody knows the answer. If I don't know it, nobody knows [laughter]. Ah, no, I don't know the answer, sorry.

The two extracts which follow have been taken from Chaudron (1983). In both extracts, the lecturer is giving the same geography lesson. In one extract, the lesson is with a group of native speakers, while in the other it is with a group of ESL speakers.

As you read the two extracts, try and decide which is the explanation to the ESL group, and which is to the native speakers. You might like to think about what the differences are between the two extracts. Which is the clearer to you, and why?

Extract 1

... this article I was reading made the point that in North America in general, uh, that – people started out with the idea of equal opportunity, you know that everybody who came here, because there was such abundance ... because there was equal opportunity to become rich. It wasn't like Europe, where you had your family an' your social class an' your education an' all this sort of thing, against you, or for you. But in Canada an' in the United States you could work away, and if you had the proper character, if you worked hard, you would make it. And therefore, of course, as the reverse of that, uh, the idea developed that if you didn't make it, then that was a reflection on your character! But then in a sense this is a result of the individualism and uh, abundance that's here in North America. So that although it's not true, we still have this myth that everybody who works hard can get ahead. And, uh, when the Depression came along of course it was a great shock to people. 'N' they therefore, made everything individual, 'n' they said, these people can't get jobs because they are lazy, because they are no good as individuals, because they have failed, not because social conditions beyond their control, have led to ... their loss of work. But I think th-that is in fact a very important point about North American society that we have such a strong belief in individual competition and hard work and so on, that naturally, those (who) don't get jobs are judged in that way, (kind o') as person-personal failures rather than (as) social accidents.

Extract 2

... aspect of uh, the book is interesting, as far in connection with what people have said about North American society. Uh, Canadian and American, but particularly American. Uh, in Europe, everyone of course was divided into social classes. Uh, you probably did what your father was going to do, uh, if you were a peasant, you accepted that ... But when, when America was was developed, people came here, there was all this land, lots of opportunity for making money, gaining wealth. And, because there was more than people needed, uh, everybody could have a lot. And therefore, people thought, if you could work hard, you would be rewarded! You would get ... what anybody would get if they worked hard and tried to make money. And this tradition has continued in North American society. And even though now ... there isn't endless opportunity, not everybody in American ca-can be rich! We can't all be millionaires. But there's still this feeling in North America that if you're unemployed, if you're poor, it's your own fault somehow. So they have a – this particular I mean this is perhaps true in many societies, but uh its exaggerated in uh, North America because of the uh, abundance, the wealth, that was here. So that everybody, so it was thought, could be rich ... That's why during the Depression, they – people did not get together, and try to help the people who were suffering from the Depression. They just thought, it's their fault, they're lazy, there's work if they would only take it. And, of course, in the Depression there wasn't work ... And they get – they have people come up to the – the streets and say, you lazy things, you could work if you wanted to. An' that's still a – still a common idea in Canada actually, isn't it? Not quite so bad now because we have unemployment [meaning insurance]. But now the idea is that you know people are lazy and want to take unemployment ... And yet, people because of this tradition blamed the people individually instead of saying, social conditions have produced general unemployment. That we should do something about that. They thought it's your fault. Not the fault of social conditions, you know ... in spite of ... the fact that this attitude still exists to a certain degree

... you know the – they would think that if you're unemployed it's your own fault, uh, because you can't keep a job, you wouldn't work hard enough and so on. That's still, still a common attitude (from Chaudron 1983: 139–40).

Extract 1 is with the native-speaking class, while Extract 2 is with the ESL group. Chaudron contends that the explanation to the native speakers is clearer than the one to the ESL group, that with the ESL speakers, the lecturer is more disorganised, that there are more digressions, that the interconnections between the ideas are difficult to interpret because of the fragmentation and lack of topic maintenance, and because the ESL explanation is about twice as long as the native-speaker explanation.

In attempting to acount for the difficulty of the ESL version of the geography lesson, Chaudron points out that there are great demands on content teachers working with non-native speakers at school and university level. They must present significant and coherent ideas to learners who lack fundamental linguistic competencies. He suggests that it is because of this that teachers can be led into producing discourse which is actually more difficult to follow than the language addressed to native speakers.

A variety of instruments have been developed for analysing teacher talk. We shall look at these in Chapter Four. They are designed to identify such things as the amount of time spent on explaining, questioning, modelling, correcting, providing feedback, etc.

Questions

One aspect of teacher talk which has received quite a lot of attention is that of teacher questions. Comparisons have been made between the types of questions addressed to learners in a classroom and those addressed to them outside the classroom. Studies have also looked at the didactic function of questions, and the relationship between different question types and learning outcomes.

Several recent studies have looked at teachers' use of display and referential questions. A display question is one to which the questioner knows the answer, whereas a referential question is one to which the person asking the question does not know the answer. It has been observed that, in contrast with interactions in the world outside, classroom interaction is characterised by the use of display questions to the almost total exclusion of referential questions. For example, Long and Sato (1983) compared the types of questions asked by teachers in class with the types of questions used by native speakers when communicating with second-language speakers in non-classroom contexts. Outside the classroom, virtually all of the questions addressed to learners were referential, while in class, the opposite was the case.

In another study, Brock (1986) investigated the effects of referential questions on ESL classroom discourse. The study was carried out with four experienced ESL teachers and twenty-four non-native speakers; two of the teachers were trained to incorporate referential questions into their classroom instruction, while two were not. Each of the teachers taught the same lesson to six of the non-native speakers and the lessons were recorded, transcribed and analysed. Brock found that the two teachers who had not been trained to use referential questions 'asked a total of 141 questions, only 24 of which were referential and 117 of which were display. The treatment group teachers, on the other hand, asked a total of 194 questions, 173 of which were referential and only 21 of which were display.' It was found that the learners in the groups in which more referential questions were asked gave significantly longer and more syntactically complex responses. Brock concludes from her study:

> That referential questions may increase the amount of speaking learners do in the classroom is relevant to at least one current view of second language acquisition (SLA). Swain (1983), in reporting the results of a study of the acquisition of French by Canadian children in elementary school immersion classrooms, argues that output may be an important factor in successful SLA (Brock 1986:55).

Van Lier has questioned the value of drawing a distinction between display and referential questions, pointing out that:

> Such [display] questions have the professed aim of providing comprehensible input, and of encouraging 'early production'. I suggest that, by and large, what gives such question series their instructional, typically L2-classroom character is not so much that they are display rather than referential, but that they are made with the aim of eliciting language from the learners (van Lier 1988:222).

Seen in this light, questions by the teacher about the colour of a student's eyes or hair or dress may be referential for some students and display for others. However, this may be unimportant in interactional terms as the function of the question, to provide input and elicit verbal responses, is the same for all students. According to van Lier, the important distinction between questions in the classroom and those outside the classroom is not their referential or display nature, but the fact that classroom questions of whatever type are designed to get learners to produce language.

What distinguishes instructional questions from conversational (non-instructional) ones is therefore not their referential or display nature, but rather their eliciting function. In interactional terms, the difference between the following (constructed) elicitations may be minimal (van Lier 1988:223):

(a) Prompt or cue:
   T   go to the theatre.
       yesterday. Martha.
   L   yesterday, I went to the theatre
(b) Display question:
   T   (pointing to a picture) Where did Martha go yesterday?
   L   She went to the theatre (yesterday)
(c) Referential question:
   T   Where did you go yesterday Martha?
   L   (yesterday) I went to the theatre.

Research into the relative effects of display and referential questions is in its initial stages, and only further work will show whether or not it is worth pursuing. While van Lier's criticism is a perfectly valid one, it is not inconceivable that the effort involved in answering referential questions prompts a greater effort and depth of processing on the part of the learner. This, in turn, may well be a greater stimulus to acquisition than the answering of display questions. However, it is also obvious that other factors such as the topic area, the learner's background knowledge, and contextual and interpersonal variables will also be operating, and thus having an effect. These have not been adequately controlled for in the rather crude experiments which have taken place up to now (in using the term 'crude', I do not mean to disparage the research; whenever a new line of investigation is opened up, initial studies are invariably crude). The real danger, it seems to me, is in attempting to manipulate discrete linguistic features such as question types in isolation from the educational and interactional contexts in which they occur.

Error correction

Error correction, along with formal instruction, is the classroom activity which most people think of as one of the language teacher's most important functions. It is often commented that one of the things which distinguishes classroom interaction from interaction outside the classroom is the existence of error correction. Regardless of the desires of learners, social norms dictate that we do not correct non-native speakers when they make mistakes in the course of interacting socially outside the classroom.

Despite the perceived importance of error correction, and notwithstanding the considerable amount of research on the subject, there is still a good deal of controversy on some key questions, including the following:

When should errors be corrected?
How should they be corrected?
Who should correct errors?
To what extent should self-correction be encouraged?
Which errors should be corrected?

There is even controversy over whether errors should be corrected at all. Krashen (1981, 1982), for instance, claims that error correction, like grammatical explanations, is of little benefit for long-term acquisition. He bases this claim on the belief that acquisition is a subconscious process, while error correction and grammatical explanations are conscious processes. From the learner's perspective, however, there is little doubt that error correction is expected. Cathcart and Olsen (1976), for example, surveyed 149 adult learners of English as a second language and found a strong preference for error correction. Willing's (1988) study of learning preferences of 517 adult learners also found that 'error correction by the teacher' was the second most highly regarded classroom activity after 'practising the sounds and pronunciation of English'.

Deciding when and which errors to correct causes problems for teachers who are trying to encourage communicative interaction in their classrooms. As Chaudron points out:

> The multiple functions of feedback, and the pressure to be accepting of learners' errors, lead, however, to the paradoxical circumstance that the teacher must either interrupt communication for the sake of formal TL [target language] correction, or let errors pass 'untreated' in order to further the communicative goals of classroom interaction (Chaudron 1988: 134–5).

He also makes the point that many attempts at error correction are patently unsuccessful, a point taken up by Allwright (1975) in an important paper on teachers' classroom error-correction practices.

Allwright suggests that the classroom fulfils a valuable function not generally available in the world outside, namely that it enables learners to form and test hypotheses about the way the target language works. From this perspective, error correction provides learners with negative evidence about a particular language rule. In addition, the correction of a single student provides evidence, not only to the student making the error, but to all other students who happen to be paying attention.

Allwright makes a strong claim for the study of error correction (and, presumably, other aspects of classroom interaction) in the classroom context in which it occurs. His ethnographic approach contrasts with other, more recent studies in which the errors are extracted from and analysed outside of the pedagogical and social context in which they occur. From his observations, he is led to the following conclusions:

1. Teachers are imprecise in their treatment of learner error, tending simply to repeat the correct model rather than telling the student precisely where the error occurred and why it was incorrect.
2. Teachers are also inconsistent in their treatment of learner error, correcting errors made by some learners but not by others. While this inconsistency is understandable, teachers need to be aware of the potential they have for creating confusion in the minds of learners, given the typical lack of precision on the one hand and the apparently inconsistent treatment on the other.

Allwright has been a consistent champion of classroom teachers, pointing out the complexities of their task. In the case of error correction, this can be illustrated by the following options confronting the teacher in the face of a learner error.

Treatment type

A. Basic options:
    1. To treat or to ignore competely.
    2. To treat immediately or delay.
    3. To transfer treatment or not.
    4. To transfer to another individual, a subgroup, or to the whole class.
    5. To return or not to the original error-maker after treatment.
    6. To call upon, or permit, another learner (or learners) to provide treatment.
    7. To test for efficacy of treatment.

B. Possible features:
    8. Fact of error indicated.
    9. Blame indicated.
    10. Location indicated.
    11. Opportunity for new attempt given.
    12. Model provided.
    13. Error type indicated.
    14. Remedy indicated.

15. Improvement indicated.
16. Praise indicated.

Let us take a look at how errors are dealt with in a piece of classroom interaction. The extract and the commentary are from Allwright (1975).

l.176   T   I start at Essex on the fifth of October. When did you start? [*nominates by gesture*]

     S4   I start in Excess since the eleventh of January.

     T   When did you arrive? You arrived on the eleventh of January, did you? You must have started the next day, did you?

180   S2   the eleventh of January
           the twelfth

     S5   No, I we start at thirteenth

     T   on the thirteenth of January
          When did you start at Essex? [*nominates by gesture*]

185   S1   I start at Essex on the thirteenth of January.

     T   On the thirteenth of January.

     S1   Yes.

     T   Again.

     S1   I start at Essex on the thirteenth of January.

190   T   Eulyces [*pause*]
         I started

     S2   I stotted

     T   started

     S1   start

195   S2   I ... ( ) [*aside to S1 in Spanish*]
         I start on on Essess eh fourteen January

     T   I

     S2   Fourteenth January

     T   I started at Essex on the thirteenth of January.

200   All right, Eulyces: on the thirteenth of January ...

     S2   On the th–

     T   Thirteenth

     S2   On the fourteenth of January

     T   Of January

205   S2   of January

     T   on the thirteenth of January

     S2   On fourteenth of January

     T   All together ... on the thirteenth

     SSS   on the thirteenth of January

210   on the thirteenth of January

     T   All right. I started at Essex [*gesture for choral response*]

     SSS   I started at Essex on the thirteenth of January.

     T   Good. Good
         Were you at university before?

Commentary on the extract

l.177   There are many errors – a relatively weak student has been chosen.

178	The grammatical errors are ignored, but the teacher picks up the factual error concerning the date.
180–2	Learners are sorting out the correct date. Errors of person, number and tense form are ignored subsequently.
183	The teacher provides a model of the full correct data phrase.
185	Learner makes a tense form error.
186	The teacher confirms the correct phrase and ignores the tense form error.
188	The teacher requests the learner to repeat.
189	Tense form error occurs again.
190	The teacher ignores the above error and calls on another student.
191	The student hesitates, and the teacher models the start of the utterance.
192	A pronunciation error occurs.
192–3	The teacher remodels, but so does another student, repeating his/her earlier error.
195–6	S2 seeks S1's help, in Spanish, then copies S1 rather than the teacher.
198	S2 spontaneously self-corrects 'fourteen' to 'fourteenth'.
199	The teacher remodels the full correct utterance. There is no emphasis on the factual error.
200	The teacher acknowledges S2's difficulties and remodels the final phrase.
201	S2 pauses after 'th'.
203	S2 repeats the factual error.
204	The teacher ignores the factual error and repeats what the student got right.
206	The teacher remodels the full correct utterance.
207	The student repeats the factual error, and omits 'the'.
208	The teacher transfers treatment to the whole class.
231–4	The teacher praises the satisfactory choral response and changes to another sub-topic.

2.5 Conclusion

In this chapter, we have looked at aspects of the language classroom which centre on teacher behaviour. We have looked, in particular, at teacher questions, explanations, speech modifications and treatment of error. The aim of the chapter has been to demonstrate the range of issues which might be looked at, and to give some idea of how these have been dealt with already.

In my introduction to the chapter, I suggested that one should collect samples of classroom data, study these, and let issues, ideas and problems emerge from the data. Hopefully the chapter has suggested some of the things one might focus on at the second and third stages of investigation.

In the next chapter, we shall look at the classroom from the perspective of the learner. In particular, we shall look at the nature of learner language, the type of language stimulated by different types of classroom tasks, and turn-taking and topic nomination by learners. We shall also look at work done in the area of learning strategy preferences.

2.6 Questions and tasks

1. Review the data in Table 2.1. How realistic are the issues nominated by teachers for investigation? (i.e., do you think teachers have the necessary expertise, time and support to carry out investigations such as these?)
2. Using the example of learner data provided in the chapter, or data relevant to your own context, ask a number of colleagues for their opinions on such things as how the learners should be grouped, what goals and objectives should be set, what teaching materials, tasks and resources would be suitable. Then record which data teachers used in making their judgements. What similarities and differences did you find?
3. With reference to the various studies and issues outlined in this chapter, draw up a list of all the aspects of your own behaviour about which you would like to find out more. Formulate these as investigative questions, for example:

    What percentage of available time do I talk, and how much talk do I allow my learners?

    In what ways do I modify my language to learners? With what effect?

    What types of question do I ask?

4. Review the research areas set out in Figure 2.1. Which of these might form a point of departure for your own research? Select two or three of these, and formulate a number of research questions.
5. Research shows that teachers do most talking in the classroom by far. How much talking do you think you do in class? Express this as a percentage. Now record and review 30–40 minutes of a lesson. How accurate was your estimate?
6. Study the lesson extract from Allwright. How adequate, in your opinion, are the explanations by the teacher? Look at the points at which there are misunderstandings or communication breakdowns. What is the cause of these?

    Find examples of teacher explanations in the extracts included in Appendix A. How satisfactory are these?

7. Record several instances of giving instruction and explanation in your own classroom, or a classroom to which you have access. How clear are the explanations? Do the students appear to understand the points you are making? Are there any ways in which you might have given clearer instructions and/or explanations?
8. Record a segment of your classroom interaction and do a running commentary of the learning errors and your own treatment of these along the lines of the Allwright extract.

Chapter Three

Looking at Learners

3.1 Introduction

Since the principal reason for having language classrooms is to facilitate language learning, it is obvious that learner behaviour is of paramount importance. Here we concentrate on those aspects of learner behaviour which we can study and thereby enrich and extend our understanding of the language classroom. Obviously, there are some aspects of learner behaviour which it is not feasible for us as teachers to investigate fully, and we do not spend a great deal of time considering these. In selecting issues for investigation, I have been guided by the fact that our principal focus is on reflective, research-based teaching, and not simply on grafting classroom research onto current practice.

In this chapter, we focus on three aspects of learner behaviour. These are the nature of second-language development, the learner and classroom tasks, and learning strategies. Table

TABLE 3.1 *Aspects of learner behaviour which might be investigated in the classroom*

Issue	Sample investigative question
Learner language: developmental features	In my teaching, I generally provide an application task to follow up a formal presentation. Which language items do learners actually use in the application task?
	Do learners learn closed class items (e.g. pronouns/ demonstratives) when these are presented as paradigms, or when they are taught separately over a period of time?
Learner language: interaction	In what ways do turn taking and topic management vary with variations in the size and composition of learner groups?
	Are learners more effective at conversational management when techniques such as holding the floor, bringing in another speaker, etc., are consciously taught?
Tasks	Which tasks stimulate the most interaction?
	Which tasks work best with mixed-ability groups?
Strategies	Is there a conflict between the classroom activities I favour and those my learners prefer?
	Do my best learners share certain strategy preferences which distinguish them from less efficient learners?

3.1 sets out, in summary form, some of the aspects of learner behaviour which might be investigated in the classroom.

3.2 Learner language: developmental features

As the primary purpose of teaching is to bring about language learning, it may seem surprising that the systematic study of learner language is a comparatively recent phenomenon. For many years, it was assumed that, given learners with the appropriate attitudes and the requisite amount of intelligence, and teachers with the appropriate skills, teaching would result in learning. In other words, it was assumed that a simple one-to-one relationship existed between teaching and learning. However, over the last fifteen years or so, studies in second-language acquisition, research on learning styles and on discourse development, and work on sociocultural and affective aspects of language development have shown such assumptions to be rather naive.

During the 1970s, a series of studies were carried out which became known as the morpheme-order studies. Most of these studies utilised a data-collection instrument known as the Bilingual Syntax Measure which consisted of a series of pictures. These were used by the researcher to conduct a structured conversation with the learner about the things and events in the cartoon pictures. The researcher then studied a recording of the conversation and identified which of a predetermined list of grammatical morphemes the learner used. (The Bilingual Syntax Measure was designed to stimulate the production of morphemes such as articles, plural 's', third person 's' and irregular past tense forms.)

The early studies showed that certain grammatical morphemes such as third person 's' and the progressive '-ing' were acquired in a certain order. This order seemed to be the same for learners regardless of their first-language background. More significantly for language teachers, this order seemed to be impervious to instruction. In other words, learners would acquire a particular grammatical item at a time determined by their own internal 'syllabus' rather than at the time the item was taught.

Largely as a result of this research, certain claims were made about classroom practice. For example, it was claimed that syllabuses and teaching should follow the 'natural order' as revealed by the Bilingual Syntax Measure. It was also suggested that second-language acquisition was largely a subconscious process that could be best brought about by exposure to natural communication in the target language rather than through tasks in which there was a conscious focus on language form (for a detailed description of the morpheme studies and their implication for practice, see Dulay *et al.* 1982).

In recent years, the morpheme-order studies have been largely discredited, and studies in second-language acquisition have become much more sophisticated. Nevertheless, the notion that certain aspects of the language will be acquired at certain stages regardless of instruction has been supported, and there have been follow-up studies which show that one cannot simply go into a language class, teach any item one wishes, or thinks might be appropriate for the learners, and expect the learners to learn.

If learners do not learn what teachers teach, the question arises – is there any value in instruction? This question was addressed by Long (1983) who, after an exhaustive review of studies available at the time, concluded that while instruction might not affect the order in which grammatical items were acquired, it did seem to speed up the rate of acquisition. Compared with learners who tried to pick up a language naturalistically in the street, instructed learners learned faster and progressed further. I should point out that the investigations referred to so far have been confined to the acquisition of grammar. There has been a comparative neglect of other aspects of language development, such as the acquisition of pragmatic and functional skills. Future research may, in fact, show that these are amenable to instruction.

A recent study in second-language development is that of Johnston (1985). The study was given the acronym SAMPLE, which stands for Syntactic and Morphological Progressions in Learner English. The aim of the project was to describe the syntactic development of adult learners of English as a second language. Johnston began with the assumption that while the language produced by second-language learners obviously differs quite markedly from the language used by native speakers, it was nevertheless systematic. In other words, he assumed that the mistakes learners made were not random, nor were they pathological deviations from the language used by native speakers. He felt that learners have their own systems, and that by studying these systems, we might obtain insights into the processes of second-language acquisition and the nature of language itself.

Johnston wanted to collect 'naturalistic' samples of learner language to analyse. Therefore, instead of using elicitation instruments (such as the Bilingual Syntax Measure, which was used in the earlier morpheme-order studies) he collected his data by interviewing twenty-four ESL learners at varying levels of proficiency. Each subject was interviewed for about an hour on two different occasions. This gave him an enormous amount of material, and a great deal of time was then spent on transcribing the interviews before any analyses could actually be carried out.

Johnston studied the development of a wide variety of morphological and syntactic features, including verb morphology, modals, negation, questions, articles, quantifiers, prepositions, pronouns and connectives.

Following the work of the ZISA group in Germany, Johnston concluded that linguistic elements could be divided into two dimensions or groups. The first dimension contains developmental features whose acquisition is governed by speech processing constraints. The second dimension contains variational features. These are linguistic items which are not constrained by limits on short term memory, but which may be leared at any time.

Speech processing consists of mental operations. In order to speak a language fluently, these must become largely automatic, in the same way as the physical operations in breathing, walking, running and driving a car must become automatic in order to carry out these actions competently. Because speech-processing operations are very complex, and also because the time available for speaking or comprehending is limited, it is only possible to focus on a limited part of the whole speech-processing operation at any one time. Learning a language, then, is a matter of gaining automatic control of these complex mental routines and subroutines.

At the present time, Johnston believes he has identified six developmental stages which are determined by the limits on memory as already described. These are as follows:

Stage 1 Production of single words, phrases and formulae (formulae are utterances such as 'I don't know' and 'What's your name?' which are learned as chunks and cannot be broken down into their separate elements).

Stage 2 Production of simple sequences or 'strings' of words following regular word order rules – e.g. subject + verb + object combinations such as 'I like rice'.

Stage 3 Ability to identify the beginning and end of strings of elements, and to attach and move elements from the beginning to the end of strings and vice versa. For example, attaching adverbs to the beginning or end of strings as in, 'Yesterday, I go home'.

Stage 4 Ability to identify and manipulate particular elements within a string. At this stage, the learner can form questions by moving the verb to the beginning of a string as in, 'Can you swim?'

Stage 5 Ability to shift elements around in an ordered way within strings, as in, 'Where are you going tonight?'

Stage 6 Ability to break down elements within strings into substrings, and to move elements out of substrings and attach them to other elements. At this stage, learners will be able to do things such as form double subject complements as in, 'He asked me to go'.

What are the implications of this research for teaching? There have been a number of different, even contradictory responses to the finding that some aspects of grammar are impervious to instruction (in other words, that instruction cannot change the order in which they are acquired). As we have already seen, one suggestion made as a result of the morpheme-order studies was that we should abandon all attempts to grade syllabuses grammatically and to teach grammar systematically. Rather, learners should be immersed in communicative activities in which the focus is firmly on meaning rather than form. An alternative suggestion is that syllabuses should still be grammatically sequenced but that the sequencing should follow the 'natural order'. These conflicting suggestions underline the fact that research is often neutral as to its implications for practice. Because of this, Johnston believes we need to test these ideas in the classroom to determine their effects on acquisition.

There are, in fact, a number of difficulties which emerge when one attempts to apply the results of research such as this. If one is to follow a natural order of instruction one must have classes consisting of learners who are all at the same developmental stage. It is also necessary for these learners to all progress at the same rate. While these conditions might obtain in some foreign-language contexts, they might cause problems in second-language contexts. Additionally, in second-language contexts, we need to consider the possibility that learners may need to learn some language items (such as question forms) as formulae to enable them to communicate at early stages of their second language development.

Another point which needs to be considered is the long term effect of instruction. It may well be that even though learners are incapable of reproducing a particular item at the time it is taught, systematic exposure over a period of time will speed up acquisition in the long run (this is certainly one of the implications we can derive from Long's 1983 study).

As a result of his work in second-language acquisition, Johnston makes a number of suggestions for classroom practice. Four of these are reproduced below. You might like to look at these and consider ways in which they might be tested in your own classroom.

1. Learners should not be forced to produce grammatical items that are beyond their current processing capacity. Grammatical items should be graded according to their complexity in terms of speech processing.
2. Learners have great difficulty in learning at one time sets of items that are closely related (e.g. pronoun paradigms).
3. Similarly, lexical opposites (e.g. tall/short) can be confusing for learners if they are introduced at the same time.
4. Learners tend to equate a single form with a single meaning. Words that have more than one function (e.g. 'there' which can function as either a demonstrative or 'dummy' subject – 'There is a book over there') should not be introduced at the same time.

3.3 Learner language: interaction

In this section we look at some of the discourse features of classroom interaction which have been investigated in first- and second-language classrooms, and which might provide suitable topics for investigation. The framework for this section comes from discourse and interaction analysis. It was only when researchers began to record and analyse interactions that they came to appreciate the complexities of the rules and regularities underlying interpersonal communication. An important implication of this research is that there is much more to learning a first or subsequent language than simply learning the grammar and vocabulary. In terms of oral communication, one needs to learn when it is appropriate to speak, what it is appropriate to speak about, to whom it is permissible to speak, in which circumstance, how to gain the right to speak, how and when to change the topic, how and when to invite someone else to speak and so on.

Some of the questions which are suggested by research into classroom discourse and interaction include the following:

1. To what extent is the language produced by my learners predetermined by me, the teacher? Does this vary from learner to learner, or according to the type of lesson being taught? Can types of language and interaction be expressed as percentages? Can they be varied? By what means, and to what effect?
2. What is the relationship between control and initiative in my classroom? What are the conditions, points in the lesson, task types, etc., which favour control, and vice versa? Can the patterns be modified? How? When? With what result?
3. What is the mix of topic/activity interaction types in my classroom? What characteristic interaction-type sequences are there in my classroom? What do they tell me about what is happening in my classroom?

Turn-taking

A great deal of theoretical and empirical research has been devoted to the identification and analysis of turn-taking, which is an essential part of managing interactions. The first problem we encounter, when studying turn-taking behaviour, is to decide what a turn is, and to identify when one turn has ended and another one has begun. This problem of identifying what, on the surface, are 'common garden' concepts is not so unusual. The problem of identifying instances of a concept with which we have varying degrees of familiarity is a common one. It underlines the fact that concepts such as 'interaction' and 'turn' (and even 'cat' and 'dog') are 'constructs'. That is, they have been 'invented' or 'constructed' by us to assist us make sense of the world and operate in it. Not so long ago grammarians had trouble dealing with concepts such as 'sentence' and 'word'. At present discourse analysts are having problems with concepts such as 'turn'.

During the course of an interaction, it may not be too difficult to identify an on-going turn by pinpointing the person currently speaking. However, when someone else interjects, we may have problems deciding whether or not to accept this as a new and separate turn. This and other problems arise when we try to fit 'turns' into hierarchical models of communication such as those devised by Sinclair and Coulthard (1975).

You might like to examine the following classroom extracts and consider where you think one turn begins and another ends. Extract A is taken from the beginning of a lesson in which the teacher is interacting with the whole class. Extract B has been taken from the middle of a small-group interaction in which several students are discussing the topic 'bad habits'. Is it, in fact, possible and/or useful to isolate different turns in extracts such as these?

Extract A

T The questions will be on different subjects, so, er, well, one will be about, er, well, some of the questions will be about politics, and some of them will be about, er ... what?
S History
T History. Yes, politics and history and, um, and ...?
S Grammar.
T Grammar's good, yes ... but the grammar questions were too easy.
S No.
S Yes, ha, like before.
S You can use ... [*inaudible*]
T Why?
The hardest grammar question I could think up – the hardest one, I wasn't even sure about the answer, and you got it.
S Yes.
T Really! I'm going to have to go to a professor and ask him to make questions for this class. Grammar questions that Azzam can't answer. [*laughter*]
Anyway, that's, um, Thursday ... yeah, Thursday. Ah, but today, er, we're going to do something different ...
S ... yes ...
T ... today, er, we're going to do something where we, er, listen to a conversation – er, in

fact, we're not going to listen to one conversation. How many conversations are we going to listen to?

S   Three?

Extract B

S1   My next door neighbour ... he make eh very noisy, very noisy [*yeah*]. I can't tell him because he's very good people.

S2   You can't say.

S1   He's very good neighbour.

S2   You can't say, because if you say, maybe will feel different.

S3   Yes, you don't like it ...

S1   I don't like.

S3   Independence ... Those people probably very protective.

S2   Yes, I think so.

S1   In my time, when I go to sleep ...

S2   ... go to bed [*yes*]

S1   These people is very good.

S2   ... you don't want to say anything because you might get upset, of course. Me do the same thing because I've got neighbours in my place and always you know do something I don't like it but I don't like to say bad because I thing maybe you know make him upset or ...

S4   I've got bad neighbour but I feel embarrass ...

S2   ... to say something of course, like everyone ...

S4   They always come in and see what I'm doing – who's coming. [*no good*] [*yeah, that's no good*] They want to check everything. If they see I buy something from the market they expect me to give them some. [*oh yeah*]. [*oh that's not nice*] But I ... it's difficult.

S2   It's a difficult, yeah, but sometime it's difficult ...

S4   They can't understand, I bought them and I gave money ... [*laughter*] [*yeah*]

S   You know sometime difficult to the people because sometime I can't speak the proper, the language, and little bit hard to give to understand ... and that's sometime feel embarrass then, I can't say it, you know?

S1   Sarah, you tell [*you tell now*]

S5   My ,er, for example, my sister in law she all the time snores in her sleep [*oh, yes*] And my brother say, 'Oh, I'm sorry, we must sleep separate' [*separate beds*] [*laughter*]. They did. [*good idea*] A good idea because she couldn't sleep.

You probably found that it is not always possible to state with certainty when one turn has ended and another has begun. In discourse there are overlaps, interjections, false starts, etc., all of which make it difficult to demarcate speaking turns.

Topic

Topic, like turn, is a fuzzy concept. While, in retrospect, we can examine classroom transcripts for the existence of topics, sub-topics, topic boundaries and so on, these are not brought along to an interaction ready-made for the participants to drop conveniently into the interaction at some appropriate moment. Rather, topic initiation, development and change are processes which are negotiated and jointly constructed by the participants in the course of an interaction.

Brown and Yule (1983) suggest that while an understanding of 'topic' seems to be essential to the discourse 'relevance' and 'coherence', formal attempts to pin the concept down are probably doomed to failure. While most of us have an intuitive feeling for the concept, it is, according to Brown and Yule, 'the most frequently used, unexplained, term in the analysis of discourse'.

Van Lier (1988) develops a useful topic/activity framework for analysing classroom interactions ('activity' here refers to the type of interaction – whether it is a casual conversation, a lecture, a joke, etc.). He suggests that at different times in a lesson different emphases on activity-orientation and topic-orientation will be evident. He postulates the existence of four interaction types as follows (van Lier 1988:155–6):

1. Less topic-orientation, less activity-orientation.
   Examples: small talk, general conversation over a cup of coffee, etc.
2. More topic-orientation, less activity-orientation.
   Examples: announcements, instructions, explanations, lectures.
3. More topic-orientation, more activity-orientation.
   Examples: elicitation (teacher–learner 'recitation'), interviews, reports, summaries, discussions, debates, jokes, stories.
4. Less topic-orientation, more activity-orientation.
   Examples: repetition and substitution drills, pair work, role taking, games.

The four following extracts exemplify the four interaction types (van Lier 1988:157–9):

Interaction type 1

1	T	okay ... right, you had a – singsong last night didn't you?
2	L1	yes
3	T	was it good?
4	LL	//yes//oh yes/
5	T	was it just – just the e:rm Teleac or were there other students
6	L	only the Teleac group
7	T	only the Teleac group
8	L1	e:h – ja
9	L1	and later in the evening eh the: hoe heten die ((unint)) ((tr: what are they called))
10	L	(Arabians)
11	L	Saudi Arabians

Interaction type 2

1	L7	and one bus . is going back at six o'clock?
2	T	yes . well we still need to find out this bec'z we need to find out how many people sign up for tickets and if there are: enough people *not* going to the theatre then one =
3	L	((unint))
	T	= bus or coach will come back here a bit earlier but it depends on the numbers ... really
4	L9	yes

Interaction type 3

1	T	any other ways?
2	L3	uh can you help me?
3	T	yes. good okay
4	L5	please can you help me?
5	T	can you help me uhuh ((write on board))
6	L4	may I ask you?
7	L5	dat heb ik net gezarg ((tr: I've just said that))
8	T	you've just said that yes

Interaction type 4

1	T	good. David have you got any questions for somebody . . . . . .
2	L8	Felix . . . Felix
3	L	why ((softly))
4	T	Felix
5	L8	why did you . . . why did you decide to come here
6	T	why did you decide to come here
7	L	oh
8	L	no?
9	L1	my parents eh: sent me here
10	T	okey

In terms of classroom research, the topic/activity framework provides a way of analysing the particular style of individual classroom teachers. Based on his extensive analysis of classroom transcripts, van Lier suggests that these patterns of interaction can be generalised across a range of lesson types, and seem to override such things as methodology. In other words, the four types are likely to occur in classrooms regardless of the methodological labels assigned to such classrooms. He also claims that Type 4 interactions (drills, pair work, role play, etc.) form the core of language lessons, which contrasts sharply with non-classroom discourse. Here is yet another example of how the language encountered by the learner in class differs from that encountered out of class (we have already seen that the types of questions addressed to learners differ in class and out of class). What we need to decide is whether or not this is a good or a bad thing. If we decide it is undesirable for learners to encounter in class types of language and patterns of interaction which differ from that encountered outside, we then have to decide what, if anything, we intend to do about it.

In this section, I have only been able to refer briefly to aspects of learner classroom interaction. If you are interested in following these ideas further, see Brown and Yule (1983) and van Lier (1988).

3.4 Learning tasks

One of the most interesting areas for classroom observation and investigation relates to the type of language which is stimulated by different types of learning tasks. This is also an area which has been investigated by a number of second-language acquisition researchers. The SLA research has been concerned with identifying those types of communicative tasks which seem to stimulate processes of second-language acquisition. The researchers have looked, in particular, at the amount of negotiation of meaning which is stimulated by tasks of different types. As yet, the research has not shown a direct relationship between input and output. In other words, it has not been demonstrated that tasks which prompt more negotiation of meaning actually result in superior learning over tasks which do not promote negotiation of meaning. The reasoning behind the research is as follows:

> **If** we acquire a second language by comprehending messages in that language, and **if** negotiating meaning makes language more comprehensible, then tasks which stimulate students to negotiate meaning **should** promote acquisition.

As we can see, there are two big ifs here and, like a lot of research, the relationship between learning processes and products is an inferred one.

Before going any further, I should clarify what is meant by 'negotiation of meaning' or, as it is sometimes called, modified interaction. In the research literature, it refers to those instances in an interaction in which the speaker and listener work together to determine that they are talking about the same thing: in other words, when the speaker carries out comprehension checks ('Know what I mean?') to determine whether he/she has been correctly understood, and when the listener requests clarification ('What do you mean, she's silly?') or confirms that he/she has correctly understood ('You stopped because you didn't learn anything?').

You might like to study the following classroom extract and see whether you can find examples of meaning negotiation, or conversational modification. Who does most of the negotiating, the teacher or the students?

T   Ahh, OK Anastasia, in Greece, did you have a bicycle when you were little? [*no, no*]
    When you were a little girl?
S   No, no.
T   No? What about you Hing?
S   Yeah, my son.
T   Your son has a bike? What about you? [*indicates to another student*]
S   Yes.
T   Yes? When you were a little girl. Mmm, same.
S   Yeah.
T   Yes. Bicycle?
S   Bicycle. [*inaudible*]
T   Many Australian children have bicycles.
S   Chinese, er, bicycle, er, different.
T   Oh.

S   Different. [*speaks in Chinese*]
T   I don't understand, Dai Cheng, I'm sorry.
S   Chinese bicycle is Australian bicycle er different.
T   Chinese bicycles are different from Australian bicycles?
S   Yeah.
T   But, er, two, two wheels?
S   Yes, two wheels.
T   Two wheels. And pedals?
S   Pedals. Pedals, yes.
T   And handles?
S   Handles different.

One recent study utilising the notion of negotiation of meaning is reported in Doughty and Pica (1986). In this study, the researchers set out to explore the effects of task type and participation pattern on language classroom interaction. The subjects for the study were adult students and teachers from intermediate ESL classes. The research hypothesis was that information-gap tasks in which participants had to exchange information for the successful completion of the task would generate more modified interaction than tasks in which the exchange of information was optional (as in one-way tasks in which one student has all the information and must convey this to the other student(s) in a group). It was also hypothesised that there would be more modified interaction when students worked in pairs than in small groups, which in turn would generate more modified interaction than when the task was carried out with a teacher and the whole class.

The required information-exchange task was carried out in three interactional patterns: teacher-fronted, small groups and pairs. In each of the interactional patterns, each participant (and in the teacher-fronted interaction this included the teacher) was provided with a felt board 'garden' and loose felt cut-out shapes which represented

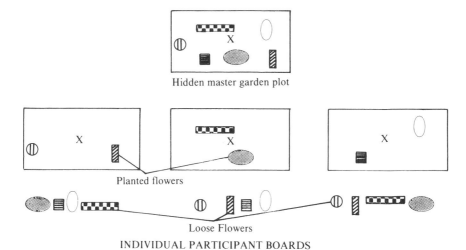

Hidden master garden plot

Planted flowers

Loose Flowers

INDIVIDUAL PARTICIPANT BOARDS

FIGURE 3.1 *Required information exchange task. (Note that this is a reduced version, using abstract figures to represent the flowers used in the task).*

flowers and which were to be arranged or 'planted' on the felt board. Each felt board contained some flowers which had already been planted, although no two boards were the same (see figure 3.1). No participant was allowed to see another's board.

The object of the exercise was to replicate the master plot, which was not shown to the participants until each had arranged their loose flowers in consultation with the other participant(s). As each participant possessed part of the solution (i.e., those parts of the master plot which had already been planted), it was necessary for all members of the group to contribute, and for participants to comprehend each other, if the solution was to be arrived at successfully.

As a result of the study, the researchers concluded that:
on the basis of our combined research, it appears that group work – and for that matter, pair work as well – is eminently capable of providing students with opportunities to produce the target language and to modify interaction. In keeping with second language acquisition theory, such modified interaction is claimed to make input comprehensible to learners and to lead ultimately to successful classroom second language acquisition . . . however, groupwork activities do not automatically result in the modification of interaction among the participants. To be effective, group interaction must be carefully planned by the classroom teacher to include a requirement for a two-way or multi-way exchange of information. Thus, the teacher's role is critical not only in providing students with access to grammatical input, but also in setting up the conditions for successful second language acquisition in the classroom.

3.5 Learning strategies

Another area of research receiving considerable attention is that of learning strategies. Familiarity with this work can greatly enhance our understanding of what goes on in classrooms. The thrust of much of this research has been to identify those strategies which characterise the 'good' language learner. Rubin and Thompson (1982) suggest that 'good' or efficient learners tend to exhibit the following characteristics as they go about learning a second language.

1. Good learners find their own way.
2. Good learners organise information about language.
3. Good learners are creative and experiment with language.
4. Good learners made their own opportunities, and find strategies for getting practice in using the language inside and outside the classroom.
5. Good learners learn to live with uncertainty and develop strategies for making sense of the target language without wanting to understand every word.
6. Good learners use mnemonics (rhymes, word associations, etc. to recall what has been learned).
7. Good learners make errors work.
8. Good learners use linguistic knowledge, including knowledge of their first language in mastering a second language.
9. Good learners let the context (extra-linguistic knowledge and knowledge of the world) help them in comprehension.

10. Good learners learn to make intelligent guesses.
11. Good learners learns chunks of language as wholes and formalised routines to help them perform 'beyond their competence'.
12. Good learners learn production techniques (e.g. techniques for keeping a conversation going).
13. Good learners learn different styles of speech and writing and learn to vary their language according to the formality of the situation.

Recently, I investigated forty-four 'good' language learners in order to find out whether there were any common patterns in their learning experiences. The learners had all learned English as a foreign language in a variety of Southeast Asian countries. They were all 'good' learners in that they had all attained bilingual competence in the language. During the investigation, they were asked to record what they found most helpful, and what they found least helpful in learning English as a foreign language. Here are some of their responses. While these were provided as free-form responses, I have classified them under several headings. As you read them, you might like to consider whether or not you find the responses surprising, given the fact that all of the respondents acquired their language in fairly traditional learning environments.

What did you find most helpful in learning another language?

1. *Form-focused activities*
   • Constant drilling.
   • When the teacher talked to the class clearly with correct pronunciation.
   • When I had my own textbook and made notes from teacher explanations.

2. *Applying skills to communicative-language use outside class*
   • Contact with native speakers.
   • The following helped me most: reading all kinds of printed materials; listening to native speakers through media – radio, TV, cinema; writing; studying grammar books; receiving instruction from my mother who was head of the English department in a public school.
   • In general: reading newspapers, magazines and books in English. Also, listening to the radio and TV.
   • When I had someone to practise with outside the classroom, at home to foreigners (native speakers).
   • I listened to songs and sang songs myself and watched TV, videos and movies; when I read interesting novels, and read other media such as newspapers, magazines, advertisements, booklets, all for pleasure; visiting English-speaking countries where I could communicate with native speakers.
   • Practising through conversations and using the media, especially TV with subtitles and newspapers. You must have someone who is proficient in the language to speak with in order to learn the language sufficiently well.
   • Social interactions (exposure and practice in the use of the language) at home and with friends.

- Language taught inside the classroom is not sufficient to make a person a competent speaker in the real world. Children still make mistakes as they follow the structure of their language or make inferences from known languages. In some cases students are good at talking or story telling but not good at written language work. I wonder whether the topics for conversations they make could be starting points for syllabus development and the development of other language skills?
- The language environment, the fact that my family knew and used English, and the radio and television programmes in English all helped.
- The most useful things I found were practice with other students and exposure to the community using the language (i.e., the target community).

3. *Communicative-language use in school*
   - There was a rule in our high school that the only language to be used was English.
   - Everyone spoke English during class and during outdoor activities (e.g., PE, gardening, etc.). I also read a lot of books from the library.
- Reading and proper modelling helped me much in learning another language. Furthermore, whenever rules were given, these were followed by illustrations and realia. To top it all, the exposure to media – both printed and visual, contributed a lot to my learning of the second language.
   - Guidance from the teacher and interactional practice with other students.
   - In general, these helped most; literature (storybooks/storytelling sessions at an early age and self-access reading later on); when it is used as the medium of instruction in all subjects (unconscious [*sic*] learning); media.

4. *Affective factors*
   - Motivation. I find that motivation is vital in the success of learning a foreign language. I learned Japanese in the university because I had a very close friend who was a Japanese. I was also fascinated with the Japanese culture and people in general. So I found it such a thrill to learn the language and to be able to communicate with my Japanese friend in his own tongue. Although most of our conversations were in English, those times when we spoke in Japanese were helpful. Motivation and the opportunity to use the language are the two most helpful elements in my learning experience.
   - In general, liking the language was most helpful.
   - Strong interest, sheer determination and motivation to learn a second language.
   - I think it's necessary to integrate all four skills in teaching a language. Our basic senses – sight, smell, sound, touch and taste – should be stimulated too when we learn a language. This will make the learning experience a very personal one and we will not feel somewhat detached from the language. Most of the time it's reading ink marks from the book or worksheet – it's too 'cognitive'. I feel it's more exciting to touch something or taste something or see something besides ink marks and learn the language simultaneously. In that way, we can relate to the language in a more natural and ultimate way and we might remember new words/expressions better.

5. *Factors relating to the teacher/teaching*
   - Resourceful teachers who provide interesting ideas and useful background and explanations to, for example, a literature text.

What did you find least helpful in learning another language?

1. *Form-focused activities*
   - Reading from textbooks.
   - Grammar lessons during class.
   - Enumerating rules of the language and memorising such rules didn't help – it only resulted in parroting.
   - Language notes from the teacher about grammar, lists of words, reading aloud, one by one around the class.
   - Memorising verb patterns, words and conversations.
   - Doing grammar exercises; boring and monotonous classwork/activities.

2. *Learning mode*
   - Learning by myself.

3. *Factors relating to the teacher/teaching*
   - I would say 'teacher's talk'. Looking back, I wish he had given me more opportunities to use the language in class, especially speaking it in and outside the classroom. It did help to have him explain everything to us, but it would have been more fun and meaningful had we been given the chance to use the language in more creative ways. Come to think of it, it would have been more fun and challenging if I was thrown into the deep end!
   - Negative criticism (oral) and punishment for wrong answers; dull teachers who do not encourage creativity or who are inactive/cannot be heard clearly.

The most striking thing about this study was the fact that despite the diverse contexts and environments in which the subjects learned English practically all agreed that formal classroom instruction by itself was insufficient. Motivation, a preparedness to take risks, and the determination to apply their developing language skills outside the classroom characterised most of the responses from these 'good' language learners. In terms of classroom learning, most subjects stressed the importance of communicative language tasks. Another significant factor to emerge was the importance of affective factors in the classroom.

Willing (1988) carried out a large-scale study into the learning styles of adult immigrant learners of English as a second language in Australia. In all, information was collected from 517 learners. The principal means of data collection was a questionnaire to which learners responded during an interview. Low-proficiency learners were interviewed in their first language. The questionnaire was as follows:

HOW DO YOU LIKE TO LEARN BEST?

1. In English class, I like to learn by reading.	no	a little	good	best
2. In class, I like to listen to and use cassettes.	no	a little	good	best
3. In class, I like to learn by games.	no	a little	good	best
4. In class, I like to learn by conversations.	no	a little	good	best
5. In class, I like to learn by pictures, films, video.	no	a little	good	best
6. I want to write everything in my notebook.	no	a little	good	best
7. I like to have my own textbook.	no	a little	good	best
8. I like the teacher to explain everything to us.	no	a little	good	best
9. I like the teacher to give us problems to work on.	no	a little	good	best
10. I like the teacher to help me talk about my interests.	no	a little	good	best
11. I like the teacher to tell me all my mistakes.	no	a little	good	best
12. I like the teacher to let me find my mistakes.	no	a little	good	best
13. I like to study English by myself (alone).	no	a little	good	best
14. I like to learn English by talking in pairs.	no	a little	good	best
15. I like to learn English in small groups.	no	a little	good	best
16. I like to learn English with the whole class.	no	a little	good	best
17. I like to go out with the class and practise English.	no	a little	good	best
18. I like to study grammar.	no	a little	good	best
19. I like to learn many new words.	no	a little	good	best
20. I like to practise the sounds and pronunciation.	no	a little	good	best
21. I like to learn English words by seeing them.	no	a little	good	best
22. I like to learn English words by hearing them.	no	a little	good	best
23. I like to learn English words by doing something.	no	a little	good	best
24. At home, I like to learn by reading newspapers, etc.	no	a little	good	best
25. At home I like to learn by watching TV in English.	no	a little	good	best
26. At home, I like to learn by using cassettes.	no	a little	good	best
27. At home I like to learn by studying English books.	no	a little	good	best
28. I like to learn by talking to friends in English.	no	a little	good	best
29. I like to learn by watching/listening to Australians.	no	a little	good	best
30. I like to learn by using English in shops/CES/trains ...	no	a little	good	best

One of the major aims of the investigation was to explore possible learning-style differences attributable to different learner biographical variables. It is widely accepted by teachers that such things as ethnicity, age, etc., will have an effect on preferred ways of learning. The variables investigated by Willing were:

Ethnic group
Age group
Level of previous education
Length of residence in Australia
Speaking proficiency level
Type of learning programme (e.g. whether in full-time or part-time courses).

The study came up with several surprising findings. In the first place, there were certain learning activities which were almost universally popular. In several instances, these were activities which did not enjoy similar popularity amongst teachers, error correction being a case in point.

> It appears that error-correction is considered by learners to be a very important aspect of the teacher's role. It may be that the current selective practice of indicating errors only when these are 'causing serious communication problems' needs to be re-examined. Learners seem to be indicating a strong desire for accuracy; and while current 'communicative' theory tends to downplay the importance of accuracy, the long-range learning effects of this should perhaps be considered. Much communicative methodological theory comes from the foreign-language teaching context, where it is crucially important to 'get them talking'. In an ESL context it may be advisable to reconsider the socio-cultural consequences of poor syntax and bad accent in addition to the communicative barriers which these create. Learners themselves seem to perceive the status implications of poor English, and correctly see that in the real world mistakes are a more serious matter than they often are in English class. In any case, learners' high rating of error correction, whether soundly based or not, constitutes in itself a reason for reconsidering the issue.

Perhaps the most surprising finding was that none of the biographical variables correlated significantly with any of the learning preferences.

> ... none of the learning differences as related to personal variables were of a magnitude to permit a blanket generalization about the learning preference of a particular biographical sub-group. Thus, any statement to the effect that 'Chinese are X' or 'South Americans prefer Y', or 'Younger learners like Z' or 'High-school graduates prefer Q', is certain to be inaccurate. The most important single finding of the study was that for any given learning issue, the typical spectrum of opinions on that issue were represented, in virtually the same ratios, within any biographical subgroup.

One final finding of note was that learners could be categorised by type according to the pattern of their responses on the questionnaire.

Type 1: 'Concrete' learners
These learners tend to like games, pictures, films, video, using cassettes, talking in pairs and practising English outside class.

Type 2: 'Analytical' learners
These learners like studying grammar, studying English books and reading newspapers, studying alone, finding their own mistakes and working on problems set by the teacher.

Type 3: 'Communicative' learners
These students like to learn by watching, listening to native speakers, talking to friends in English and watching television in English, using English out of class in shops, trains, etc., learning new words by hearing them, and learning by conversations.

Type 4: 'Authority-oriented' learners
These learners prefer the teacher to explain everything, like to have their own textbooks, to write everything in a notebook, to study grammar, learn by reading, and learn new words by seeing them.

3.6 Conclusion

In this chapter, we have looked at aspects of language learning which centre on the learners themselves. In particular, we have looked at developmental aspects of learner language, learner interaction in the classroom, communicative tasks and the language they promote, and learner strategies.

When it comes to observing and investigating one's own classroom, I have suggested that in the first instance you simply monitor your teaching over a period of time and let the issue or issues emerge from this initial observation. Naturally, your own beliefs, attitudes and ideology about language teaching and learning will colour your perceptions. However, as long as you are aware of these beliefs and attitudes, this will not be a problem. It is not crucial, as some teachers believe, that you have a burning issue which demands investigation. The main thing, as Kemmis and McTaggart (1981) suggest, is that you have a general feeling that existing practice might be improved.

If there is a gap between the intention or ideal (what we would like to happen in the classroom) and actual practice, the following questions can act as a point of departure in helping us formulate issues.

- What is actually happening in my classroom now? Are there any problems and, if so, is there anything I can do about it?
- What do my learners actually do in class? What are they learning? Is this what I intended them to learn? Is it worthwhile?
- Is there anything I am puzzled or irritated about in relation to my teaching or my pupils' learning?
- Are there any new ideas I would like to try out in my classroom?
- What do I actually do in class? Is there a difference between what I think I do and what I actually do? Is this a problem and, if so, is there anything I can or should do about it?
- What have I learned/what would I like to learn about myself as a teacher? How might I go about this?
- Is there a difference between the way I see myself as a teacher and the way others (e.g. colleagues, learners, superiors) see me? How might I find out about this?

For more detailed suggestions on getting started, see Kemmis and McTaggart (1982).

In the next two chapters, we shall take these ideas forward by looking at some of the data-collection methods we can employ in our research.

3.7 Questions and tasks

1. Which of the research suggestions made by Johnston might you investigate in your own classroom?
2. Can you think of any ways in which you might obtain information about where your learners are 'at', in terms of grammatical development?

3. Teach a language item or items which you think your learners are ready for. Now set up a communicative task in which you would expect the item(s) to occur. Record some of your learners as they carry out the task. Do they use the pre-taught item(s)?

4. Look again at the two classrooms extracts in the section on turn-taking. Identify the different turns and mark each turn off from its neighbours. What problems did you have? Were there any pieces of interaction where you were unable to decide when a particular turn had been completed? What differences are there between the two interactions in terms of how turn-taking and speaker-change are arranged?

5. Record and transcribe a piece of your own classroom interaction and analyse it according to van Lier's topic/activity framework.

6. Johnston's SAMPLE study utilised interviews rather than elicitation instruments in order to obtain 'naturalistic' samples of learner language. How representative do you think the resulting language was of the type of language learners might use in genuine communication outside the classroom? What language item(s) would you expect not to occur in teacher/student interviews?

7. Compare and contrast the characteristics of good learners from Rubin and Thompson with those revealed by the EFL speakers set out in section 3.4. What generalisations would you make about the 'good' learner as a result of the information presented in the section?

8. Administer Willing's survey to some of your learners. Are you surprised at the responses? Talk to your students about how they like learning and how they feel they learn best. Are there any major points of similarity or dissimilarity?

Chapter Four

Collecting Data

4.1 Introduction

This is the first of two chapters focusing on different methods which might be used in investigating classrooms. These chapters outline methods which are basically qualitative in nature (although, as we have seen, it is not always possible to draw a hard and fast distinction between interpretive–qualitative and experimental–quantitative methods). For those readers who are interested in quantitative research, Appendix C looks at the experimental method and provides an introduction to the use of statistics in research. While the methods presented in Chapters Four and Five will be of greater use in setting up investigations than the information in Appendix C, and while it is unlikely that you will want to set up formal experiments, the appendix will enable you to read and make sense of published studies which employ statistics.

This chapter and the next are complementary. In this chapter we look at a range of methods for collecting information inside and outside the classroom. In particular, we look at the use of diaries, journals, field notes, questionnaires, interviews, case studies and protocol analysis. In Chapter Five, we shall be concerned with classroom observation.

4.2 Diary studies

Journals, diaries and field notes are becoming increasingly popular as tools for gathering information about teaching and learning. While it may be possible to distinguish between them, I treat the three terms 'journal', 'diary' and 'field notes' interchangeably. Following Bailey (1989), I define a diary study as 'a first-person account of a language learning or teaching experience, documented through regular, candid entries in a personal journal and then analysed for recurring patterns or salient events'.

From the definition, you can see that diaries can be employed to monitor either the learning process or the teaching process or both. Diaries kept by learners about their learning experiences can provide information and insights into language learning which is unlikely to be obtained by other means. This can be seen in the following case study of a second-language learner.

Schmidt and Frota (1986) describe the development of conversational ability in

Portuguese by Schmidt (referred to in the study as R), a native speaker of English, during a five-month stay in Rio de Janeiro, Brazil. Data for the case study were a series of tape-recorded conversations between Schmidt and Frota, and a record of his subjective experiences made on a daily basis by Schmidt. In this illustrative study, we shall focus principally on the diary study.

R arrived in Brazil with virtually no ability in Portuguese, and, over a period of twenty weeks, attained roughly a pre-intermediate level of proficiency (i.e. he was able to cope with casual conversations on familiar topics). His experience as a language learner is divided into three unequal stages as follows:

Stage 1 (3 weeks)   No instruction and no interaction.
Stage 2 (5 weeks)   Both instruction and interaction.
Stage 3 (14 weeks)   Interaction but no instruction.

The following extracts illustrate the types of diary entry made by R.

Stage 1 (no interaction/no instruction)

> P [R's teenage son] and I have been alone almost all the time we've been here ... We've been spending a lot of time at the beach, which requires no language, and exploring the neighbourhood, which requires a little more. When we want to go somewhere, I ask at the hotel desk first, repeat whatever I was told to the cab driver, and read the meter to see how much it cost. Buying necessities and eating require a bit more. The night before we left Honolulu, X and Y gave me a dictionary and a phrase book [Figueirdo and Norman 1979], both pocket-sized, and I carry them everywhere. So when I went to a pharmacy the second day I could ask for a *pasta de dente* instead of just pointing at the toothpaste. When a clerk says how much something costs, I try to understand the price (so far I cannot) before handing over a bill I've already calculated to be more than enough ... My solution in restaurants: order something I don't know, and I'll know what it is the next time. I've been frustrated at breakfast, though, because the waitress always brings my coffee with milk, which I detest. She always asks first *cafe com leite*? and I've tried saying *leite nao*, meaning that I want it black, but it still comes with milk or not at all.

During the remainder of stage 1, virtually all of R's journal entries report non-comprehension of Portuguese and a strong sense of frustration at not being able to break into the language system.

Stage 2 (interaction plus instruction)

> P and I started class yesterday ... The teacher is young and very good. She introduced herself to us (in Portuguese): I am X, my name is X, I am your teacher, I am a teacher, I am a teacher of Portuguese ... She went around the class asking the same kinds of questions ... For the rest of the class we circulated, introducing ourselves to each other and talking until we exhausted the possibilities. At the end of the class, X put the paradigm for SER on the board, plus a few vocabulary items. Great! This is better than *bom dia* and then silence.

R was then moved to a new class and a different teacher.

> When I sat down a drill was in progress. SER again, which must be every teacher's lesson one. Teacher asks, student responds: *Voce e americana*? ['Are you an American?']: *Sou sim*

['I am, yes']. When it was my turn the question was *Voce e casando*? ['Are you married?'], so I said *nao*. L corrected me: *sou, sim*. I objected: *eu nao sou casando*. L said [in English], 'We are practising affirmative answers.' I objected again, I'm not married, and L said, 'These questions have nothing to do with real life.' My blood was boiling, but I shut up.

[two weeks later] L and I are still giving each other a hard time. Today in class, K's sentences in a substitution drill had a negative before the verb, followed by *nada*. I wanted to find out whether other double negatives are possible, so when it was my turn I said *eu nao conhecia ninguem* ['I don't know anyone']. This wasn't the sentence I was supposed to produce. I don't know whether L corrected me to *alguem* or not. I only remember her annoyance that I was not performing the drill as I was supposed to, so I didn't find out what I was after.

Stage 3 (interaction only)

H and I ate dinner at Caneco 70. He complained non-stop about his job. I tried to say 'you don't seem comfortable' with the job *sinto que voce nao esta comfortavel*, and his face showed complete non-comprehension. I grabbed my dictionary. 'Comfortable' is *comfortavel*, but it flashed through my mind that perhaps you can only say chairs are comfortable, not people. A few minutes later, H said something with *nao deve*. I was taught DEVER as 'have to' or 'must' and I've been thinking that *nao deve* + Verb would mean 'must not', but H's remark obviously meant 'should not'. So I learned something, but in general H is a terrible conversationalist for me. He doesn't understand things that I say that everyone else understands. When I don't understand him, all he can ever do is repeat.

Last night I met X, who's just come back from Argentina. Before we were introduced, I overheard M and U talking to X about me at the other end of the table. X: *ele fala portugues*? ['Does he speak Portuguese?']. U: *fala mal* ['He speaks poorly']. M said I make lots of mistakes, and mentioned *marida* and *pais*. X saw me looking at them and said: *mas voce entende tudo*? ['But you understand everything?']. I wanted to let them know I had been listening, so I replied: *entendo mal tembem* ['I also understand poorly'].

These short extracts demonstrate the fascinating insights into the struggle to learn a second language inside and outside of the classroom. R's diary is a rich source of data on language learning, and provides insights which it would be difficult to obtain in any other way. In particular, they underline the intensely personal nature of second-language learning − something which is not immediately apparent in other forms of data collection, and underline the psychological vulnerability of the learner. We also obtain insights into R's preferred learning strategies and can see the problems which arise for the learner when these conflict with the teacher's preferred teaching strategies. One can readily imagine that such frustrations might have caused a less persistent and committed learner to abandon classroom learning at an early stage.

While the Schmidt and Frota study shows some of the insights which can be revealed by learner diaries, a great deal about the teaching/learning process can also be revealed by teacher diaries, journals and field notes.

Hopkins (1985) makes the following observations on the keeping of field notes:

Keeping field notes is a way of reporting observations, reflections, and reactions to classroom problems. Ideally, they should be written as soon as possible after a lesson, but can be based on impressionistic jottings made during a lesson. The greater the time-lapse between the event and recording it, the more difficult it becomes to reconstruct problems and responses accurately and retain conscious awareness of one's original thinking. Many teachers I know keep a notebook open on their desk or keep a space in their day books for jotting down notes as the lesson and the day progresses. Keeping a record in this way is not very time consuming and provides surprisingly frank information that is built up over time. (Hopkins 1985:59)

As we have already seen, diaries and field notes can take several different forms. They can be kept either by learners or teachers, and can focus on a particular issue or problem such as the effect of particular question types on learner output, or be used more generally to create an impressionistic record of a particular classroom world. In the second instance, the teacher would keep an ethnographic account of the classroom, recording all significant events immediately after the class in which they occurred, rather than restricting the record to such things as question types or patterns of interaction. They can also be used, along with a range of other techniques, to provide data on a particular learner which can be incorporated into a case study (we shall look in greater detail at case studies later).

Hopkins suggests that diaries have the following advantages:

1. They are very simple to keep, and there is no outsider needed.
2. They provide a good on-going record which can provide good continuity.
3. The first-hand information they provide can be studied conveniently in the teacher's own time.
4. They act as *aides-mémoire*.
5. They help to relate incidents and can be used to explore emerging trends.
6. They are very useful if the teacher intends to write a case study.

Against these advantages are the following disadvantages:

1. There is often a need to fall back on aids such as question-analysis sheets, tapes and transcripts for specific information.
2. Conversation is impossible to record through field notes.
3. A notebook record can be kept of a small group, but not with the whole class (of course, this depends on what it is that the teacher wants to record).
4. They are initially time-consuming to keep.
5. They can be highly subjective.

Bailey and Ochsner (1983) outline a procedure for conducting a diary study which can be used to document either learning or teaching. The procedure is illustrated in Figure 4.1.

The crucial thing about diary studies is that the entries should be as honest as possible. Such honesty is something which needs to be learned by the novice diarist. I have included the five-stage outline from Bailey and Ochsner to illustrate the importance of creating in the first instance an uncensored record which can be censored at a later date for public consumption if this is felt desirable. In a recent comment on the procedure, Bailey (forthcoming) says that:

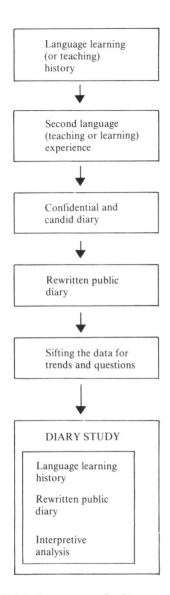

Language learning (or teaching) history	1 The diarist should provide an account of his personal language learning or teaching history.
Second language (teaching or learning) experience	2 The diarist should systematically record events, details, and feelings about the current language experience in the diary.
Confidential and candid diary	
Rewritten public diary	3 The diarist revises the journal for the public version of the diary. In the process, meaning is clarified.
Sifting the data for trends and questions	4 The diarist studies the journal entries, looking for patterns and significant events. (Also other researchers may analyse the diary entries.
DIARY STUDY Language learning history Rewritten public diary Interpretive analysis	5 The factors identified as being important to the language learning or teaching experience are interpreted and discussed in the final diary study. Ideas from the pedagogy literature may be added at this stage.

FIGURE 4.1 *Activities involved in a second-language diary study (Bailey and Ochsner 1983:190).*

In actual practice, events that are embarrassing or painful when they occur often lose their sting after weeks of reflection, and can be discussed openly and objectively in the analysis.

She also notes that not all steps are obligatory. A teacher may, for instance, decide to omit step 1 (although compiling a learning or teaching history can be illuminating, particularly for teachers in training, who may find that their teaching reflects the way they were taught, rather than the way they are being taught to teach).

Being analytical and critical, and committing to paper comments which we might feel reveal less than flattering aspects of our personality, is not particularly easy. Candlin (personal communication) also points out that being able to write metacommunicatively and metacognitively (i.e. writing about communicative and thinking processes) is also difficult, but that it is ultimately a rewarding skill to develop as it can greatly enhance one's professional self-development.

4.3 Interviews

Collecting information from learners (and teachers) through various forms of interview is a commonly used method in both ethnographic and quantitative research. Interviews can be relatively structured or unstructured. A structured interview is one which is orchestrated around a set of predetermined questions, whereas an unstructured interview is more like a free-flowing conversation between the interviewer and interviewee. Structured interviews can also be combined with other data-collection techniques such as formal questionnaires. Interviews can be used to investigate a range of issues including developmental aspects of learner language and learning-style preferences.

In the following study, Aslanian (1985) interviews students as a follow-up to a reading test. The purpose of the research was to study the relationship between responses on objective language tests (in this case, a fill-in-the-gap reading test) and learners' comprehension of the test passage as revealed by follow-up interviews. As we shall see, the procedure provides a great deal of valuable data which can be incorporated into subsequent classroom instruction.

Aslanian (1985) set out to study the reading comprehension of three high-intermediate level ESL students. Her point of departure was the belief that reading comprehension is too complicated a phenomenon to be measured only by the sorts of objective, standardised tests which are commonly used. In the study, she had her subjects complete a multiple-choice test and then she interviewed them about their responses.

The test passage and questions for the study were as follows:

Instructions
Read this passage and choose one of these words for the blanks. After you finish reading and filling out the spaces, I will ask you to give me reasons for your choices. Then you will tell me what you have understood from the passage. You can read the passage as many times as you wish to.

Bridges
Bridges are built to allow a continuous flow of highway and railway traffic across water lying in their paths. But engineers cannot forget the fact that river traffic, too, is essential to our economy. The role of (1) . . . . is important. To keep these vessels moving freely, bridges are built high enough, when possible, to let them pass underneath. Sometimes, however, channels must accommodate very tall ships. It may be uneconomical to build a tall enough bridge. The (2) . . . . would be too high. To save money, engineers build moveable bridges.

1. (a)   wind   (b) boats   (c) weight   (d) wires   (e) experience
2. (a)   levels   (b) cost   (c) standards   (d) waves   (e) deck

Analysis of the interview transcripts (or 'protocols', as they are called) revealed that students who provide the correct response on objective tests do not necessarily have a better understanding of the test passage than those who have provided incorrect answers. In fact, in one instance, the subject providing an incorrect response had a better grasp of the gist of the passage than one who got the answers correct.

Qualitative analysis of the interview transcripts also provides interesting insights into language learning and patterns of language use. Here is part of one of the transcripts. (O = observer; S = subject).

O   What about question (2)?
S   I picked levels. They are talking about ... it's talking about how to build tall enough bridges.
O   Could you read the sentence with your choice
S   'The levels will be too high. To save money, engineers ...' OK. The cost will be too high.
O   What made you change your mind?
S   OK. I changed my mind because to save money engineers build movable bridges. So we're talking about money. So it could be cost.
O   Why do you think levels was not the correct answer?
S   'Cause we are talking about the uneconomical, so it has to do with money.
O   Now, tell me everything you understood from this passage.
S   I think this passage is about the economy with traffic in ... you see, they're trying to build boats but feel boats are too expensive because of the economy, the traffic, I guess; they feel that because we have too many traffic, the boats are very important, you know. Because of the river traffic we need more boats.
O   What else?
S   It's saying that we need tall ships that could be economical. Like what's the use of having too many ships if you can just have a big tall ship and get everybody in their and no too many ships to take up traffic.

Aslanian comments:

Here we have a student who is very fluent in oral English, speaks pretty correctly and is quite verbose. To the listener she might sound like an advanced ESL student. Yet, when we read her replies to questions and her 'retell' of the passage, we conclude that her arguments are all mixed up and sometimes contradictory; moreover, they are frequently irrelevant. She talks and talks but does not seem to be making much sense. After some faltering, she picks out the correct words for the slots, but gets stuck in the rephrasing of the passage. She say things that are not even hinted at in the passage.

Aslanian claims that the technique of getting students to talk about why they gave the answers they did can be a powerful diagnostic tool:

The reason why ESL teachers often feel powerless to help their students is that, though they have the best intentions, they are not fully aware of their students' individual problems, which could range from limited literacy in the mother tongue to linguistic and sociolinguistic problems with the second language, and attitudes towards the new culture and to language learning in general. To solve problems ... the teacher should start, not with the text and vocabulary, but with the reader herself.

Finally, Aslanian suggests that the technique can be used as a useful communicative classroom activity. Students are placed in small groups of three or four and have to come to a consensus about the correct answers. One representative from each group then summarised the group discussion.

The interview technique used by Aslanian allows her to obtain insights into the reading competence of her students which were not revealed by either a formal test or unstructured observation. By using such a technique, it is possible for her to adopt a more individualised approach to diagnosing and remedying students' problems. In terms of teacher-research, it is a technique which could be used, along with other methods such as observation, to track the development of individual students, and to investigate central issues in second-language learning (for example, the relationship between reading strategies and learning outcomes).

4.4 Questionnaires and checklists

Questionnaires and checklists come in many shapes and forms, and can be utilised to investigate practically any aspect of the teaching or learning process. We saw in Chapter Three, for instance, the questionnaire used by Willing to investigate the learning preferences of adult learners of English as a second language. Figure 4.2 shows a questionnaire from Nunan (1985) which is used to collect information from learners which in turn is used as the basis for course design. Questionnaires and checklists can also be used to obtain information from teachers about their teaching practices. Figure 4.3 shows questionnaires which were used by Nunan (1988) in a large-scale investigation of the curriculum practices of classroom teachers. Forsyth and Woods (cited in Walker) analysed four types of questionnaire; their study is summarised in Table 4.1

Questionnaires and checklists can provide a great deal of information in an economical form. Data so provided are also amenable to various forms of quantification. For example, we can compare percentages and frequencies of responses from different learners much more readily from questionnaire data that from the sorts of free-form responses obtained in unstructured interviews. The problem with questionnaires is that, having developed our categories and questions before collecting the data, we may predetermine, to a large extent, what we actually find. Another problem (and one which is not restricted only to questionnaires) is that of trying to obtain information in the target language from low-proficiency learners. If one is working with such learners, it is advisable to have one's questionnaire translated, or obtain bilingual assistance during the data-collection phase.

4.5 Protocol analysis and stimulated recall

Protocol analysis and stimulated recall are designed to get teachers to reflect on their teaching in order to come to conclusions and make generalisations about the teaching and

SAMPLE NEEDS ANALYSIS FORM

This form was developed for use at the Pennington Migrant
Education Center, South Australia. Students complete the form
with assistance from bilingual information officers.

Date: _____ ASLPR _____

                                                    L S R W
Name: _____ Address: _____
Age: _____Country of Origin: _____
Family: M.S.W.D. No. of Children: _____ Ages: _____
Other relatives in Australia: _____
Elsewhere: _____
Education: No. of years: _____Qualifications: _____
             Why study finished: _____
             English study: _____
Employment: Main occupation: _____
             Other jobs held: _____
             In Australia: _____
             Type of work sought: _____
Interests: e.g. hobbies, sports, leisure activities: _____
             Skills: _____
First language: _____Others spoken: ___
                                             Others studied:
Language learning:
A. Do you like to learn English by READING
                                    WRITING
                                    LISTENING AND SPEAKING
                                    OTHER
    Which do you like the most? _____
B. Do you like to study grammar
                 learn new words
                 practise the sounds and pronunciation?
    Which do you like the most? _____
C. Do you like to learn English by:
                 _____ cassettes
                 _____ games
                 _____ talking to English speakers
                 _____ studying English books
                 _____ watching TV
Which is the most important (1–5) to you? _____
D. Macroskills
    1. Reading:
    (a) Can you use a dictionary?
        – a little _____ very well _____
    (b) What can you read in English
                      simple stories
                      newspapers
                      forms: bank
                             P. O.
                             C.E.S.
                      advertisements: shopping
                                      housing
                                      employment
                      bus timetables
                      maps/directories
                      school notes
    (c) What are the most important for you to learn
        now?

2. Writing:
   (d) do you ever write letters?
                   write notes to teachers?
                   fill in forms?
   (e) Which is the most important for you to learn
       now _____

3. Listening and speaking:

(f) Who do you speak with in English?	(g) How much do you understand?
	0 a little–a lot 100%
Shop assistants	
Neighbours and friends	
Bus drivers	
Medical people	
Teachers	
Employers	
Others	

   (h) Who is it most important for you to learn to
       speak with now? _____
   (i) Do you watch TV?
             listen to the radio?
   (j) How much do you understand?

E. How do you learn best?

	No	A little	Good	Best
alone				
pairs				
small group				
class				
outside class				

F. What do you feel are the most important things for you to
    learn in the short term? _____
                    long term? _____

G. How much time is available for study now?
        per day _____
        per week _____
    Where would you like to study:
        I.L.C. _____
        Home _____

H. Agreement:
    Length——/——/—— to ——/——/——
    How often do you want supervision?

I. Date of first supervision ——/——/——
    Comments (may include impressions of interviewer/interpreter):

J. Interviewer: _____
    Interpreter: _____
    Date: _____

FIGURE 4.2 *Collecting information from learners (Nunan 1985).*

SURVEY QUESTIONNAIRE: ON 'TRADITIONAL' AND 'COMMUNICATIVE' ACTIVITIES

Instructions:

Please rate each of the statements according to the following key:

1. Virtual non-use. This principle or activity forms little or no part of my teaching methodology.
2. Trivial incidental use. This principle or activity forms a limited part of what I do, but I tend to reject its use more than I favour its use. Somewhat disagree with use.
3. Neutral.
4. Important supplementary use. This principle forms an important supplementary part of my teaching. Somewhat agree with use.
5. Essential use. This is essential to what I do, and it forms an essential part of my practice. Use or agree with use.

1. Drills involving manipulation of formal aspects of the language system are used. ....

2. The development of fluency is more important than formal accuracy. ....

3. Activities focus on whole-task rather than part-skill practice. ....

4. Comprehension activities precede activities requiring production ....

5. 'Grammar' is explicitly taught. ....

6. Learner errors are corrected. ....

7. Activities are selected because they are interesting/enjoyable rather than because they relate to course objectives. ....

8. Activities are derived in consultation with the learner. ....

9. Activities are developed which require the learner to simulate, in class, behaviours needed to communicate outside class. ....

Comments

....

SURVEY QUESTIONNAIRE ON CAUSES OF LEARNER FAILURE

Below are listed some possible causes of learner failure. Which of these, in your opinion, are significant factors in the failure of learners to achieve course objectives? Circle the appropriate numbers.

1   Inefficient learning strategies
2   Failure to use the language out of class
3   Irregular attendance
4   Particular macroskill problems
5   Inappropriate learning activities
6   Inappropriate objectives
7   Faulty teaching
8   Poor attention in class
9   Personal (non-language) problems
10 Learner attitude

RESPONSIBILITY FOR CURRICULUM TASKS SURVEY FORM

Indicate by giving a rating from 1 to 6 (1 = most important) who, in
your opinion, should be primarily responsible for carrying out the
following curriculum tasks. Give a rating from 1 to 6 for each curriculum
task.

Key:
A   Counsellor   D   Teacher-in-charge of centre or program
B   Bilingual resource person   E   Classroom teacher
C   Curriculum advisor   F   Outside curriculum specialist

Curriculum processes	*A*	*B*	*C*	*D*	*E*	*F*
Initial needs analysis						
Goal and objective setting						
Selecting/Grading content						
Ongoing needs analysis						
Devising learning activities						
Instructing learners						
Monitoring/Assessing progress						
Course evaluation						

SURVEY QUESTIONNAIRE ON CONTENT SELECTION

Which of the following learner groups have you never *worked with
before? (Circle the appropriate number.)*

A   Zero proficiency learners who are illiterate in their own language.
B   Advanced students who want a pre-tertiary course.
C   Learners who are studying in the English-in-the-Workplace
    program.
D   Fast track On-Arrival students.
E   Mixed level students in the Community Program.

*Imagine you have been assigned one of the groups you have circled.
How would you go about determining course content? Select three of the following options.*

1   Devising learning activities and tasks
2   Drawing on knowledge of language and language learning
3   Consulting other teachers with relevant experience
4   Selecting a coursebook
5   Determining post-course communication needs
6   Analysing other relevant language courses
7   Selecting appropriate materials
8   Consulting and negotiating with learners on course content

FIGURE 4.3   *Assessing curriculum practices of classroom teachers (Nunan 1988).*

learning which goes on in their classrooms. This line of research is predicated on the
assumption that what teachers do in class, the judgments and decisions they make, is
affected by their beliefs and attitudes about the nature of language and language learning.
Once again, this technique has tremendous potential for providing insights into the life of
language classrooms.

TABLE 4.1 *Questionnaire analysis (after Forsyth and Woods)*

Type	Administration and equipment	Advantages	Disadvantages	Notes
I	Outsider/teacher Question sheet	1. Easy to administer 2. Quick to fill in 3. Relevance of questions 4. Easy to follow up 5. Provides direct comparison of groups and individuals	1. Time-consuming analysis 2. Extensive preparation to get clear and relevant questions 3. Outsider must have clear object 4. Difficult to get questions that explore in depth 5. Who is suitable outsider? 6. Suitable outsiders are difficult to obtain	Relevant to groups rather than to individuals – one questionnaire about one teacher irrelevant. Adv. – tells teachers about other teachers/pupils
II	Teacher/child Question sheet	1. Feedback to teacher re.: (a) attitudes (b) resource adequacy (c) assess. of adequacy of teacher help (d) preparation for next session 2. Quick to fill in 3. As teacher is involved he is better able to effect and analyse questions 4. Data are quantifiable	1. As method above 2. Effectiveness depends on reading ability of child 3. Child may fear answering candidly 4. Child will try to produce 'right' answers	Anonymity encourages candour, but individual problems cannot be followed up
III	Outsider/child Question sheet	1. As method II above 2. Outsider is more likely to be unbiased	1. As method II above 2. Difficult for outsider to do any detailed follow-up work 3. Children can be put off by strangers 4. Availability of suitable outsiders	Outsider should consult teacher regarding contents of questionnaire

Name: _____   Week of: _____

Class (language): _____   Level _____   Period: _____

This is an inventory that asks you to identify how many times you used a given teaching practice in a particular class in a given week. Please use this key in responding to the following statements relating to different aspects of grammar presentations.

> 0 = Never   This is something I did not do in this particular class this week.
> 1 = Infrequently   This is something that I did once this week in the class.
> 2 = Sometimes   This is something I did two or three times a week in this class.
> 3 = Regularly   This is something that I did four or five times this week in this class.

In presenting a grammar teaching point for the first time I:

_____ 1.   Presented the teaching point both orally and with visual aids.
_____ 2.   Used pictures and diagrams to convey the meaning of the teaching point.
_____ 3.   Presented the teaching point indirectly in the context of spoken language, but did not formally teach it.
_____ 4.   Presented the teaching point indirectly in the context of written language, but did not formally teach it.
_____ 5.   Presented the teaching point indirectly in the context of spoken language and pointed it out to the students.
_____ 6.   Presented the teaching point indirectly in the context of written language and pointed it out to the students.
_____ 7.   Presented the teaching point using only the target language.
_____ 8.   Reviewed with the students relevant, previously presented grammatical structures.
_____ 9.   Gave the students several examples of the teaching point, and guided them in discovering the grammatical rule.
_____ 10. Gave the students several examples of the teaching point, before supplying them with the grammatical rule.
_____ 11. Translated examples of the teaching point to be certain that the students understood.
_____ 12. Assisted the students in participating in a target-language conversation, then drew the teaching point from the language that the students themselves had generated.
_____ 13. Spoke only in the target language, but modified the structure, vocabulary and speed so that the students could understand easily.
_____ 14. Did not focus on grammar in the teaching of the language.
_____ 15. Based new teaching points on previously presented grammatical structures.
_____ 16. Gave only one example of the teaching point and did it orally.
_____ 17. Embedded the teaching point in a command designed to elicit a non-verbal response from the students.
_____ 18. Relied on gestures and mime to convey the meaning of the teaching point.
_____ 19. Drew the teaching point from dialogues that the students had memorised.
_____ 20. Explained the teaching point in English.
_____ 21. Conducted oral drills on the teaching point before presenting it formally.
_____ 22. Wrote the grammatical rule on the board/overhead before beginning to explain it.
_____ 23. Gave the students the general grammatical rule, then wrote examples of the rule on the board/overhead.
_____ 24. Allowed students to look at the explanation in their textbook while I was presenting the teaching point.
_____ 25. Had the students read a grammar explanation in their texts before I presented it in class.

FIGURE 4.4 *Monitoring and evaluating the teaching of grammar in the classroom (Koziol and Call 1988).*

The methods which are subsumed under this heading can vary from the straightforward to the elaborate. The use of self-report inventories is one of the more straightforward techniques. These have been developed for use in language-teacher education and research by Koziol and Call (1988), who have created inventories for a wide range of teacher behaviours. The inventory illustrated in Figure 4.4 was developed for teachers to monitor and evaluate the teaching of grammar in the classroom. One interesting feature of the inventory is the attempt to quantify precisely what is meant by terms such as 'infrequently' and 'regularly'.

Another technique, and one which we looked at in Chapter Two, is to provide colleagues with a set of learner data and ask them to exercise their professional judgment in making pedagogical decisions about the learners. We can record their responses and then analyse these to obtain insights into those learner factors which teachers feel are most likely to facilitate or impede learning. We may find, for example, that certain teachers group learners on the basis of years of formal education, believing this to be an important factor in the rate at which learners will acquire the target language. Other teachers may prefer to group learners on the basis of their communicative goals, believing that it will be easier to select content for the groups so formed.

In stimulated recall, teachers listen to an audiotape or view a videotape of their teaching and describe what they are doing and why. This can be set out as a running commentary parallel to a transcript of the lesson (an example of the stimulated recall technique is provided in the next chapter).

In order to collect data systematically, checklists and observation schedules of various kinds are extremely useful. We shall look at observation schedules in Chapter Five, and any of the samples provided there can also be used for the analysis of videotaped (and, to a lesser extent audiotaped) lessons.

Yet another technique involves teachers in sorting statements about teaching into different categories. This technique allows the researcher to compare teachers' belief systems with their actual practice. The following illustrative study on the effect of teachers' implicit theories about reading on teaching practice is from an unpublished study by Duffy as reported in Clark and Yinger (1979). The study illustrates how classroom observation can be combined with out-of-class data-collection techniques to research particular issues.

[Duffy and his colleagues] had approximately 350 teachers engage in an exercise of sorting propositions about reading. The teachers were asked to sort thirty-six propositions about reading and reading instruction into five categories ranging from 'most like me' to 'least like me'. These propositions, drawn from an analysis of the literature on reading, were identified with five major conceptions of instruction in reading: basal text, linear skills, natural language, interest and integrated whole. An additional category (confused–frustrated) was added, and six propositions consistent with each of these conceptions of reading were generated.

From among the 350 teachers who completed the exercise, thirty-seven who manifested clear and strongly held beliefs about reading were asked to take a variation of Kelly's Role Concept Repertory Test (REP Test) in order to refine and specify more clearly their conceptions of reading.

In the second phase of this study, eight teachers who evidenced strong belief patterns on the sorting of propositions and on the REP Test were observed teaching on ten different occasions. Ethnographic field notes and post-observation interviews were used to determine the extent to which the teachers' instructional behaviour reflected their conceptions of reading. The investigators found that only four teachers consistently employed practices which directly reflected their beliefs; these included two teachers who had structured beliefs (basal-linear skills), a teacher who had an eclectic view, and one of the teachers having an unstructured belief system (natural language-interest-integrated whole). Of those whose practices did not reflect their beliefs, two of the teachers having strong unstructured belief systems were found to be smuggling elements of unstructured practices into an administratively imposed program reflecting a structured view. Two other teachers holding unstructured views, however, did not consistently reflect their beliefs; one of the teachers employed practices which, to a large degree, were counter to the unstructured belief system she espoused, while a second teacher operationalized unstructured beliefs only some of the time with some pupils and some activities.

This study shares certain features with the one carried out by Swaffar *et al.* (1982) into the relative efficacy of different language-teaching methodologies. Both studies demonstrate the importance of collecting information from a variety of sources. In this instance, as in the Swaffar study, we find a discrepancy between what teachers believed they were doing and what they were actually doing in the classroom. In particular, we see how important it is to collect data directly from the classroom itself. Techniques for collecting such data are presented in Chapter Five.

In their major survey of research on teachers, Shavelson and Stern provide the following comments on methods of obtaining information on teachers' decision-making processes:

> In a process-tracing study, typically, subjects are asked to 'think aloud' while performing a task, solving a problem or reaching a decision. For example, Peterson, Marx and Clark (1978) asked teachers to think aloud while they planned a social studies lesson. The resultant verbal protocol becomes the data to be analysed. The analysis may take the form of a traditional content analysis where the researcher counts the number of times a teacher refers to behavioural objectives while planning a lesson. Or it might take the form of a flow chart modeling the teacher's thought processes ... Stimulated recall is typically used when the process-tracing technique would interfere with the subject's performance on a task. For example, asking a teacher to 'think aloud' while conducting a lesson usually is not feasible. So, the researcher usually either audio- or videotapes the lesson. After the lesson (or after school, depending on scheduling), the tape is played back to the teacher by the researcher and the teacher is assisted in recalling the covert mental activities that accompanied the overt behaviour (Shalvelson and Stern 1981:458).

4.6 Case studies

A case study is an account of a single instance of whatever it is we are investigating. We can thus have case studies of a single teacher, a single learner or a single school. Case studies can utilise any or all of the methods already discussed as well as those relating to direct classroom observation which will be discussed in the next chapter. The investigation by Schmidt and Frota cited earlier is a case study of a single learner which utilises a range of methods, although we only looked at the data provided by the diary.

There is controversy over the status of data yielded by case studies. Researchers who take a quantitative approach to research question the extent to which we can generalise from a single instance. In the case of Schmidt and Frota, for example, they would probably question the conclusion reached that learners must notice the gap between their current competence and the target form of a particular structure (see Section 4.8) for that structure to become a candidate for acquisition. This is because they are essentially concerned with 'samples' rather than particular instances (the logic behind this reasoning is outlined in Appendix C).

The notion of identifying a particular learner and studying that learner in detail, rather than attempting the huge task of studying all learners in a given class or group, has been put forward at different times. In 1980, Allwright published an important paper in which he argued strongly for the adoption of a case-study approach to the investigation of learners in the classroom.

> Learners are interesting, at least as interesting as teachers, because they are the people who do whatever learning gets done, whether it is because of or in spite of the teacher ... since it is learners who do the learning, we should take a close look at what the learners actually do. Curiously, the case-study approach, so central to the methodological baggage of first and second language acquisition researchers, has not, typically, been thought sensible for learners in class. (Allwright 1980).

He goes on to outline a procedure for studying a single learner's participation in classroom interaction and management of learning. In macro-analytical terms, we can look at *samples* or instances of the target language – *guidance* – that is, instances of communication concerning the nature of the target language, and *management activities* 'aimed at ensuring the profitable occurrence of samples and guidance'. In relation to these three elements, we can look at their relative proportion in a given lesson, their distribution between teachers and learners and between learners and learners, their sequencing and the actual language used.

At the level of mocro-analysis, we can look at particular aspects of classroom interaction. (We looked at a range of these in Chapter Three.) Allwright illustrates the value of conducting case studies of particular aspects of classroom interaction with a study of 'Igor', a low-level ESL learner at the University of California, Los Angeles.

In his study, Allwright focuses on turn-taking. Data were collected by audiotaping two parallel ESL classes for two hours a week over a period of ten weeks. These were then analysed for the turn-taking patterns according to the following analytical categories:

1	Turn-getting	
1	Accept	Respond to a personal solicit.
2	Steal	Respond to a personal solicit made to another.
3	Take	Respond to a general solicit.
4	Take	Take an unsolicited turn, when a turn is available.
5	Make	Make an unsolicited turn, during the current speaker's turn without intent to gain the floor.

6	Make	Start a turn, during that of the current speaker, with intent to gain the floor.
7	Make	Take a wholly private turn at any point in the discourse.
0	Miss	Fail to respond to a personal solicit, within whatever time is allowed by the interlocutor.
2	Turn Giving	
–		Fade out and/or give way to an interruption.
0		Make a turn available without making either a personal or general solicit.
P		Make a personal solicit.
G		Make a general solicit.

Table 4.2 summarises turn-getting by the teacher and students over the course of an hour.

TABLE 4.2

Turn-getting category						Participant							
	T	S1	S2	S3	S4	S5	S6	S7	S8	S9	S10	S?	Total
1	18	3	18	8	5	4	7	2	1	3	5	1	75
2	1	—	3	3	—	—	—	—	—	1	—	2	10
3	—	—	6	4	2	2	1	—	—	5	1	38	59
4	160	—	14	6	—	3	—	2	1	6	1	36	229
5	7	1	1	3	1	—	2	—	—	1	—	7	23
6	12	—	1	—	—	—	—	—	—	—	—	—	13
7	—	—	—	1	—	—	—	—	—	—	—	1	2
0	—	—	1	—	—	—	—	—	—	—	—	—	1
?	6	—	3	—	—	1	—	—	—	—	2	62	74
Total	204	4	47	25	8	10	10	4	2	16	9	147	486

What do data such as these tell us about the turn-taking in general and about any given learner in particular? Allwright makes the following observations:

> In terms of the categories of analysis, the most striking finding is the preponderance of 4s – discourse maintenance in the absence of a solicit. As one might expect, the great majority of 4s are attributed to the teacher, who has a vastly disproportionate number of turns overall compared with the other participants. The teacher also does most of the interrupting, and is even among those guilty of turn-stealing. Of course, one of the reasons the teacher's figures are so high is the fact that her voice, as a native speaker, was distinctive, and we have probably identified all but a very few of her contributions. The voice of S2 (a student from the USSR, whom we shall call Igor) was not so distinctive, and yet he also has a wholly disproportionate share of the identified turns. This is the starting point for the case-study approach, where one learner stands out as of particular interest. S1 did have a quite

TABLE 4.3

Turn-giving category		Participant											
	T	S1	S2	S3	S4	S5	S6	S7	S8	S9	S10	S?	Totals
—	5	—	5	2	1	1	—	—	1	3	—	7	25
O	80	4	34	19	7	7	9	4	1	10	8	71	254
P	76	—	8	3	—	1	1	—	—	3	1	2	95
G	75	—	—	—	—	—	—	—	—	—	—	—	75
?	3	—	—	1	—	1	—	—	—	—	—	67	72
Totals	239	4	47	25	8	10	10	4	2	16	9	147	521

distinctive voice, and we are confident that the turns attributed to her represent fairly the full extent of her participation. She is of interest, also, although the sparseness of her data will make the interpretation problematic.

When we look at data on turn giving, some additional interesting points emerge (see Table 4.3).

From Table 4.3, we see that:

> Igor seems to follow the general pattern for learners, by disposing of most of his turns without making a solicit of any kind. We can also see that the teacher's turn-giving differs radically from that of the learners in that, as one might expect, it includes a great many solicits addressed to the whole class, almost as many as are addressed to individual students, instead of an overwhelming preponderance of unmarked turn giving.

The turn-taking analyses enable the researcher to explore a range of preliminary hypotheses about Igor's interactive behaviour. For example:

1. The teacher called on him most (Category 1)
   The evidence is certainly consistent with this hypothesis, given that Igor is recorded as having been asked by the teacher to contribute no fewer than eighteen times, as often as the teacher, in fact, and twice as often as any other learner, and only one other learner is recorded as getting more than eighteen turns in any way.
2. He stole most turns (Category 2)
   The evidence is not so convincing, given that stealing was rare, and that Igor's three 'steals' (the largest number for any individual, including the teacher) is equalled by S3.

Allwright's study illustrates just one approach to case study. It is of interest because Allwright combines quantitative and qualitative data. A comprehensive study of Igor would include data from a variety of sources including some or all of the following:

1. A teacher's journal in which running comments were kept by the teacher.

2. A learner's diary kept by Igor.
3. Interview transcripts or summaries.
4. Questionnaire data (for example, a version of the Willing questionnaire on learning preferences (Chapter Three) could be administered to Igor two or three times during the course of his studies, and correlated against classroom events.

4.7 Conclusion

In this chapter, we have looked at some of the techniques which might be employed in investigating language learning and teaching. In particular, we have looked at the use of interviews, questionnaires, diaries, journals and field notes, protocol analysis and stimulated recall. We also looked at the case study, which may utilise a range of methods.

In the next chapter, we shall turn our attention to the classroom itself, and look at some of the tools and techniques which can help us in carrying out classroom observations.

4.8 Questions and tasks

1. What sort of generalisations about language learning do you think diaries such as Schmidt and Frota's permit? What generalisations would you make about R as a language learner?
2. Schmidt and Frota came to the following conclusion (among others):

   Krashen proposes that (1) new forms may be presented to the language learner in two ways, via input that is understood or through the creative construction process. Either of these two processes can present the acquirer with an $i + 1$, a potential new rule. (2) for acquisition to occur, acquirers need to notice a difference between their current form or competence i and the new form or structure $i + 1$. (3) If the comparison of i and $i + 1$ shows a gap, the $i + 1$ form becomes a candidate for acquisition. If it turns up in input with some minimum frequency, it can be confirmed and acquired. If it does not turn up, it is a transitional form and will eventually be discarded.

   ... it seems to us that the process of comparative operations and the principle that learners must 'notice the gap' are extremely important and potentially useful additions to the theory of second language acquisition that Krashen has been developing for more than ten years. However, we propose to make a significant modification of the principle, with which Krashen would surely not agree.

   While Krashen proposes that both the product and the process of acquisition are subconscious, and specifically that differences between competing forms i and $i + 1$ are noticed at a subconscious level (Krashen 1983:140), we propose instead that in the particular case of a nontargetlike form i and a targetlike form $i + 1$ a second language learner will begin to acquire the targetlike form if and only if it is present in comprehended input and 'noticed' in the normal sense of the word, that is, consciously (Schmidt and Frota 1985:311).

   How might you set up a diary study to test this hypothesis?
3. Use the Koziol and Call self-report grammar inventory, or an adaptation of it in several of your classes over a week or two. What did you discover about your teaching? What similarities or differences were there from one class to another?

4. Develop and trial a similar self-report inventory for another aspect of your teaching such as error correction, instruction giving or classroom management.

5. In addition to the two hypotheses about Igor's behaviour in Allwright's study, the following hypotheses are also suggested. From an inspection of the tables in the study, what observations or comments would you make?

Hypotheses:

He responded most frequently to general solicits (category 3).
He did most discourse maintenance (category 4)
He made the most 'concurrent' comments (category 5)
He interrupted most (category 6)
He spoke most to himself (category 7)
He missed turns least often (category 0)
He made most solicits (categories P and G)

Chapter Five

Classroom Observation

5.1 Introduction

There is no substitute for direct observation as a way of finding out about language classrooms. Certainly, if we want to enrich our understanding of language learning and teaching, we need to spend time looking in classrooms. Given the fact that classrooms are specifically constituted for the purposes of bringing about learning, it would be surprising if this were not the case. The classroom is 'where the action is', and we shall now look at ways of recording and investigating that action.

A great deal has been said and written about classroom observation and, in this chapter, we shall only be able to touch on selected aspects of an intensely interesting area of investigation which has generated a range of methods and techniques.

5.2 Basic orientations

It is important to realise from the outset that our preconceptions about what goes on in the classroom will determine what we see. It is extremely difficult (some would say impossible) to go into a classroom and simply observe what is there in an objective way without bringing to the observation prior attitudes and beliefs. Even people who have never taught have beliefs about what a classroom is and what constitutes legitimate classroom activity.

Different players in the classroom drama will also have different views and interpretations of a given lesson or piece of interaction. Malamah-Thomas gives the following fictional account of the way a classroom interaction can develop into conflict when the expectations and agendas of the participants differ, particularly when there are different ideologies on what is legitimate classroom activity (Malamah-Thomas 1987:8–10).

> Here is a lesson plan aimed at bringing about a co-operative atmosphere in a classroom. The teacher is a young man, with several years' experience of teaching in his own country, who has just secured a job overseas. He is taking his first class, an evening class of about sixteen adults, who all did some English at school, but who now want to improve their reading skills in English for both career and leisure purposes. The new teacher is keen to establish a strong feeling of group solidarity in the class and good student–teacher relationships.

Lesson plan
1. *Relaxation*: eyes closed for three minutes.
2. *How much do we know about each other?*
   The label game: each student has six sticky labels and writes a different adjective on each, for example *clever, clumsy, witty, nice, ambitious*, etc. Students then circulate, sticking their adjectives on to the jackets of classmates they most appropriately fit . . .

Now look at the interaction which might arise from the execution of this lesson plan:

Teacher	*Class*
1. Let's see how they take to relaxing . . .	What is this man doing? We're here to learn English, not to relax. I don't understand. Is this some new method?
Mmm. They don't seem too happy. Perhaps I'd better explain more full the importance of relaxing for a friendly atmosphere . . .	We were all quite relaxed before. I don't know why he's wasting time like this!
2. OK. I'd better get on with the Label game, and let them see the point of my approach . . .	Aha! A vocabulary exercise, good. We write adjectives . . . but why on labels? We'll soon see . . .
They seem happy, but they think this is just a language exercise. I'll explain what they are to do with the labels . . .	My goodness. He can't be serious. *Clever, witty* . . . all right. But who shall I stick *bad-tempered* or *nasty* on to? And what shall I do if anyone puts a bad adjective on me?
They don't like it. They're afraid. But they have to be honest with each other if we are to get a good class atmosphere going . . .	He can't force us to play this ridiculous game. But perhaps a few adjectives will humour him . . .
That's better. They're playing the game. If I encourage them, they might get into the spirit of things and use the bad adjectives too . . .	This is ridiculous! We are here to learn English, not insult each other. This young man needs a lesson . . . oh look, Frau Schmidt is going up to him with a label.
Good. Frau Schmidt is coming to me with a label. What is it? *Stupid*. She's stuck *stupid* on me.	*Stupid*! Good for her. Serves him right. She's told him what she thinks of him.
My God. Is she being rude? A fine way to welcome a new teacher. What a cheek!	Oh dear. He's gone red. Maybe she shouldn't have done that. But he did ask for it, making us do such stupid things.

The tools and techniques which we use to help us document classroom interactions will also strongly influence, if not determine, what we see. They provide the same sort of mental blinkers as our own preconceptions. Consider, for example, the tally sheet of a piece of interaction, illustrated in Figure 5.1.

By inspecting the tallies made on observation charts such as this, we can make certain inferences about what was going on in the class in which the observation was made. We can infer, for instance, that it took place near the beginning rather than the end of the lesson, judging by the number of instructions and directions which are given, and the fact that students ask referential questions (something which, as we saw in Chapter Three, they rarely do during the lesson).

The advantage of using a tally sheet such as this is that the observations can be made

	Tallies	Total
1. Teacher asks a display question (i.e. a question to which she knows the answer)	///	3
2. Teacher asks a referential question (i.e. a question to which she does not know the answer)	////	4
3. Teacher explains a grammatical point		0
4. Teacher explains meaning of a vocabularly item		0
5. Teacher explains functional point		0
6. Teacher explains point relating to the content (theme/topic) of the lesson	/	1
7. Teacher gives instructions/directions	⤙⤙⤙ /	6
8. Teacher praises	/	1
9. Teacher criticises		0
10. Learner asks a question	///	3
11. Learner answers question	////	4
12. Learner talks to another learner		0
13. Period of silence or confusion		0

FIGURE 5.1 *Tally sheet for analysing classroom interaction.*

by someone with appropriate training in real time. There is no need to go through the laborious task of recording and transcribing the interaction. However, there is a price to pay. Most obvious is the fact that the actual language used has been lost.

The following is a narrative account of the same interaction. Notice how different the perspective is.

The teacher enters the classroom in conversation with one of the students. 'Of course I had lunch', he says. 'Not enough. Why? Why?'

The student gives an inaudible response, and joins the rest of the class who are sitting in a semicircle. There are eighteen students, in all. They are a mixed group in both age and ethnicity.

The teacher deposits three portable cassette players on his table, and slumps in his chair. 'Well, like I say, I want to give you something to read – so what you do is, you have to imagine what comes in between, that's all ...' He breaks off rather abruptly and beckons with his hand, '... Bring, er, bring your chairs a little closer, you're too far away.'

There is some shuffling as most of the students bring their chairs closer. The teacher halts them by putting his hand up, policemanwise, 'Er, ha, not that close.' There is some muffled laughter. The teacher is about to speak again, when a young male student breaks in with a single utterance 'Quiss?' The teacher gives him a quizzical look. 'Pardon?'

The student mutters inaudibly to himself and then says, 'It will be quiss? It will be quiss? Quiss?' Several other students echo, 'Quiss. Quiss.'

The teacher grins and shakes his head, 'Ahm, sorry. Try again.' The student frowns in concentration and says, 'I ask you . . .' 'Yes?' interjects the teacher. '. . . You give us another quiss?'

Slowly the light dawns on the teacher's face. 'Oh quiz, oh! No, no, not today. It's not going to be a quiz today. Sorry . . .But, um, what's today, Tuesday it is?'

'Yes', says the student.

The teacher frowns and flicks through a notebook on his desk. 'I think on Thursday, if you like. Same one as before. Only I'll think up some new questions – the other ones were too easy.'

The students laugh, then the teacher, holding up the daily newspaper, continues, 'Um OK, er I'll take some questions from, er, from newspapers over the last few weeks, right? So – means you've got to watch the news and read the newspaper and remember what's going on. If you do, you'll win. If not, well, that's life.'

One of the woman students, a Pole in her early thirties says, 'Will be better from TV.' There is laughter from several of the students.

'From the TV?' echoes the teacher. 'What, er, what programmes . . .'

'News, news,' interject several of the students.

There is an inaudible comment from one of the students. The teacher turns sharply and begins, 'Did you say . . .?' He breaks off abruptly. 'Oh, OK. We'll have, er, it'll be the s. . ., it'll be the same.' He pauses and then adopts an instructional tone, as he attempts to elicit a response from the students. 'There'll be different . . . ? Er, there'll be different . . . ? Different? Different? The questions will be on different . . . what? Different?'

'Talks,' ventures one of the students near the front.

'Tasks? What?' says the teacher giving a slight frown.

'Subject?' suggests another student rather tentatively. The teacher gives her an encouraging look and says, 'Different sub . . .' He extends his hand and narrows his fingers as if to say

'You've nearly got it.'

'Subjects,' says the student, beaming.

The teacher beams back, 'Subjects, subjects, thank you. Right, yes.'

Here the actual language used by the teacher and students, as well as interpersonal dynamics and affective climate of the classroom are brought out. The major disadvantages of this particular method of carrying out classroom observations are the extremely time-consuming nature of the task, and the biases inherent in the authorial comments which are woven into the narrative itself.

In a workshop on classroom observation and research, a group of teachers provided the following reactions to the observation scheme and the narrative.

Tally sheet

Advantages	*Disadvantages*
• Objective	• Likely to distort actuality
• Good for observer to use while watching class	• Does not show the human element
• Good for self-analysis by teacher	• Very abstract
• Easy to compare different interactional categories	• Focuses on quantity not quality
• Easy to focus on specific elements	• Does not indicate success or failure

- Orients one's mind set as observer

- Visual presentation – easy to overview

- Does not indicate sequences of interaction
- Open to misinterpretation

- Categories create straitjacket
- Categories are biased toward teacher
- Does not indicate length of interaction

Narrative

Advantages
- Displays significant paralanguage
- Reflects rapport between teacher and students
- Gives overall effect of interaction

- Can be used to cary out subsequent tally-sheet analysis
- Shows real nature of questions asked
- Context given to support the language

Disadvantages
- Difficult to use for clinical purposes
- Time-consuming to write

- Allows distraction by focus on unimportant detail
- Open to emotive reporting

- Inadequate on its own
- Cannot be done in real time

- Requires high-quality recording equipment

Let us look at the interaction a third time, this time at a transcript. The transcript has been coded using a scheme devised by Bowers (1980). Bowers' interactive categories are as follows:

Responding   Any act directly sought by the utterance of another speaker, such as answering a question.

Sociating   Any act not contributing directly to the teaching/learning task, but rather to the establishment or maintenance of interpersonal relationships.

Organising   Any act which serves to structure the learning task or environment without contributing to the teaching/learning task itself.

Directing   Any act encouraging non-verbal activity as an integral part of the teaching/learning process.

Presenting   Any act presenting information of direct relevance to the learning task.

Evaluating   Any act which rates another verbal act positively or negatively.

Eliciting   Any act designed to produce a verbal response from another person.

T   of course i had lunch ... not enough ... why? why? (*sociating*)
   well, like i say, i want to give you something to read (*organising*)
   – so what you do is, you have to imagine what comes in between, that's all ... (*organising*)
   ... bring, er, bring your chairs a little closer, you're too far away
   er, ha, not that close (*organising*)

S   quiss? (*eliciting*)
T   pardon? (*responding*)
S   it will be quiss? it will be quiss? quiss? (*eliciting*)
Ss   quiss ... quiss (*eliciting*)
T   ahm, sorry ... try again (*eliciting*)
S   i ask you ... (*eliciting*)
T   yes?
S   you give us another quiss? (*eliciting*)
T   oh, quiz, oh! no, no, not today ... it's not going to be a quiz today ... sorry ... but, um, what's today, tuesday is it? (*eliciting*)
S   yes (*responding*)
T   i think on thursday, if you like ... same one as before ... only i'll think up some new questions – the other ones were too easy ... um, ok, er i'll take some questions from, er, from newspapers over the last few weeks, right? so – means you've got to watch the news and read the newspaper and remember what's going on ... if you do, you'll win ... if not, well, that's life (*organising*)
S   will be better from TV (*sociating*)
     [laughter]
T   from the TV? ... what, er, what programmes ... (*eliciting*)
Ss   news, news (*responding*)
T   did you say ...? oh, ok, we'll have, er, it'll be the s..., it'll be the same ... there'll be different ...? er, there'll be different ... ? different? different? the questions will be on diferent ... what? different? (*eliciting*)
S   talks (*responding*)
T   tasks? (*evaluating*)
     what? (*eliciting*)
S   subject? (*responding*)
T   different sub ... (*eliciting*)
S   subjects (*responding*)
T   subjects, subjects, thank you ... right, yes (*evaluating*)

Here, the authorial intrusions have been removed. The record is therefore less rich, but also less biased. At the same time, the actual language has been preserved.

The first decision which needs to be made when selecting research methods for observing and analysing classroom interaction is whether or not to adopt an observation scheme. Such schemes, as we have seen can tell us a great deal about the interaction being recorded, and enable us to uncover patterns and regularities which might otherwise have gone unnoticed. Once we have adopted a particular scheme, however, we are from that moment operating with a pair of mental blinkers which may well obscure other significant features of the interaction. In addition, in many schemes, the actual language used in the interaction is lost.

We may decide against the use of an observation scheme, in the first instance, because of the factors mentioned above, and decide to base our study on an analysis of the actual interactions themselves. In order to do this, we shall need an audio or videotaped record. We may also require a transcript of the interaction. We shall deal with the question of observational schedules in the following section. In Section 5.4, we shall look at some of the shortcomings of using observational schedules, and consider the alternative, the adoption of an ethnographic approach to classroom observation.

5.3 Observation schemes

Before we can identify the particular observational tool we are going to use, it is desirable to think about what we want to look for or at. If possible, we should clarify the nature of the problem or issue we wish to investigate. This should be formulated as precisely as possible as an investigative question. The next step is to decide why observation is likely to help us find answers to our question or resolve our problem. It is also useful at this point to consider the relevant characteristics of the setting, including space and equipment, in which the behaviour will be observed, and the constraints imposed by the physical setting. The following questions have been adapted from Boehm and Weinberg (1977).

1. What are the physical arrangements of the various components of the setting that might need to be considered?
2. What people will be present in the setting?
3. What characteristics of the individuals or group being observed need to be considered?
4. Given the particular focus of your observations and given your knowledge of the problem area, what is the universe of behaviours that you intend to consider?
5. What units of behaviour or clearly defined categories of behaviour will you focus on?
6. Is there a previously developed observational schedule which might be used?
7. Is it more appropriate to use a sign or a category system?
8. Are the categories or signs employed mutually exclusive?
9. Are they exhaustive of the universe of behaviours you wish to consider?
10. What sampling procedures (time or event) will most effectively enable you to record representative observations?
11. Will all of the people in the setting be observed, or will you select a representative sample?
12. How frequently across time should you observe so that your conclusions have adequate observational support?
13. To what extent does the subject of the observation need to be viewed in a variety of settings and activities within the school in order to deal adequately with the particular problem or question?
14. How confident are you that your observation schedule facilitates reliable observations?
15. How might you verify this?
16. What inferences or conclusions can you make on the basis of your collected observation data?
17. Have you realised the goals for which your observations have been made?
18. If not, can you redefine your problem more clearly and focus on different behaviours, and from a different perspective?
19. Did you consider the role that methods of enquiry other than systematic observations (e.g. psychometric testing, controlled experimentation or developmental histories) might play in dealing with your problem?

Deciding on an observation instrument is made all the more difficult because of the large number of such instruments which have made their appearance over the last few years. It seems that every researcher who wants to investigate classroom interaction has felt bound to devise his/her own scheme. Long (1983c) lists twenty-two instruments developed for the analysis of interaction in second-language classrooms alone (Chaudron 1988 adds a further three to these). In addition to these, there are schemes for the analysis of interactions in L1 classrooms. Each instrument is classified according to the following categories:

Recording procedures – whether a sign or category system is employed (a category system allows the observer to code a particular behaviour every time it occurs, whereas a sign system requires an observation to be made at regular time intervals, e.g. every three seconds).

Item type – indicates whether the observer is required to make high, low or mixed inference observations (student hand raising or teacher use of display questions would be examples of low-inference behaviours; high-inference observation, e.g. *teacher encourages*, require the observer to interpret the behaviour.

Multiple coding – does the scheme allow a particular observation to be assigned to more than one code?

Real-time coding – indicates whether the instrument is intended for use in direct coding or coding of video/audiotapes.

Source of variables – have the categories been derived from an explicit theoretical or empirical base, a modification or synthesis of existing systems, or original categories derived by the author?

Intended purpose – indicates whether the scheme is intended principally for research, teacher training or both.

Unit of analysis – whether the scheme is based on an arbitrary time unit or an analytical unit such as a move, cycle or episode.

Focus – the different aspects of classroom interaction and behaviour focused upon; these may be verbal, paralinguistic, non-linguistic, cognitive, affective, pedagogical, content or discourse.

An excellent introduction to the use of observation schemes in investigating language classrooms if provided by Allwright (1988), who reproduces and provides a critique of several key papers which have been published over the last twenty years.

The first widely used observational instrument was developed by Flanders (1970), for use in content classrooms. The Flanders' Interaction Analysis Categories (FIAC) classified classroom language into one of the ten categories. The categories are as follows:

Teacher talk
1. Accept feelings.
2. Praises or encourages.
3. Accepts or uses ideas of pupils.
4. Asks questions.
5. Lectures.

6. Gives directions.
7. Criticises or justifies authority.

   Pupil Talk
8. Pupil talk: response.
9. Pupil talk: initiation.

   Silence
10. Period of silence or confusion.

From these categories, it can be seen that the instrument is heavily biased in favour of the teacher. This reflects the teacher-dominated nature of classrooms during the time when the instrument was developed. It can also be seen that the categories themselves are rather crude. The linguistic behaviour of pupils, for example, is restricted to *response, initiation* and *silence* or *confusion*. It is worth considering, from one's own perspective, what has been omitted from the categories.

In 1971, Moskowitz published her own adaptation of FIAC. Her FLINT system was designed specifically for analysing language classrooms, and was more sophisticated than FIAC, expanding the original ten categories to twenty-two categories and subcategories. Her categories are as follows:

Teacher talk

Indirect influence
   1. *Deals with feelings*: In a non-threatening way, accepting, discussing, referring to, or communicating understanding of past, present or future feelings of students.
   2. *Praises or encourages*: Praising, complimenting, telling students why what they have said or done is valued. Encouraging students to continue, trying to give them confidence. Confirming answers are correct.
2(a) *Jokes*: Intentional joking, kidding, making puns, attempting to be humorous, providing the joking is not at anyone's expense. Unintentional humour is not included in this category.
   3. *Uses ideas of students*: Clarifying, using, interpreting, summarising the ideas of students. The ideas must be rephrased by the teacher but still recognised as being student contributions.
3(a) *Repeats student response verbatim*: Repeating the exact words of students after they participate.
   4. *Ask questions*: Asking questions to which an answer is anticipated. Rhetorical questions are not included in this category.

Direct influence
   5. *Gives information*: Giving information, facts, own opinion or ideas, lecturing, or asking rhetorical questions.
5(a) *Correct without rejection*: Telling students who have made a mistake the correct response without using words or intonation which communicate criticism.
   6. *Gives directions*: Giving directions, requests, or commands which students are expected to follow.

6(a) *Directs patterns drills*: Giving statements which students are expected to repeat exactly, to make substitutions in (i.e. substitution drills), or to change from one form to another (i.e. transformation drills).

7. *Criticises student behaviour*: Rejecting the behaviour of students; trying to change the non-acceptable behaviour; communicating anger, displeasure, annoyance, dissatisfaction with what students are doing.

7(a) *Criticises student response*: Telling the student his response is not correct or acceptable and communicating by words or intonation criticism, displeasure, annoyance, rejection.

Student talk

8. *Student response, specific*: Responding to the teacher within a specific and limited range of available or previously shaped answers. Reading aloud.

8(a) *Student response, choral*: Choral response by the total class, or part of the class.

9. *Student response, open-ended or student-initiated*: Responding to the teacher with students' own ideas, opinions, reactions, feelings. Giving one from among many possible answers which have been previously shaped but from which students must now make a selection. Initiating the participation.

10. *Silence*: Pauses in the interaction. Periods of quiet during which there is no verbal interaction.

10(a) *Silence-AV*: Silence in the interaction during which a piece of audio-visual equipment, e.g. a tape recorder, filmstrip projector, record player, etc., is being used to communicate.

11. *Confusion, work-oriented*: More than one person at a time talking, so the interaction cannot be recorded. Students out of order, not behaving as the teacher wishes, not concerned with task at hand.

12. *Laughter*: Laughing, giggling by the class, individuals, and/or the teacher.

e *Uses English*: Use of English (the native language) by the teacher or the students. This category is always combined with one of the 15 categories from 1 to 9.

Non-verbal: Non-verbal gestures or facial expressions by the teacher or the students which communicate without the use of words. This category is always combined with one of the categories of teacher or pupil behaviour.

When deciding on an observation instrument, a number of considerations need to be borne in mind. Not the least of these is the complexity of coding interactions in real time, rather than from audio or videotape, when using a system with a large number of categories. Obviously there is a trade-off between the relative crudity of an easy-to-use instrument with few categories and the sophistication of a complex instrument with many categories.

One of the most sophisticated instruments yet developed for analysing interactions in the language classroom is the COLT scheme. COLT, an acronym for Communicative Orientation of Language Teaching, was originally devised for a large-scale investigation of second-language acquisition by children (see Frohlich *et al.* 1985). Recently it has been used by Spada (forthcoming) for observing classroom behaviours and learning outcomes in different second-language programmes.

The instructional contexts explored by Spada include the following:

1. Regular English and French as second-language programmes for children.
2. Intensive ESL programmes for adults and children.
3. French immersion programmes for children and adolescents.

In her study, Spada was looking for differences in instruction across various L2 programmes and for relationships between any instructional differences identified and learning outcomes.

The COLT scheme contains two sections: part A, which describes classroom activities in organisational and pedagogic terms, and part B, which categorises verbal interactions. Part A analyses the classroom in terms of activity description, participant organisation, content, student modality and materials. Theses categories and the subcategories below them

> were designed to capture those aspects of classroom instruction which are more or less typical of instruction within a 'communicative language teaching' (CLT) approach. For example, classroom organisation which is student-focused with an emphasis on meaning-based practice and the use of authentic materials in which extended texts predominate, are considered to be more communicatively-oriented than a classroom which is teacher-centred, where the language itself is the focus of instruction and where most materials are pedagogic with little extended text.

Part B analyses teacher and student verbal interaction and captures things such as the existence of an information gap, the extent to which participants engage in sustained speech, the extent to which teachers ask referential or display questions, the ability to initiate discourse, etc.

Spada applied the COLT scheme to thirteen classes in order to determine whether it could capture instructional features in a variety of second-language programmes with different pedagogical orientations. Classes, which lasted from 30 to 100 minutes were visited and coded according to the COLT scheme. Spada predicted that the core French programme would emerge as less communicative than either the extended French programme or the ESL programme which would, in turn, be less communicative than the French immersion programme.

In general, the results of the study confirmed the predictions about the relative communicative orientations of the different programmes. There were, however, some exceptions. For example, the ESL programme *was* considerably less teacher-centred than the other groups, but this did not turn out to mean that the ESL students were involved in more group interaction as anticipated, but rather, that they were involved in individual seat work a considerable amount of the time. ' . . . the ESL program . . . was the most heavily oriented toward explicit language instruction with comparatively little time spent on meaning-based instruction'.

While process-oriented studies such as those described above provide a great deal of useful information, they do not tell us whether differences in instruction result in differences in learning outcomes. In order to test for such differences, Spada used the COLT instrument to document three adult ESL classes. While the three classes were all purportedly 'communicative' in their orientation, they all varied in a number of ways, particularly in terms of the amount of time spent on explicit language practice. In particular, class A received more formal language instruction that classes B or C. These differences led Spada to examine 'whether relative degrees of form and meaning-based instruction contributed differentially to various aspects of learners' L2 proficiency'.

In order to carry out this part of the study, Spada used statistical analyses to compare the mean scores of the three groups on tests of language proficiency (some of the more commonly used statistical procedures in language research will be explored in Chapter Six). She found that the

> type of instruction accounted significantly for differences in improvement on the listening and speaking tests in the first comparison (i.e. class A compared with classes B and C) and on the discourse test in the second comparison (i.e. class B compared with class C). Further analyses indicated that learners in classes B and C improved significantly more than learners in class A on the listening test ... In addition, while learners in classes B and C improved on the speaking test (although not significantly for class C), learners in class A got worse ... there was a difference between the means of class A and classes B and C on the grammar test, indicating higher scores for class A. This did not reach statistical significance.

In commenting on the results of the listening test, the investigator states that she

> examined both quantitative and qualitative differences in the listening practice offered in the three classes. The quantitative results revealed that class A spent considerably more time in listening practice than the other two classes yet class A improved the least. However, because the listening practice in this class did not prepare learners for the listening input as carefully as the listening comprehension instruction did in classes B and C, the investigator concluded that qualitative rather than quantitative differences in instruction seemed a more plausible explanation for significantly more improvement in listening comprehension in classes B and C.

The Spada study is of interest for several reasons but of particular interest is her attempt to link teaching processes with learning outcomes. In order to do this, the researcher adopts both qualitative and quantitative research methods. By using a sophisticated observational instrument, and combining this with statistical analysis, Spada is able to generate insights into the instructional process which would have been difficult to arrive at using one procedure on its own. This mix of quantitative and qualitative measures illustrates the point made in Chapter One that it is not always easy to label empirical studies as either 'qualitative' or 'quantitative' as many studies employ a mix of procedures.

5.4 Classroom ethnography

One of the problems with the use of observational schedules and schemes is that the various categories comprising the schedules are predetermined by the researchers before they actually go into the classroom to collect their data. Admittedly, the schedules are developed over many painstaking hours, involving a great deal of classroom observation.

They also reflect current theoretical perspectives on the nature of language learning and use. However, there is no denying the fact that they predetermine what we should look for, and to that extent are likely to condition what we see.

Van Lier (1988) has criticised the use of a single observational scheme, no matter how comprehensive. He argues that such schemes could be valuable if they are simply one of a number of tools which might also include lesson plans, field notes and interviews. However, constraints of time and money often preclude the use of a comprehensive array of tools and techniques. In addition, a broad ethnographic approach is sometimes devalued by those who favour the use of measurement and statistics. Amongst such researchers, it is the fashion to equate excellence with the hard-nosed hypothesis-testing methods of the natural sciences. Those who advocate the tabulation of classroom interaction using observational schedules, and the subjection of the resulting data to statistical analyses are falling into the trap of equating quality is research with measurement, according to van Lier.

> Observed facts that are relevant in terms of the [predetermined] categories are coded and tabulated, and the result is a score of classroom performance of some kind, whether it be expressed as 'classroom climate' (Flanders 1970), 'communicative orientation' (Allen *et al.* 1984), or whatever. The results can be compared for several classrooms, correlated, and statistical tests of significance will support or reject claims that classroom A has a better climate or is more communicatively oriented than classroom B (van Lier 1988:43).

While van Lier admits the attraction of such schemes, and the fact that they are a great improvement over anecdotal reports and the like, he questions whether they actually add to our knowledge and understanding of what goes on in the classroom. They are all based on a prior selection of categories which are determined by ideological beliefs about the nature of learning; they focus on the observable, countable, and, usually, low-inference, behaviours; they assume that more equals better, and they are based on the following piece of logical circularity (van Lier 1988:44):

Procedure	*Problems*
1. The 'good' classroom is characterised by certain features.	What is meant by 'good'? Are these features all equally relevant? Some more than others?
2. These are the features that are relevant.	What is meant by 'relevant'? Who decides? Why?
3. Translate them into categories that are clear and unambiguous.	Is the translation valid? Are all the features translatable? When you reduce ambiguity, what else do you reduce?
4. These are the classroom behaviours that fit into each category.	How well do they fit? Do some fit in more than one category, or in none at all?
5. Add them up.	Is 'more' necessarily better?
6. Compare.	What does this say about lesson quality? Answer: Back to Procedure 1

Van Lier's alternative is to record, transcribe and engage in the close textual analysis of classroom interactions. In other words, we should allow structures to emerge from the data rather than being imposed on them. This alternative, however, is not without its price. Recording and analysing classroom data can be extremely tedious. If one is working from audiotape, rather than videotape, it is difficult to decipher all student contributions and, if one is listening to more than four or five speakers, it is almost impossible to identify which speakers are making particular contributions. While sophisticated electronic equipment, such as the pedal-operated recorders stenographers use, can greatly facilitate the transcription process, it is doubtful whether most teachers have access to such equipment.

Van Lier's stricture that issues should emerge from the data also needs to be tempered by the fact that there is no such thing as theory-free observation. Even without formal and predetermined observation schedules, we bring with us our own interior 'observation schedule' which will be framed in terms of our own beliefs, attitudes and ideologies about language, learning and teaching. Being implicit, this covert 'schedule' might in some ways be even more dangerous than explicit schedules.

You might like to examine the following extracts from a classroom transcript and consider which issues 'emerge'. What do you think might warrant further investigation in this particular classroom? (The complete transcript of the lesson is included as Appendix A).

Note: The teacher and students are working with a sequence of five pictures showing an accident between a boy on a bike and a milk delivery float which has been caused by the milkman braking to avoid hitting a dog. The students' task has been to work in small groups and put the pictures into the sequence in which the incidents portrayed might have occurred in real life. The teacher then initiates the following discussion session on the content of the pictures.

T   Where are they?
Ss Where are they?
T   Where are they? Inside, outside?
S   Department.
T   Department?
S   Department store.
T   Mmm. Supermarket. They're in the street. In the street. They're in the street. Outside. They're in the street. The bicycle, and the van – where are they? Where are they? What's this?
Ss Street.
T   In the street. OK. Is this a man or a woman?
Ss Man.
T   A man?
S   Woman.
S   Woman.
S   Man.
S   No man.
T   She's a woman there.
Ss Woman, woman, man, woman.
S   Boy.
T   Boy? Maybe a boy. Boy?
S   Boy.

[*inaudible*]

T   Boy, boy, boy? OK. What's, what's he riding? What's he riding?
Ss Bicycle. Bicycle.
T   A bicycle. A bicycle.
Ss Bicycle.

    .
    .
    .

T   Er, what's this?
S   Hospital car. No.
T   Hospital car. Name?
S   No, I don't know?
T   Ambulance.
S   Ambulance.
T   Ambulance. Hospital car. Ambulance.
S   Ambulance.
T   Ambulance.
S   Ambulance.
T   Ambulance. (Ambulance). Is this a woman? (Woman). Yes? Yes, it's a woman. What's she doing?
S   Car, er, car.
T   What's she doing? This woman. (Car, car). No, yes, Seng. That woman. Seng. That woman. (Woman, woman). What's she doing?
Ss Go to [*inaudible*] Help.
T   Help.
S   Help.
T   Help (help). She's helping the boy (boy, boy, boy)
S   Is help the boy in, er, in the ...
T   In the ambulance, into the ambulance.
S   Into ambulance (ambulance, ambulance) OK? (ambulance, ambulance, police)
T   Police or maybe the ambulance driver.

    .
    .
    .

T   Ah, in Australia, motor bike, yes. Yes, yes, yes. Bicycle, yes, good (oh). Children, special helmet (helmet) Helmet, mmm. Special helmet.
S   Erm, China, er, there are many, many [*gestures*]
T   Many, many accidents.
S   Accidents.
T   And Greece?
S   No.
T   No? In China many bicycles. Have you ever? Have you seen an accident? Have you seen an accident?

Even from these brief extracts, it is possible to identify many different issues and questions for closer examination and investigation. A few that suggest themselves are as follows:

1. How does the teacher deal with failure on the students' part to answer questions? Does she repeat herself, restructure the question or answer the question herself?

2. What happens to the patterns of interaction when the teacher switches from asking display questions to asking referential questions?
3. Is there more negotiation of meaning when the teacher switches from asking display to referential questions?
4. Is there evidence of learner uptake – i.e. instances where learners build language the teacher uses into their own output?
5. How are errors dealt with? What types of errors are treated? With what effect?
6. In what ways does the teacher modify her speech? When? With what effect?

It will be seen that these questions have all been dealt with in preceding chapters. They are in fact partly a product of my own background as a researcher and teacher, and serve to demonstrate that I do not come to the analysis and interpretation of classroom interaction with a completely open mind.

If one is carrying out an ethnographic inquiry on or with a colleague, it is usually extremely informative to use the stimulated recall technique described in Chapter four. It is even more interesting if one can get a parallel commentary from one or more learners in the class. The transcripts and student and teacher commentaries can then be juxtaposed, to provide illuminating insights into teaching and learning processes.

This process is illustrated in the following transcript and commentary. I obtained these data by videotaping the teacher, showing the videotape to the teacher and audiotaping her commentary. Both the videotaped lesson and the audiotaped commentary were then transcribed.

Transcript

T Once you've got a set of pictures ... Bo, are you listening? I'm waiting for people to listen. Still waiting.

Ss Listen. Listen.

T When you've got a set of pictures, go anywhere in the room. Anywhere. Don't have to sit in a circle. Go anywhere. Find, find your own personal space. Now, how many pictures should you have? How many?

S Nine. Nine.

T All right. Nine.

S Nine.

Commentary

At this stage in the lesson I was trying to set up an extended listening activity. The students really lack confidence, and need the opportunity to hear lots of input. I've read people like Krashen and Asher, and was trying to put some of their ideas into practice – I mean these students are really slow track. They came to me after an on-arrival course – I suppose they'd had well over a hundred hours of instruction, and couldn't even answer questions like 'What's your name?' That was a real shock to me. Their previous teacher said that they were incapable of learning, but I just don't accept that.

I can hear from the audiotape that I was a bit irritated at this point at just how long they were taking to each get a set of pictures. Just getting them to pay attention to simple classroom instructions is really hard work.

I also realised from the tape that I make these little asides – I mean, 'personal space' really! Not that they'd be able to pick it up, but it could come across to someone else you know, another teacher, as patronising. It's quite incredible

T And they should all be different. Now this time, this time ...

All right, this time it's going to be, this time it's going to be difficult because I'm not going to speak. The ... instructions will come from the cassette. So you must listen very carefully, all right? You must listen for the picture to find and hold it up, then you have to listen where to put it ... On top of ... on top of (Ss on top of). Underneath. On the right, on the left. Between.

T Is everybody ready? ... How could you possibly not ... ? What were you doing? Talking? (*laughter*)

S No, I give to ...

T Oh, you gave them away. ... turning off the ... nine ... there you are. You can go over there if you like.

what you find out about your own teaching by listening to a tape – frightening really.

I had to pause here as some of the students discovered that they didn't have enough pictures after all. It was really important for them to concentrate because I was trying to do something new. Before, they'd been listening to me describe a picture, and they'd have to find which one I was describing and hold it up. Now, they were having to listen to a tape. It's much more difficult. We'd done a lot of work on adverbials of place and prepositions, too, and I built those into the activity.

I had to stop again because one of the students *still* didn't have the right cards. I was starting to get a bit cheesed off – shows how important it is to give them time and find out what's going on. It turned out she'd given her cards to her friend who's much weaker than she is. I counted out a set of picture cards for her and put her on the other side of the room so her friend would have to work by herself. One of the things I've found with this comprehension approach is that the students tend to switch off, and not process the language at all if you're not directly addressing them. And the weaker ones don't seem to process the language at all – they just watch what the better ones are doing and copy them.

It is obvious from this small sample how much richer the picture becomes if we can include a teacher commentary. The commentary provides us with insights into what is happening which would otherwise not be accessible to us (as already noted, an even richer picture would emerge if we were able to include a learner commentary, although, with low-level learners such as these, it would be necessary to obtain the commentary in the learner's first language and have it translated). The technique is also an excellent one for throwing up issues and questions which might form the basis of a classroom investigation.

Another technique which offers an alternative to the use of observation schemes is 'pattern analysis'. This has been used by Ireland and Russell as a method of helping teachers make sense of their own teaching. The procedure for carrying out pattern analysis is as follows:

1. Make an audiorecording of a class and transcribe a portion of the tape.
2. Read through the transcript and look for patterns, regularly recurring behaviours or forms of interaction which occur repeatedly.
3. Write down the patterns in descriptive terms (see examples A–K below).

Pattern analysis is a technique for looking at what happens in classrooms. One of the most constructive applications is its use to provide 'feedback' which is otherwise not readily available to teachers. Pattern analysis is an 'open-ended' technique, rather than a preconceived set of categories for analysis. It is amenable to a variety of different points of view and is probably most useful to teachers who have already identified particular aspects of their teaching which they wish to examine.

A. To every student response, the teacher replies with the phrase, 'O.K., very good.'

B. When the teacher proposes an idea, the students elaborate it.

C. When the teacher asks students to read a book, students may choose from several titles.

D. Virtually all questions are asked by the teacher.

E. When the teacher records responses on the board, the responses are recorded in precisely the language used by the students.

F. When students propose an idea, the teacher elaborates it.

G. When students make no response, the teacher never waits more than three seconds before speaking again.

H. After the teacher speaks, a student speaks; then the teacher speaks again, then a student and so on.

I. The teacher often sits behind the desk when speaking to the entire class.

J. To every student response, the teacher replies by saying 'Yes, ..., but ...'

K. Students usually wait to speak until the teacher calls on them.

(Ireland and Russell 1978:21)

5.5 The social organisation of the classroom

In this section, we shall look at some alternative ways of exploring language classrooms. In particular, we shall look at the use of seating charts, sociograms and so on for tracing patterns of classroom interaction.

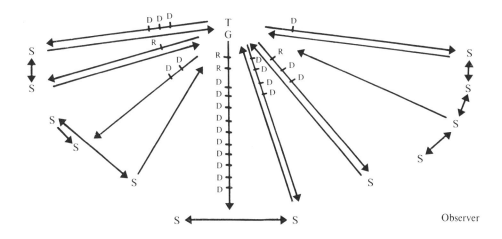

FIGURE 5.2 *An example of a seating chart for an ESL class.*

Acheson and Gall (1987) use the acronym SCORE to refer to seating-chart observation records. They provide a diagrammatic representation of the physical arrangement of the classroom and allow the observer to record a range of behaviours, including the amount and type of interaction between different classroom participants. Figure 5.2 is an example of a seating chart for an ESL class. This particular seating chart shows the number and direction of display and referential questions by the teacher, whether these were directed to the class in general or to specific individuals, and learner responses. It also show interactions between learners.

Seating charts such as these allow a great deal of information to be presented on a single page. They also enable interactions between individual students and the teacher/other students to be documented and examined while keeping track of the behaviour of other students in the class.

Day (1990) has made extensive use of seating charts in second-language teacher education. He claims that SCORE instruments are particularly helpful in three aspects of teacher preparation: in documenting teacher/student talk or 'verbal flow'; keeping a record of time-on task; and in recording movement patterns.

Verbal flow documents the frequency with which different individuals interact. Day's students have used it to record experienced teachers' questioning and praising behaviour, and for coding student questions and responses. While SCORE does not preserve the actual language used, it enables us to record the extent to which a teacher addresses questions generally or to specific students, and whether students sitting in particular parts of the room (e.g. towards the front) receive more opportunities to interact than others.

Time-on-task, which has been correlated with achievement in mainstream classrooms, can also be captured using SCORE instruments, although there are problems here in that some behaviours associated with on-task work require inferences on the part of the observer:

> it is a high-inferential task to decide if students talking during a group work activity are at- or off-task, unless the observer is close enough to hear the speech. It is also a high-inferential task to determine if a student who is writing something in her notebook during a conversational class is off-task, as she could possibly be writing down a vocabulary item which came up during the lesson (Day 1989).

Recording teacher and student movement patterns allows for the generation of hypotheses about classroom management. Day points out that coding teachers' movements during a lesson can provide insights into possible discipline problems and their resolution as well as indicating biases towards certain students, in the same way as verbal flow.

Hopkins (1985) uses similar techniques to those proposed by Acheson and Gall for documenting questioning techniques and observing on-task and off-task behaviours. In Figure 5.3 the numbers represent the questions answered by pupils sitting in that particular position, i.e. the first question asked was answered by the student sitting in the far right position/front row. The 'V' indicates pupils who have volunteered answers, while the 'A' identifies students who have been asked to respond.

Sociometry is used to obtain an indication of the interpersonal dynamics and social structure of a group. Conducting sociometric surveys can be a threatening thing for

Teacher				
28	11	24	0	1
VA	VA	A	A	VA
16	10/23	3/4	2/27	29
A	V	V	AV	V
17	9/22	5/18	6/12	7/13
AV	VA	AV	AV	V
30	0	10/26	20/21	8
V	—	AV	V	A
0	0	0	25	14/15
A	—	—	A	A

FIGURE 5.3 *A seating chart observation record showing pupil response patterns to teacher questions.*

learners, and need to be undertaken with care. It is particularly important that confidentiality be preserved and that the participants in the process are aware of this. The process can be carried out through the following steps:

1. Students are told that a procedure is to be carried out to find out who will work with whom in undertaking a class project, or small group assignment.
2. Each student writes his/her name at the top of a slip of paper.
3. On one side of the paper, students rank those students they would like to work with, the person they would most like to work with being at the top. They can list as many or a few as they like.
4. On the other side of the paper, they write the names of those they would not like to work with. Once again, they can write as many names as they like or none at all.
5. The pieces of paper are collected and used to draw up a sociogram. This is done by identifying the most chosen student, and adding symbols for pupils who have reciprocated choices. The example in Figure 5.4 from Hopkins, shows a sociogram with some commonly used terms associated with it.

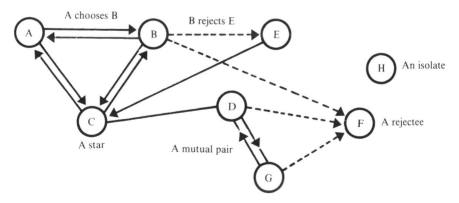

FIGURE 5.4 *An example of a sociogram (Hopkins 1985:77).*

In relation to this sociogram, Hopkins suggests that:

> pupils E, F and H are unpopular and this information encourages the teacher to act to remedy this situation; action that can also be monitored through other classroom research techniques. The sociogram is a useful method for teacher–researchers who wish to explore the social structure of their class and the relationship between pupils. It also provides a starting point for action and further research. (Hopkins, 1985)

5.6 Conclusion

In this chapter we have looked at some of the techniques available for carrying out classroom observation. We have seen that the choice of instrument or technique will have a large bearing on what we actually find in the classroom.

While I have chosen to contrast the use of various schemes for recording classroom interaction with less structured classroom ethnography, I should, at this stage, point out that these are not necessarily mutually exclusive, and that a range of techniques can be brought to bear on a particular research problem or issue.

5.7 Tasks and questions

1. One of the disadvantages of observational instruments is that they act as mental 'blinkers' on the user. They also encapsulate their author's ideological beliefs about the nature of teaching and learning.
   What assumptions about the nature of instruction are revealed about the authors of FIAC and FLINT, which we looked at in Section 5.3? What assumptions about the nature of language learning are inherent in the FLINT scheme? In what ways is the FLINT scheme more satisfactory than FIAC?
2. What are the ideological assumptions and beliefs about language learning underlying COLT, as these are revealed by Spada (1989)?
3. Analyse the observation schemes included as Appendix B. Rank them from most to least manageable.
4. Evaluate the arguments adduced by van Lier against the use of observational scales. How convinced are you by these?
5. Study the classroom transcript included as Appendix A and write out a set of investigative questions similar to the ones prompted by the extract in Section 5.4.
6. Consider again the transcript and commentary in 5.4. What insights does the commentary yield which are not immediately apparent from the transcript itself? What investigate questions suggest themselves?
7. Following the pattern-analysis procedure of Ireland and Russell, analyse one or both of the lesson transcripts in Appendix A. Make a list of the patterns identified. What research questions suggest themselves as a result of this exercise?
8. Use a seating chart to document interactions in your own classroom or that of a colleague. What does this reveal about the class you observed? Is it suggestive of follow-up research?
9. Draw up a sociogram for one of your classrooms, or a subgroup of students. What does this reveal about the class you observed? Are you surprised by the outcome? Is it suggestive of follow-up research?

Chapter Six

Teacher-research and Professional Development

6.1 Introduction

A major benefit of the observational and investigative activities outlined in this book is that they provide a powerful professional development tool. Having considered these activities and ideas, the logical next step is for teachers to apply them to their own classrooms through their own personal research agenda. In this chapter, I shall try to outline in some detail the benefits of incorporating a teacher-research component into professional development programmes. I shall also outline an in-service workshop programme for introducing teachers to the concept and for providing them with basic skills and techniques for establishing their own research projects.

6.2 A rationale for teacher-research

The growing interest in clasroom-oriented research, and indications by teachers that they would like to carry out their own research, are signs of maturity within the language-teaching profession. They mark a departure from the 'follow the right method' approach, with its implication that somewhere there is a correct method waiting to be discovered which will work for all learners in all situations and circumstances.

Despite their diversity, 'designer' methods such as the Silent Way, Suggestopedia, Community Language Learning and the Natural Approach all share a particular orientation:

> common to all of them is a set of prescriptions as to what teachers and learners should do in the language classroom. There are prescriptions for the teacher as to what materials should be presented, when it should be taught and how, and prescriptions for learners as to what approach they should take towards the teaching materials and classroom activities ... The teachers' job is to match their teaching styles, as well as the learners' learning styles to the method (Richard 1987:12).

In contrast with the 'follow the method' approach, a teacher-as-classroom-researcher orientation encourages teachers to approach methods and ideas with a critical eye, and to adopt an experimental approach to incorporating these ideas into their classrooms. Rather than adopting new methods, materials of ideas and judging their efficacy on intuitive grounds, it is far more satisfactory, and professionally rewarding, to establish a small-scale classroom experiment to monitor, observe and document the effect of the new methods or materials on learner language, learning outcomes, classroom climate, patterns of group interaction and any of the other issues we looked at in Chapters Two and Three. In addition, this alternative orientation seeks to derive principles for teaching from the close observation and documentation of what actually happens in the classroom rather than uncritically importing and applying ideas from outside.

In Chapter Two, we looked briefly at a study of Scherer and Wertheimer (1964). This was an example of a large-scale study designed to evaluate the claims of two competing methodologies. We saw that studies such as these seem doomed to failure. An alternative which developed at about the same time was the search for the 'effective' teacher. This line of research, which was imported into language teaching from mainstream educational research, was similar in its aims to the 'search for the right method' approach, but it attempted to derive principles of practice from the classroom, rather than from some external theory or set of propositions. One of the most carefully devised investigations in the search for the 'effective' teacher was carried out by Politzer (1970), who videotaped seventeen high-school teachers of French. He then tested these teachers' students and grouped them according to their performance on the test. The next step was to come up with a list of characteristics of the 'effective' teacher by comparing the observable behaviours of the teachers with the level of achievement of their learners.

The results of Politzer's study are extremely revealing. Teaching behaviours which correlated positively with student achievement included use of conversion drills, allowing free responses, the frequency with which teachers switched from controlled to free drills, the use of visual aids and the introduction of a variety of structures. Interestingly, in light of the current communicative orthodoxy, student/student interaction showed significant negative correlation.

In commenting on Politzer's study, Bailey (1988) concludes that it

> was well designed and well executed, but it illustrates some of the problems associated with the use of student achievement data as criteria for evaluating teachers. We cannot be sure, since it was a correlation study, what really caused the observed gains. Furthermore, since it relied exclusively on observable data, we cannot know what sorts of motivation, hidden effort, and social relationships contributed to the learning that was measured. If someone were to go back now to the same videotapes, and choose different observational categories, motivated by current theory and practice, would we find surprisingly different results? If we could go back in time and interview the students and teachers, or ask them to keep diaries, what else might we discover about the teaching and learning that went on in those classrooms. (Bailey 1988:7).

Politzer's study has been described here because it underlines an important point. This is that isolating and counting instances of particular classroom practices is unlikely to result in a list of behaviours which aggregate to the 'effective' teacher. While the study represents a step forward, in that the behavioural categories are derived from the classroom, rather than being imported from outside, it is still predicated on what appears to be a fundamental misconception, i.e. that somewhere or other there exists a way of teaching which will result in effective learning for all learners in all contexts.

An alternative to this approach is one in which teachers are encouraged to develop skills in observing, analysing and critiquing their own classrooms. With appropriate support, they can use the skills and knowledge acquired as a springboard for conducting their own classroom-oriented research.

An extremely useful model for how this might be done is provided by Ramani (1987). She suggests that incorporating classroom observation and analysis into teacher-training programmes is an ideal way of integrating theory and practice. As we saw in Chapter One, this integration is one of the most crucial issues in the professional development of language teachers. Ramani outlines a methodology for raising teachers' awareness of theory by encouraging them to conceptualise what they do in the classroom. This, in consequence, helps them to narrow the gap between theory and practice. In promoting her approach, she criticises conventional ways of updating teachers' knowledge. These include lectures from trainers and reading assignments which cast the teacher into the role of passive recipient of other people's ideas. However, their own perceptions are rarely engaged or strengthened. Her alternative is to encourage teachers to observe a live or recorded lesson and to get them to deduce the theoretical underpinnings of the lesson.

Ramani cites as an example a lesson observed by her trainees in which learners listened to a dialogue and were then required to put into the correct order sentences from the dialogue which were written on strips of paper. At the conclusion of their observation, trainees were encouraged to reveal their own assumptions about the nature of language and learning by considering questions such as the following:

1. Does the sentence reordering exercise involve only recall from memory?
2. What knowledge does it demand of the learner – knowledge of real-life conversations, discourse structure, logical organisation?
3. What kind of skills might this exercise help to develop?
4. Is it more effective for this exercise to be done individually or in groups? Why?
5. At what stage in the lesson should this exercise be done?

I believe that the directions signalled by Ramani can be extended to second-language-teacher education in general, and I should like to propose that the philosophy enshrined in her approach can be captured by the rubric of 'reflective' rather than 'effective' teaching. In the rest of this section, I should like to outline what I see as some of the salient characteristics of 'reflective' teaching. I shall derive these characteristics from an analysis of two exemplary teacher-education programmes. The first has been developed for the in-service education of foreign-language teachers, while the second has been devised as a graduate programme for second-language teachers.

Breen *et al.* (1989) describe an in-service programme for secondary-level teachers of English as a foreign language. They claim distinctiveness for the programme on the basis of eight characteristics. These are as follows:

1. The programme is long rather than short term, thereby facilitating a cyclical rather than 'one shot' in-service experience.
2. Continuity has been assisted by the ongoing involvement of the same four trainers.
3. Teachers apply on a voluntary basis to undertake the programme.
4. Teachers come from the same or neighbouring regions, and are therefore able to network outside the formal in-service sessions.

5. The programme is articulated within a general (rather than specifically language) teaching context, and participants are therefore able to relate their in-service language training to a broader educational context.
6. The programme emerged from the felt needs of the client group, rather than being imposed from the outside.
7. The actual training workshops took place on only two and a half days a year.
8. Follow-up meetings facilitated by the local trainers maintained the momentum of the annual workshops.

Initially, the workshops, which were developed by the two trainers from abroad, were conceived within a transmission model of educational change. The experts were 'bringing the good news' about communicative language teaching.

In evaluating the initial workshop, it became clear that there were problems with the transmission model; less than half of the participants followed up on the ideas presented and less than a quarter actually tried out the materials which emerged from the workshop with their students. The trainers concluded that there were several fundamental weaknesses with the transmission model, and noted five weaknesses in particular.

1. It represents a top-down approach in which content is derived from 'sources other than classroom practice'.
2. It cast participants into a passive role in which they are relating to ideas rather than action.
3. Problematic issues such as how to introduce the innovative materials in mixed-ability classes were thrown up.
4. Follow-up support to teachers having difficulty implementing the ideas was not available.
5. There is a large gap between the security of the workshop situation and the insecurity of the classroom.

As a reaction to the perceived weaknesses of the transmission model, the trainers adopted a problem-solving model in which they relinquished the role of transmitter of knowledge to that of consultant. The workshops were now built, not on the trainers' knowledge, but the teachers' problems with their classroom practice and a consideration of learning processes. While the problem-solving model represented an advance on the transmission model, it too had weaknesses. In particular, the trainers were still seen as 'experts'. The workshops threw up far more problems than could possibly be addressed.

The third and current phase in the in-service programme evolved out of the insight that trainees' classrooms and their learners are the key training resources, and that, in consequence, in-service education should be orchestrated around classroom decision-making and investigation. The purposes of the workshop were now 'to discover whether or not particular innovations are needed, and if they are, how they can evolve with direct learner participation through more explicit sharing of decision-making with teachers', and to encourage teachers to become their own classroom researchers.

The case study of the evolution of an in-service training programme described by Breen *et al.* gives empirical support to the contention that professional growth and development should grow out of the classroom experiences and problems of teachers, rather than revolving around ideas imported from outside the classroom.

From a non-award, in-service context, I should like to turn to a graduate programme for language teachers. Lange (1990) works in a very different context from Breen *et al.*, being concerned with the university education of teachers in the United States. However, he develops a set of principles for the development of a teacher-education programme which are similar to those of Breen *et al.* His model incorporates nine core features:

1. *Field-based* – pre-service teacher development takes place on-site where schools, in cooperation with collegiate teacher-development programmes, are known as teaching centres.
2. *Problem-centred* – the theory and practice of a curricular and instructional programme are organised around the resolution of identified, real problems in actual classes.
3. *Technology-driven* – computers, videotape, videodisk, satellite hook-up are key components of a problem-resolving mode of instruction in providing an informational data base, the means for analysing that information through a variety of spreadsheets, and the means for sharing decisions through word processors.
4. *Experimental sharing* – neophyte, experienced, master teachers, college/university supervisors, and professorial staff share in the identification and organisation of resolutions to curricular and instructional problems.
5. *Developmental* – the teacher-development instructional programme meets the needs of an increasingly sophisticated developing professional. It differentiates theoretical issues and performance competencies on a continuum from simple to complex depending on the capabilities and experience of the learner.
6. *Competency* – the teacher-development instructional programme, while focusing on the resolution of curricular and instructional problems, is oriented towards knowledge, skills and attitudes which are appropriate to each experiential level identified, taught, practised and evaluated.
7. *Expertly staffed* – problem resolution in such a programme comes about because of a constellation of staff who work together: school staff, university faculty, representatives of agencies, consultants from the community and the like.
8. *Critical mass* – a high concentration of professional staff within a school setting for the purpose of developing teachers through problem resolution by means of risk-taking and experimentation makes the process possible.
9. *Open-ended* – the open-endedness of the model suggests that professional development is unending, continual and life-long.

Despite the very different contexts in which they operate, Breen *et al.* and Lange come to remarkably similar conclusions about the nature of second-language teacher education. I would like to suggest that their views can be synthesised into five core principles which can be conveniently captured by the rubric of 'reflective' teaching. I believe that reflective teaching should be school-based, experiential, problem-centred, developmental and open-ended. The essential spirit of these five principles is captured in the following (adapted from Nunan 1989):

1. *School-based*

   As far as possible, both pre- and in-service programmes should be strongly linked with the communities they serve. In particular, it is crucial that strong bonds be forged and maintained between the university and the schools and other teaching institutions it serves.

2. *Experiential*

   Related to the preceding point is the notion that research and teaching should take their bearings from actual practice. Language teaching has been particularly prone to the 'guru' effect in which teaching principles are formulated from largely data-free notions of what should happen in the classroom, rather than the close examination of what actually does happen. The ideal is for theory and principles to be tested out in practice, and for this process to be documented and reported. The development of the teacher–researcher and ethnographic approaches to classroom research has done a great deal to promote this principled articulation between theory and practice.

3. *Problem-centred*

   This principle is also closely related to the first and second, and is contingent upon them. I am suggesting here that research and teaching be related to the sorts of problems which exist in real classrooms and learning environments, and that the major thrust of teaching and research be towards the identification and resolution of such problems (in mainstream education there is a rich seam of work running back to Dewey on problem-posing as well as problem-solving).

4. *Developmental*

   Programmes should recognise that teaching is a complex human undertaking, and that as a result of this, teachers will be at different stages of development. Professional programmes should recognise and cater for such differences.

5. *Open-ended*

   As an extension of 4, programmes should recognise and cater for lifelong learning and professional renewal.

In this section, I have tried to present a rationale for the notion of teacher as researcher. At the beginning of the section, I suggested that a major change is taking place in teacher education. This change is reflected in a growing rejection of the notion that principles for practice should be derived from outside the classroom itself. I used Ramani's ideas on the nexus between theory and practice to introduce two teacher-education programmes which lend strong support to the central argument of this chapter, that professional renewal and development should derive from the close observation and analysis of the classroom by teachers, and that this observation should provide a springboard for classroom action in the form of teacher-research.

In the next section we shall review a number of research techniques and explore how they can be pressed into service as professional development tools. Then, in the final major section of this chapter, I shall outline a workshop procedure for introducing teachers to classroom observation and research.

6.3 Techniques

In this section we shall revisit some of the techniques introduced in Chapters Four and Five. The aim of this section is to demonstrate how these techniques and procedures can be used from the perspective of professional development to encourage the critical, reflective approach which I argued for in section 6.2.

In Chapter Five, we saw that observation schemes can be classified according to whether they are intended primarily as research tools or teacher-development tools (some, of course, are both). Allwright (1988) provides a detailed analysis of the use of observation as a feedback tool in teacher training. He points out that while observation of trainees by supervisors has been standard practice in teacher training for many years, such observation has always been fraught with problems, not the least of which is the issue of validity.

As Allwright sees it, there are two aspects to the validity of supervisory observation. In the first place, observations should accurately and objectively capture the reality of what actually went on. It is not enough for the supervisor to observe and then make one or two general comments along the lines of, 'Not bad, but watch your questioning techniques' or 'Don't address all your questions to the three front rows'.

The second aspect of validity is much more complex and problematic. This relates to the need for classroom observations not only to be accurate records of what happened, but also to focus on those aspects of classroom behaviour which are causally related to learner achievement.

> There is not much point in objectivity for its own sake. Objectivity needed to be directed to the things that actually made a difference to learning, whatever they were. We have already seen ... that it was proving impossible to provide a 'scientific' basis for believing any one method to be the 'best', and that even where the focus was on individual teaching techniques, as in Politzer's work, it was proving impossible to 'pass any absolute judgment about what constitutes "good" and "bad" devices of teaching foreign languages' (Allwright 1988:44–5).

The problem, of course, is that the search for a set of variables which can be unambiguously linked to learning outcomes has proved as futile as the search for the right method, and largely for the same reasons.

In Chapter Five, we looked at the scheme devised by Moskowitz for documenting classroom behaviour. A year after the publication of her FLINT scheme, she published another paper arguing for the use of systematic observation in teacher training (Moskowitz 1968). However, she saw observation, not so much as a way of systematising supervisors' evaluation of trainees, but as a feedback tool for trainees. Her paper is an important one for several reasons, not the least of which (as Allwright points out) is that she makes no attempt to justify the use of observation schemes by referencing classroom behaviour to learning achievement. She therefore avoids a problem which bedevils most quantitative research, that of demonstrating a link between classroom processes and learning outcomes.

The student teachers trained by Moskowitz to use classroom observation claimed to have benefited greatly from this training. In particular, they believed that the training made them much more aware of the interaction which takes place in the classroom, that it was suggestive of specific techniques such as providing varied positive feedback, and that it encouraged a more critical reflective attitude. A similar finding is reported for pre-service teachers trained in similar techniques.

The crucial thing to note at this point is the importance of teachers recording and reviewing their teaching on a regular basis. This is something which should be encouraged regardless of whether teachers intend to undertake their own research. As Richards suggests:

> those with the greatest interest in knowing what teachers do in the classroom are teachers themselves. All teachers want to know what kind of teacher they are and how well they are doing. While supervisor's evaluations and students' grades are one way of assessing the value of the teacher's classroom practices, a more direct source of information is available to teachers through regular observation of their own teaching. While few teachers avail themselves of this resource on a regular basis, self-monitoring has much to recommend it as a component of the teacher's ongoing professional development (Richards 1989).

In the case of teacher-researchers, it is imperative that systematic observation and self-monitoring be undertaken. Such teachers need an objective record of what they actually do, rather than what they think they do, as a preliminary to undertaking classroom research. In the next section, we shall look at a workshop programme for introducing teachers to principles of classroom observation as a preliminary to setting up their own classroom-research projects.

Another useful tool for teacher-researchers to document their own professional self-development is the diary or journal. We have already seen how useful diaries are for documenting teaching and learning and they can be similarly used for teacher development. One of the most absorbing teacher diaries is Ashton-Warner's (1983) *Teacher*, which details her experiences with Maori children in New Zealand. This is a book which should be read by all teachers, not just those interested in conducting teacher research. It provides an excellent model of the reflective teacher and shows at a practical level the close symbiotic relationship between theory and practice. (Another major ethnographic investigation of language learning and teaching which should be required reading for all language teachers, as well as those concerned with the education of minority groups, is Heath 1983.)

The most accessible account of diaries in teacher education is offered by Bailey (1990), who has also written extensively on the diary as a tool in second-language acquisition research. She points out that diaries, if they are made available to others, can fulfil two functions. On the one hand they can act as vehicles for personal development (which is our principal point of interest here) and, on the other hand, they can provide research data for others.

Bailey focuses on the use of diaries in the documentation of teaching practice. Her trainees keep individual written accounts of both their immediate classroom experiences and their later reflections on the teaching/learning process. Some of the issues which have become the focus of concern for her teachers are lesson planning and creativity, time management, problems faced by the non-native teacher of English, classroom control, groupwork and student–teacher relations, issues which are all particularly amenable to investigation by the teacher. While Bailey admits that the diary entries tend to be rather sketchy and underanalysed, and that while they 'were not necessarily always gems of ethnographic investigation, they were often extremely useful for the teachers-in-training, both in generating behavioural changes and in developing self-confidence' (the procedures she advocates for keeping a diary are set out in Chapter Four).

The potential value of the diary as a professional development tool and a stimulus to research, as well as an actual research tool is captured by this quote from Telatnik (cited in Bailey):

> After having analysed myself daily I tend to see other people's analysis of my teaching more objectively. Having learned to be honest and objective in my own recording, I found it easier to be more honest and objective about other's comments. Observer Y, whom I respected and admired, reinforced some of my self-observations ... On the other hand, with Observer X, who criticised my authoritarian, teacher-dominated approach, I began to become less defensive. My resentment passed when I accepted the fact that I *did* run a teacher-dominated classroom and that was exactly what I wanted. I no longer secretly raged through our discussions. I even managed to glean from our sessions a few techniques on encouraging student participation.

Similar insights can be derived from the stimulated recall technique outlined in Chapter Four, in which a running commentary is made by the teacher in parallel with a lesson transcript.

6.4 Introducing teachers to classroom observation and research

In this section, I should like to outline a procedure for introducing teachers to the concept of teacher-research, and for providing a basic grounding in issues, methods and techniques for teacher observation and investigation in the classroom. The workshop outlined here is intended to provide about 12–15 hours of instruction, which is a minimum for getting teachers started. The objectives of the workshop are as follows:

1. To introduce participants to tools and techniques of classroom observation.
2. To provide participants with the opportunity of analysing their own teaching.
3. To introduce principles and practice of teacher research.
4. To provide participants with the opportunity of developing their own teacher-research projects.

Before attending the workshop, participants are asked to record and transcribe a 10–15 minute segment from one of their lessons in which they were trying something for the first time or in which a 'critical incident' occurred.

The first part of the workshop is designed to demonstrate to participants that observations are not value neutral, that what we see when we observe a classroom will reflect our own beliefs and attitudes as teachers about the nature of language and the

LESSON 1

	Liked	Disliked	Presuppositions
1			
2			
3			

LESSON 2

	Liked	Disliked	Presuppositions
1			
2			
3			

FIGURE 6.1 *Lesson observation sheet for identifying teacher attitudes and beliefs.*

nature of learning. In addition, the way we choose to document classroom behaviour will have an important bearing on what we see.

In highlighting the latter point, participants are presented with an observation schedule similar to those discussed in Chapter Four, on which the different interactions which have occurred for part of a teacher-fronted lesson have been recorded in tally form. Participants are asked to come up with as much information as they can about the lesson segment which has been analysed. It is surprising just how much teachers can, in fact, infer about a lesson even when they have had no experience of observation schedules. They are then given a narrative account, which includes the tapescript, of the same interaction, and are asked to compare the two ways of recording the interaction and to list the advantages and disadvantages of the two methods.

The second part is designed to get participants to reveal and confront the ideological beliefs and attitudes they hold about language and learning and to illustrate the way in which these attitudes and beliefs colour what one sees when viewing a lesson. Participants are asked to view short (10–15 minute) segments from two lessons which differ markedly in several ways (for example, one segment might be teacher fronted while the other shows small-group work, one might show a drill and practice session with a group of beginners, while the other might show a discussion between a group of intermediate learners). The initial task is simply to note on a worksheet (see Figure 6.1) three things which one likes and three things which one dislikes about the lesson segments. Participants then get into small groups and are required to reach a consensus on the three best and three worst things about each lesson. This can cause prolonged discussion, particularly if group members hold contrary views about language and learning. Conflict is something to be encouraged, as it brings participants face to face with the point of the exercise, which is that observation is not value neutral, that it reflects our beliefs and attitudes, that different people will have different beliefs and attitudes, and that these will have a major effect on our evaluation of a lesson.

The next step is more difficult as it requires participants to turn the discussion back upon themselves, and to uncover the preconceptions and presuppositions behind their value judgments. Thus, for a teacher who says that she liked the use of authentic materials in a lesson, the presupposition is that specially written materials do not go far enough in preparing learners for comprehending and interacting in the target language outside the classroom. Once they have articulated their presuppositions, participants can be asked where these have come from, if anywhere (for example, from professional reading, introspection, wisdom born of experience, etc.). In fact, it usually transpires that most of the beliefs held by teachers are based on hearsay and folk wisdom rather than hard evidence. While there is not necessarily anything wrong with this, it is something of which teachers should be aware. Often, in workshops, it is the teacher with the least evidence who clings most tenaciously to a particular belief.

The next phase in the workshop is to provide participants with the opportunity of using a range of observation instruments. The ones which follow provide a taste only. Developing skills in observing, documenting and analysing classroom interactions could be a complete course in itself, involving many hours of instruction.

In the procedure described in Figures 6.2, 6.3 and 6.4, the participants are split into

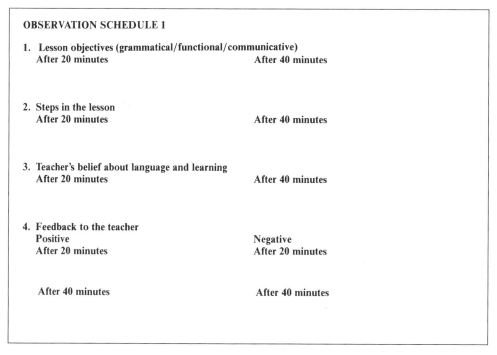

FIGURE 6.2 *Observation schedule: lesson structure.*

three groups. Each group is given a different schedule with which to view the same lesson (usually a lesson of about 40–50 minutes' duration). Halfway through the lesson, and again at the end, participants complete the schedule they have been given. After participants have completed their observations and discussed these with colleagues who have completed the same schedule, the groups are rearranged so that participants who have filled in different schedules are put together to compare the different views of the same lesson which emerge. This task completes that part of the workshop designed to introduce participants to tools and techniques for observation.

The next phase introduces issues for investigation. Participants are given short lesson transcripts and workshop guides designed to help them identify micro aspects of classroom behaviour such as question types, teacher explanations, turn-taking and other issues which we looked at in Chapters Two and Three. They are then provided with more substantial extracts such as those included as Appendix A and undertake both micro and macro analysis guided by stimulus questions such as the following.

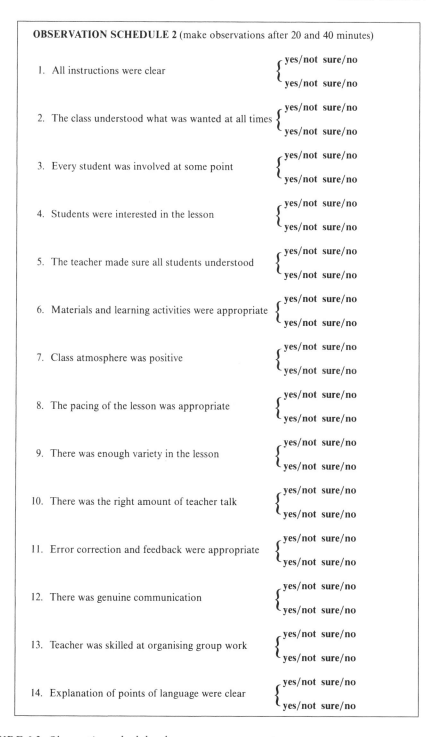

FIGURE 6.3 *Observation schedule: classroom management.*

OBSERVATION SCHEDULE 3

1. How well do you think the tasks provided by you measured up to the following criteria for 'good' language-learning tasks?

		After 20 minutes	After 40 minutes
(a)	They encouraged attention to authentic data	very well / well / not well	very well / well / not well
(b)	They addressed the real-world needs of learners	very well / well / not well	very well / well / not well
(c)	They allowed for flexible approaches to doing the tasks	very well / well / not well	very well / well / not well
(d)	They allowed for different solutions depending on different learner skills	very well / well / not well	very well / well / not well
(e)	They asked for input from learners	very well / well / not well	very well / well / not well
(f)	They involved interaction in solving the tasks	very well / well / not well	very well / well / not well
(g)	They encouraged learners to evaluate the tasks	very well / well / not well	very well / well / not well
(h)	They challenged but did not threaten the learners	very well / well / not well	very well / well / not well
(i)	They offered opportunities to talk about language use	very well / well / not well	very well / well / not well
(j)	They helped learners to discover new learning problems and solve them	very well / well / not well	very well / well / not well
(k)	They promoted information sharing	very well / well / not well	very well / well / not well
(l)	They encouraged learners to reflect critically about language and learning	very well / well / not well	very well / well / not well
(m)	They offered a high return for effort put in	very well / well / not well	very well / well / not well

2. Which tasks or aspects of tasks do you think learners would carry out in real life?

3. Which tasks or aspects of tasks in the lesson do you think learners would only carry out in the language classroom?

FIGURE 6.4 *Observation schedule: learning tasks (acknowledgement to Chris Candlin who devised this schedule).*

Transcript analysis guide

The accompanying extract is taken from a part-time, low-level new arrivals' class. At the beginning of the interaction, the students have each been given five pictures and have been asked to sequence them. This then leads into a general discussion which has been recorded and transcribed.

Read the transcript and discuss the following questions:

1. What do you think was the objective of the lesson?
2. What is revealed in the transcript about the teacher's beliefs on the nature of language and learning?
3. What is revealed in the transcript about the teacher's and learners' roles?
4. What types of questions does the teacher ask?
5. What modifications does the teacher make to her language to facilitate comprehension? Is she successful in this or not?
6. How are topics, subtopics and speaking turns determined?
7. Do any parts of the lesson work better than others?
8. What positive feedback would you provide to the teacher?
9. What negative feedback would you provide?
10. If you were advising the teacher on planning a research project, what issue would you advise her to investigate? Formulate this as a research question.

In the final, and critical, phase of the workshop, participants work in pairs or small groups to analyse the transcriptions they have made of their own classrooms. While many teachers are sensitive to the idea of colleagues examining their classroom transcripts, it is worth encouraging them to do so. Not only are two heads better than one for identifying issues and providing more than one perspective on what is actually happening in the lesson, but a collaborative approach, if it is extended to the planning, implementation and evaluation of a research project, will provide teachers with a collegiate approach to their work which most find extremely beneficial to their own professional growth (Shaw and Dowsett 1986). Kemmis and McTaggart (1982) advance the following reasons for adopting a collaborative approach to teacher research:

It encourages the development of the rationale for the practice under investigation and for others related to it.

It helps to allow the inquiry to be seen as a 'project' rather than as a personal and introspective process.

It helps to clarify unforeseen consequences and ramifications of the work.

It makes defining the issues easier because explaining the project to others demands clarifying one's own thinking.

It helps to get moral support and to see the limits of support (others may not be so captivated by the project as oneself).

It allows others to help and become involved in a constructive participatory way.

It aids reflection by providing a variety of perspectives on the effects of action and the constraints experienced. (Kemmis and McTaggart, 1982:13).

We shall look in greater detail at implementing and supporting teacher-research in the next chapter.

Participants work through their transcripts and complete the following instruction sheet.

Investigating your own classroom – instruction sheet

The aim of this session is to give you the opportunity of analysing your own teaching.
1. Select some area or aspect of teaching which interests you – it might involve one or more of the following areas:
   • teaching objectives
   • task analysis, sequencing and integrating tasks
   • learner groupings, roles of teachers and learners
   • type and quality of classroom interaction
   • materials.
2. Analyse the interaction, noting in particular issues relating to the aspect you have selected for attention. (You may like to use, in an adapted or modified form, some of the tools we used yesterday.)
3. Make notes on this worksheet so you have give a brief oral report to the rest of the group at the end of the session.

Types of student

Aim of lesson

Learner configuration

What did you look at/for in particular?

What did the analysis tell you about your current practices/beliefs?

What did it tell you about your role as a teacher?

What did it tell you about your learners' roles?

Did the analysis reveal anything surprising or unexpected?

Was there a problem? What was the nature of the problem

Has the task revealed an issue or question which might be followed up?

When all participants have completed their sheets, they meet in a plenary session to compare results. This final session is devoted primarily to the last question on the sheet and, guided by the workshop leader(s), participants develop a research proposal to follow up in their classroom.

6.5 Conclusion

In this chapter we have looked at classroom investigation from the perspective of professional development. I have suggested that the notion of reflective teachers, observing and experimenting in their own classrooms, is consonant with current directions in language teaching away from the importation of ideas from outside the classroom. In section 6.2, a theoretical rationale for the teacher-researcher is provided, and empirical support is lent by two very different professional development programmes, one dealing with the in-service training of foreign-language teachers, and the other, a graduate programme for teachers in the United States.

I have also provided, in outline, a workshop programme designed to introduce teachers to the notion of teacher-research, and to provide them with some of the basic skills and knowledge they will need to initiate action in their own classrooms.

While such a programme is a necessary prerequisite for teacher-research, for the concept itself to take root and flower, teachers need support. Supporting teachers is a major part of the next chapter on implementing teacher-research.

6.6 Questions and tasks

1. To what extent is your own teaching situation predicated on the 'follow the method' approach described in this chapter?
2. Make your own summary of the key principles behind the programmes of Breen *et al.* and Lange as set out in this chapter.
3. Record and review a lesson or lesson segment from one of your classes. What assumptions about the nature of language and the nature of learning do you think are revealed by the extract? Ask a colleague or critical friend to do the same. What similarities and differences are there in the two analyses?
4. Study the two lesson transcriptions in Appendix A. What positive and negative feedback would you give to the respective teachers involved?
5. If these teachers were looking for a classroom-research project to undertake, what issue or issues would you recommend to them?
6. Tape a 10-minute segment from one of your lessons and analyse it using one of the observation schemes reproduced in Appendix B. Now make a transcription of the same segment. What patterns emerge from the analysis which are not immediately apparent in the transcription? What is lost in the analysis? (alternatively, carry out this task on a lesson segment from Appendix A).
7. Audio- or videotape a lesson. Select a 10–15 minute segment of the lesson and ask a colleague or critical friend to review it. Ask them to write down three things they liked and three they disliked about the segment.
8. Analyse a lesson using the three observation schedules included in Section 6.4. What do the different analyses tell you about the lesson that were not immediately apparent from an unstructured observation? (for this task, you may use one of the lesson transcripts in the back of the book).
9. Analyse one of your lessons (or one of the transcriptions in the back of the book) using the instruction sheet headed 'Investigating your own classroom' in Section 6.4. Ask a colleague or critical friend to do the same. What similarities emerged?

Chapter Seven

Implementing Teacher-research

7.1 Introduction

One of the major impediments to systematic classroom observation and investigation is the lack of support available to classroom teachers. This is a major problem for teachers attempting to implement a research agenda in the isolation of their own classroom. In this chapter we look at ways in which problems inherent in isolated research might be overcome.

One obvious solution is to promote collaborative research. Such collaboration might be between teachers sharing the same interests and concerns, or it might be between teachers and researchers and even teachers and learners. In Section 7.2 we look at the possibilities offered by a collaborative approach to research, and also at some of the problems created by collaboration.

Teacher-research, whether of the collaborative or individual kind, creates problems, particularly in relation to resources, time and expertise. In Section 7.3 we look at these problems and possible solutions to them. We also look at some of the ways in which research can be disseminated to the wider teaching and research community.

7.2 Collaborative research

As already indicated, collaborative research can be much more fruitful and rewarding than individual research. The collaboration can be between teachers working together as colleagues, between a teacher and an external consultant acting as a 'critical friend', between a teacher and a member of the academic research community, or between teacher and learners.

Kemmis and McTaggart (1988) provide a number of observations on developing action-research projects, all of which have relevance for collaborative research. I have extracted pertinent observations from the list they present. I have also made a brief comment on each of their points in order to reinforce some of the ideas and issues which have already been encountered.

1. Get a research group together and participate yourself. (Comment: not only can sympathetic and like-minded colleagues be a useful source of ideas, they can provide a great deal of support when things get tough.)

2. Be content to start work with a small group. Allow easy access for others. Invite others to come when the topics that interest them will be discussed. (Comment: rather than trying to 'sell' the idea of collaborative research to sceptical colleagues, it is far better to work with a small group of people who are in sympathy with the idea of collaborative teacher-research. Once the group begins to work effectively together, the idea will sell itself.)

3. Organisationally, get things started by arranging an initial launching, identifying a nucleus of enthusiasts, negotiating meeting times and the like. (Comment: the same remarks apply here as to point 2.)

4. Start small: offer simple suggestions to get people started. For example, who talks in your classroom and who controls the development of knowledge in your classroom group? Work on articulating the thematic concern which will hold your group together and establishing agreement in the group that the thematic concern is a shared basis for collaborative action. (Comment: as we have already seen, one of the errors that is often made by people undertaking classroom research for the first time is to set themselves research projects which are far too ambitious.)

5. Establish a time-line: set a realistic trial period which allows people to collect data, reflect and report over two or three cycles of planning, acting, observing and reflecting. (Comment: the research process invariably takes longer than initially envisaged, particularly once unanticipated problems begin to appear. Time needs to be allowed for these to be worked through. By drawing attention to the desirability of working through several research cycles, the ongoing rather than episodic nature of teacher-research is emphasised.)

6. Arrange for supportive work in progress discussions in the group. (Comment: once again, the value of collaborative support is highlighted. Regular work-in-progress meetings can also serve to reassure participants that progress is, in fact, being made.)

7. Be tolerant and supportive: expect people to learn from experience and help to create conditions under which everyone can and will learn from the common effort. (Comment: collaborative research is stressful because the participants are placing themselves in a situation where their real or imagined professional shortcomings come under scrutiny by others. For this reason, it is imperative that a supportive environment be created from the beginning.)

8. Be persistent about monitoring. Collecting compelling evidence is essential to ensure that people are learning from what their experience actually is. Be suspicious of claims made without evidence. (Comment: an important initial phase in the workshop outline presented in Chapter Six was to get participants to articulate their beliefs about language and learning, and then to produce evidence for these beliefs.)

9. Plan for the long haul on the bigger issues of changing classroom practices and school structures. Remember that educational change is usually a slow social process requiring that people struggle to be different. Change is a process, not an event. (Comment: implicit in the concept of teacher-research is the notion of change. We are doing more than simply observing our classrooms to see what is going on there. We are also intervening with the hope of improving on current practice.)

10. Work to involve (in the research process) those who are involved (in the action), so they

share responsibility for the whole action-research process. (Comment: this point, once again, underlines the desirability of adopting a collaborative approach to research.)

11. Remember that how you think about things, the language and understandings that shape your action, may need changing just as much as the specifics of what you do. (Comment: one of the great benefits of involving others collaboratively in our research concerns is that it helps us identify and, hopefully, overcome the limitations of our own ways of thinking, acting and reacting.)

12. Register progress not only with the participant group but also with the whole staff and other interested people. Create a reputation for success by showing what is being done. (Comment: while it can be counterproductive to try to involve those members of the school community who are unenthusiastic about teacher-research, it is important to keep the community informed of what one is doing and the progress one is making. It is also important to avoid being seen as an exclusive, elitist group.)

13. If necessary arrange legitimising rituals, involving consultants or other 'outsiders' who can help to show that respected others are interested in what the group is achieving for education in the school. (Comment: this can be particularly useful if there is a feeling of scepticism among others in the school community who feel you are just playing at research.)

14. Make time to write throughout your project. Write at the beginning, during the project and at the various 'endings'. (Comment: the value of diary writing has been underlined here several times, but particularly in Chapters Four and Six).

15. Be explicit about what you have achieved by reporting progress. For example, you can write up an account of your research project for others. Invite them to understand your educational theorising, to try the practices you have tried, and become part of the widening community of action researchers interested in the educational issues you have addressed. (Comment: the comments made in relation to points 12 and 13 are relevant here as well.)

16. Throughout, keep in mind the distinction between education and schooling. Action research is a concrete and practical process which helps those involved to build a critique of schooling, form the perspective of education, and to improve education in schools. (Comment: it is also important to keep in mind the value of teacher-research as an aid to one's own professional development.) (Points extracted and adapted from Kemmis and McTaggart 1988:25–8.)

Collaborative research is receiving increasing attention in the language-teaching field. At the 1988 TESOL convention, for example, a research colloquium and keynote presentation were devoted to collaborative research.

Schecter (1988) describes a collaborative study between university-based and school-based researchers. The study is of interest because it reinforces some of the points made by Kemmis and McTaggart, particularly those relating to the establishment of an appropriate working climate for the conduct of collaborative research. It also carries several potent warnings for those contemplating collaborative research between university- and school-based personnel. As you read of the project, you might like to consider the points of contact between it and the observations of Kemmis and McTaggart (1988).

The study was designed as an investigation into Young Writers' Week as a socially mediated event. This was part of 'a three year longitudinal investigation of the ways in which seventy-two children from four different ethnolinguistic populations develop and adapt their uses of language in interactions in elementary school classrooms'. The aim of engaging in collaborative research with participating teachers was to enhance children's opportunities for learning. The point of departure for the research were the issues felt by the teachers 'to be most in need of constructive examination'.

The context for the research was Young Writers' Week at one of the schools, participating in the longitudinal investigation. schecter, the university-based researcher, was to collaborate with the three project teachers at the school. She made it clear at the beginning that her contribution was to be as 'on-site ethnographer', and not as 'writing expert'. Here are some extracts from the ethnographic portrait of Young Writers' Week.

> Bain school staff have been engaging in evaluating and reevaluating their vision of the role of Young Writers' Week in fostering children's identities as writers and as members of a school-wide community of writers since the event's inception in 1984. ... In the first year ... only a few students participated.... The second year saw a school-wide democratization of the event: 'We want to provide an opportunity for all children and teachers to participate in the writing process from start to finish.' Since everyone was to be involved in Young Writers' Week, the need to isolate related activities no longer existed. Seizing on the potential of the school's open architecture, the organizers set up 'centres' on unclaimed territory where equipment – computers, mounting and binding machines and so on – could be installed and supervised by auxiliary staff and volunteers.
>
> ... the librarian is continuing with her chronology, 'we're starting to stress the quality of the story rather than "let's write a book" ... We want top quality. So there's a lot of pre-preparation.'
>
> Young Writers' Week falls at the beginning of April. By this time, students have worked on their texts, with the assistance of their teachers and classmates, for over a month. Just before the week begins, by leave of their teachers ... they take their books over to the computer centre to format their title pages. They then put the finishing touches to the cover illustrations and go to the 'illustrating centre' to 'wash' their book covers with lightwater paints.

A number of issues surfaced in field notes and conversations. These included the following:

Ownership: given the considerable intervention by adults (parents, teachers and librarians) the question arose over the writer's sense of ownership of the resulting book.

Writing for an audience: the role of social mediation in introducing learners to writing skills was also a focus for the research team.

The effects on teachers: some teachers found the experience a positive one, while for others it created anxiety over roles.

Public relations versus pedagogy: there was controversy over the value of parents' night, some teachers believing that it was just a 'showy performance', while others defended it for its motivational value.

Conferencing: this was also a controversial issue. Teachers who saw themselves as being the writing 'experts' were ambivalent about the right of, for example, volunteer typists to correct the children's spelling, punctuation and sentence structure.

The conferencing issue, and the relative roles of different participants, created a dilemma for the university-based researchers who felt that their teacher colleagues 'held ungrounded notions about the discourse functions served by conversations between various adult facilitators and the children (i.e. from a sociolinguistic perspective, they were wrong) ... there was an important positive link that had been missed between what the principal was trying to accomplish and what the organisers of Young Writers' Week were in effect accomplishing'. The researchers were also irritated by the attitude of certain staff members towards the participation of linguistic-minority parents in the literacy education of their children.

The university-based researchers were confronted with a dilemma on how to resolve this problem. They did not want to take any action which would provoke a confrontation, and yet they felt morally bound to act. Finally, a meeting was held at which the issue was talked through. To Schecter and her colleague Sally's surprise, the teachers did not disagree, but commended them for their positive contribution to the school. Schecter concludes:

> I had wasted precious time proceeding on the wrong assumption, i.e. that the most serious problem confronting the team was finding a way to work toward a common perspective. And the one problem I did not anticipate materialized: The group was, in fact, consensus-oriented, and participants were reluctant to explore differences in their perspectives. ... In the end it was the 'conferencing' issue more than any other part of the investigation, which raised important questions about the nature and purpose of collaborative research in educational settings. The undertaking taught me much about the value of collaboration as a method of triangulation. For me, the most challenging and gratifying part of the collaborative process consists of reaching, not so much a common perspective, as mutually negotiated and ratified ways of expressing differences in perspective.

Schecter's footnote to her study is also worth reporting:

> Ironically, I am now officially a 'writing expert' (my formal title is Academic Coordinator of the National Center for the Study of Writing). At times, I conjecture about what my contribution might have been had I looked at the phenomenon through a different lens (a process-oriented instruction lens, perhaps?). I would no doubt have found something valuable, related to the nature and extent of true collaborative talk, in writing conferences, for example, but I might have also missed something important. The idea of bringing a packaged perspective to the study of a school community which, in the final analysis, wrestled conscientiously with the psychological and social boundaries of literacy instruction, and specifically to a group of colleagues who were unwilling to confront their own demons, and mine, is somewhat unsettling.

Schecter's study demonstrates the role conflicts which are inherent in all collaborative research, not only that between university and school personnel but also, and probably most particularly, between colleagues and between teacher and learner. Her narrative also provides a warning of the potentially stressful nature of collaborative research. Finally, the study underlines another point made at various times in this book, that different people will view the same set of events in different ways. In other words, there will be multiple perspectives on the realities of classroom life, such perspectives reflecting the training and experiences of the participants involved. Any study which proceeds on the assumption that all the participants will see things in the same way is likely to run into difficulties (I am not suggesting here that Schecter made this assumption, merely pointing out that it is something to be aware of in entering collaborate projects).

Despite the difficulties and complexities of collaborative research, particularly research between individuals who because of their various backgrounds will have sharp differences of perspective, such research is still worth pursuing. The important thing is for each participant to declare his/her interests at the outset so that each knows where the other stands.

7.3 Supporting teacher-research

Thus far, we have focused primarily on teacher-research at a local level, although the case study reported by Schecter also looks at networking beyond the immediate environment of a single educational institution.

If the major thrust of Chapter Six is accepted, that teacher-research can provide a particularly effective means of facilitating ongoing professional development and curriculum renewal, then it is worth encouraging such research at a systemic, rather than isolated, classroom level. Doing so brings added complications, but also the possibility of added rewards.

Extending the scope of any enterprise brings complications. In the case of teacher-research, these complications are compounded by the fact that the sort of research we have talked about should receive its major impetus from those directly involved in the classroom, from the bottom-up as it were. Implementing a system-wide teacher-research programme, however, implies a more centralised top-down approach (this is not a necessity of systemic change, as the Graded Level of Achievement in Foreign Language Learning (GLAFLL) project in the UK has shown; for an account of this project, see Clark 1987).

One of the dangers of an extended, collaborative approach to teacher-research is that teachers who are either apprehensive of, or simply not interested in, carrying out their own research might be coerced into the programme, or may feel that as this seems to be the 'flavour of the month', they must necessarily become involved. I should therefore like to stress at this point that while teacher-research projects and networks should receive maximum publicity and promotion along the lines suggested by Kemmis and McTaggart, care should be exercised that teachers are not drawn in whose commitment might be lukewarm at best.

Once a teacher-research initiative spreads beyond a single classroom, another problem which often arises is that some teachers who have become interested and involved may not have the necessary support available to them to assist them shape, implement and evaluate their project. For this reason, educational authorities interested in experimenting with the sort of proposal being advocated in this book need to make adequate provisions of resources, time and expertise.

Experience has shown that extended teacher-research projects need, as a minimum, the following:

1. Adequate and appropriate training for participating teachers along the lines set out in Chapter Six.
2. Time (preferably paid release) for teachers to plan and evaluate their projects.
3. An adviser who is available at short notice to support and assist individual teachers with their research projects.

See also the comments of Kemmis and McTaggart (1988) and Breen *et al.* (1989).

Key to the success of a teacher-research programme is the availability of an appropriately trained adviser or facilitator. Such a person needs the following qualities:

1. Personal experience in planning, implementing and evaluating teacher-research.
2. Familiarity with the second-language literature.
3. An ability to create a non-threatening and trusting relationship with classroom teachers undertaking research.
4. An ability to help the teacher shape an area of interest and concern into a realistic, feasible and 'researchable' question.
5. Skills in classroom observation, transcription and analysis, and an ability to draw conclusions from such observation and analysis.
6. An ability, when under pressure, to respond quickly and creatively to problems as they arise during the course of particular projects.
7. An ability to analyse and identify where and why a project is going wrong and how to remedy it.
8. A knowledge of where to go for help, if one cannot provide it oneself.
9. Skills in writing up, presenting and disseminating research outcomes.
10. Skills in evaluating other people's research.

These qualities are possessed by many teachers who act as advisers and in-service educators within school districts, and it may be possible to find individuals who can reorient the skills they already possess to teacher-research.

The other major impediment to teacher-research is lack of time. This is a serious problem and can jeopardise projects being planned by even the most committed teachers. Unfortunately, there is no easy solution. Elliot (1982; cited in Walker 1985) provides the following suggestions for dealing with the time problem. These range from the flippant to the sensible to the self-evident.

Adapt standard methods.
Be flexible.
Convince authorities of need for more resources.
Clarification of task in small group/team discussion before whole staff work together.
Check on present use of time.
Timetable for research and support activities.
Try to delegate some of your responsibilities.
Use resources of students, university, college, etc.

A proper meeting calendar.
Use parents.
Learn to manage with less sleep.
Term in which research undertaken – autumn most favourable.
Management team undertaken structured servicing of research, implementing action, etc.
Close school early one day a term.
Second staff.
Release staff using INSET money.
Be judicious in collecting data.
Seek co-operation of colleagues.
Team teaching.
Be nice to the office/clerical staff.
Don't transcribe everything.
Reappraisal of professional priorities.

Most of these suggestions entail the co-operation of others. Working in a team, for example, can be extremely rewarding in terms of both teaching and research. However, it often involves the wholesale rearrangement of timetables and teaching schedules, and can inconvenience others not directly involved in the team effort. It can also eat up disproportionate amounts of time, particularly if those involved have to negotiate to achieve a common understanding and consensus about what they are supposed to be doing.

If one is working alone, it is possible to get more out of one's day by careful planning and timetabling. The best method for doing this is to keep a diary for a couple of weeks, noting what one is doing on an hourly basis. It is surprising how many hours are lost during a teaching week on casual conversation and various activities which rank well down the productivity scale such as covering books or getting stationery from the store. I am not suggesting that such activities should not be carried out, nor that staffroom chat is not important. Rather, I am suggesting that for the period which a research project is to be carried out, less time be spent on these activities, and the time thus saved, be redirected to the research effort.

7.4 Reporting teacher-research

It would be unfortunate if the research projects which are carried out by teacher-researchers never saw the light of day, and it is therefore important to think of ways in which the outcomes, successes and failures, problems and solutions are documented and reported. All projects should have a reporting mechanism built in. Some of the ways in which research can be reported are listed and commented on in this section.

While I have chosen to discuss a number of options separately, there will be occasions when two or more of these options will be combined to report a particular project.

Written accounts

Written reports of various kinds are probably the most common means of disseminating the outcomes of a research project, and they are usually a requirement in the case of specially funded research.

Such accounts can take many different forms, the form itself being determined by the nature of the research project and the intended audience. In some cases, several different versions of a report might be prepared. For example, in the case of a project funded partly or in whole by a government body or agency, one version of a report might be prepared for the funding body, a different type of report might be prepared for one's professional colleagues, and a third type might be written for submission to a journal.

While submission to a journal, particularly one with an international circulation, might seem a rather bold step to take, it is something which should be considered if one has undertaken a substantial piece of research. If nothing else, it is an extremely good way of drawing one's research to the attention of a wide audience.

Placing an article successfully requires a lot of work. In the first place, one needs to identify the type of journal likely to accept one's paper. Most journals have particular biases. It is doubtful whether an ethnographic account of the out-of-class reading opportunities of immigrant children will have much chance of being placed in a journal biased towards psychometric studies of adult foreign-language learners. It is also important to find out the readership towards which the journal is aimed, particularly whether the target audience is made up of researchers, graduate students or practising teachers.

Most journals have a style sheet which can be obtained free of charge. Most also include in each issue an account of their editorial policy and guidance on the preparation and submission of manuscripts.

Reputable journals send submissions to outside (generally anonymous) readers who comment on the suitability of the paper for publication. Those papers which are not rejected outright will usually attract a number of critical comments which will need to be addressed before rewriting and resubmitting the manuscript. While it can be painful, at least initially, to receive such comments, it is important to realise that all authors receive such comments from time to time, that they are intended to assist the author produce a better paper, and that it is better to receive such criticism before rather than after the paper has been published.

If the research has been carried out collaboratively, it might be possible for different members of the research community to contribute their own version of the research and its outcomes. While there is generally pressure to achieve agreement and consensus on research outcomes, this might, in some instances, be neither desirable nor necessary. There is, in fact, a type of research and evaluation reporting called 'adversarial reports'. In these, two or more participants provide their differing (and sometimes conflicting) accounts of the research (see, for example, Stake and Gjerde 1974, cited in Walker 1985).

In his discussion of ways of reporting research, Hopkins (1985) argues that written reports need to be put together in such a way that:

1. The research could be replicated on another occasion.
2. The evidence used to generate hypotheses and consequent action is clearly documented.
3. Action taken as a result of the research is monitored (Hopkins 1985:117).

He provides the following framework to assist teachers in presenting their research. He suggests that the framework encourages teachers to 'stand back and examine systematically the process of making a meta-analysis of the research'.

1. Statement of intent
   (a) Clarify purpose
   (b) Rationale
2. Procedures and process
   (a) Research design
   (b) Techniques of data collection
   (c) Verification of concepts
   (d) What actually occurred
3. Results and implementation
   (a) Outcomes of research
   (b) Theoretical implications
   (c) Action taken as a result
   (d) Evaluation of action
4. Meta-analysis
   (a) Review whole process
   (b) Conclusions as to utility of research
   (c) What would you do differently next time?

Seminars and oral papers

Like written reports, seminars vary greatly in format and intended audience, from the in-house variety in which a teacher reports back to colleagues in the institution in which the investigation took place, to formal papers presented at national and international conferences.

Conference presentations also provide a good opportunity of taking one's research to a wider audience. Although obviously reaching a more limited audience than a journal, conferences have the advantage that one can engage in a face-to-face dialogue with those who have come to hear one speak. They therefore offer an excellent opportunity to develop networks of like-minded individuals.

Slide/photograph show

The use of photographs can be a powerful means of recording and presenting data. Erickson and Wilson note that:

Audiovisual documentation involves the recording of the finely shaded details of everyday life in a setting. The record permits the researcher and the researcher's audience various kinds of vicarious 'revisiting' at later points in time. Because settings of social life are so complex and their details are so numerous, the ability to revisit an audiovisual record enables us to compensate for our limited human information processing capacities and to discover, after the fact, new aspects of meaning and organization that we did not realize at first (Erickson and Wilson 1982:40).

Templin (1979) cited in Walker (1985) outlines a procedure for undertaking and presenting research projects based on the use of photographs.

1. Talk with clients, staff, audiences.
2. Select sampling method.
3. Select instances to photograph.
4. Develop programme issues.
5. Select photographer(s).
6. Discover concerns of constituents, audiences, information needed.
7. Obtain permission to photograph.
8. Negotiate access with camera.
9. Begin taking many pictures.
10. Photograph mapping shots, detail and close-up shots.
11. Select representative pictures, focus issues, topics.
12. Go back, photointerview, interview, observe, rephotograph, gather verbatim data, repeat.
13. Validate, confirm, attempt to disconfirm story, issues.
14. Rephotograph, repeat process.
15. Assemble photos, narrative materials for report.

Video report

Like photographs, video, because of its immediacy, offers a powerful means of presenting one's research. The video record can include interviews with teachers, learners and others involved in a project, as well as classroom extracts. It can also provide a picture of the physical and intellectual context in which the research took place in a way which is not possible with other types of presentation.

I have already mentioned that reports can take a 'hybrid' form, with different media being combined to capture the complexity of the teaching/learning process, and video can and should be used where possible, particularly to supplement oral presentations and seminars.

Poster display

Poster displays are also generally 'hybrids', combining written texts, photographs, extracts from students' work and so on. These can be mounted in staffrooms, school corridors and classrooms, where they can provide feedback to the participants in the research process.

Conferences are also increasingly offering poster sessions as an alternative to the more usual papers, workshops, plenaries and seminars.

Workshop

A workshop can also be an effective means of presenting the results of one's research to others. If one has the time, workshops are particularly effective with classroom colleagues.

The essential difference between a workshop and other types of oral presentation such as papers and lectures is that in the latter participants listen passively to the researcher talking about his/her research, while in the former there is the possibility of playing a more active, participatory part. For example, if the research is reporting on some aspect of classroom intervention such as the effect of different task types on learner speech, participants can be given the opportunity of listening to and analysing oral and/or written classroom extracts, drawing their own conclusions, and then comparing these with the conclusions reached by the research group.

Discussion

Another alternative to the 'stand and deliver' lecture format is a structured discussion, in which participants discuss the issues thrown up by the research, and work through the implications of the research. One technique which works well in presenting collaborative research is the 'fishbowl' technique. Here, those involved in the research (including, if possible, some of the subjects) sit in a circle and discuss the research, debate the outcomes, and talk through the implications. The audience sits on the outside of the circle and looks into the 'fishbowl'.

Another variation is to arrange for a panel discussion. Each of the participants gives a short presentation, outlining the thrust of their contribution to the research and the outcomes. The audience is then invited to comment on the presentation, or ask questions of individual panel members.

The goldfish bowl and panel discussion techniques are particularly suitable if a number of teachers have investigated a similar question, problem or issue. Each can bring their various experiences to the discussion, and points of commonality as well as points of difference and disagreement can be aired.

In this section, I have outlined some of the ways in which teacher-research can be disseminated to the wider teaching and research community. Needless to say, I have only been able to give a brief description of some of the more common ways of disseminating research, and with a little thought you will probably be able to come up with other, possibly more creative, alternatives.

In deciding on preferred ways of reporting on teacher-research, some of these questions need to be addressed:

1. Who are the target audiences for the research and how can they best be reached?
2. Within the constraints of budget, time, etc., is it feasible to have more than one form of reporting?

3. Who will be involved in the reporting procedure? Is it possible to involve learners and other teachers who might be affected by the research?
4. Is it feasible or desirable to disseminate the research beyond the immediate teaching/research community of those involved in and/or directly affected by the research?
5. What is the optimal timing for disseminating the research?
6. Is it desirable to have an adversarial reporting mechanism?

7.5 Some generalisations and implications for teacher-research

In this section, we shall examine some of the implications of the foregoing for curriculum innovation and support.

In the last chapter, we looked at an in-service programme developed by Breen, Candlin, Dam and Gabrielsen (1989). At the conclusion of their paper, they make several deductions concerning in-service training, and these are worth reporting here as they reinforce some of the points which have already been made. While Breen *et al.* make their comments in relation to in-service training, they are just as relevant for teacher-research and, to this end, I have recast them so they are presented from a classroom-research perspective.

In the first place, in-service programmes should grow directly out of the experiences and problems of the teachers taking part in the programme. The implication of this is that trainers need to devise methods for drawing out participants' experiences, assumptions and problems. Due consideration also needs to be given to how teachers will reflect on these (one is reminded of the procedure recommended by Ramani (1987), as well as the workshop outline presented in Section 7.4, both of which are designed to achieve this aim).

Breen *et al.* also make the observation that teachers attempt too much in the classroom (see also the comments adapted from Kemmis and McTaggart in Section 8.3). This is something which is also borne out by my own experiences in facilitating teacher-research projects. Initially, teachers want to undertake projects which are far too large, and which would be beyond the resources of the teacher and the teaching institution. A research facilitator can play an important part in helping teachers refine the investigation so that it is feasible and realistic in terms of time and resources.

The next observation derives from the fact that learners are a major source of information about language and learning. In-service courses should therefore provide teachers with tools and techniques for investigating language-learning processes so that theory and practice are mutually supported. While it is not the principal aim of teacher-research to contribute directly to theory building and hypothesis formation, there is no reason why this should be explicitly ruled out. In any event, facilitators should at all times help teachers link their own work to major theoretical and empirical developments in the field.

It is also important for the focus to remain firmly fixed on the daily life of the classroom itself. As Breen *et al.* point out, this requires time for classroom data to be collected and shared. It also requires that the facilitator or trainer respect the teacher's interpretations of what happens in the classroom as well as her ways of articulating these events.

The next point represents an explicit rejection of the 'deficit' model of teacher development, which suggests that current practice is to be dismissed. It is important that classroom research build on what is currently happening rather than replacing it with ideas and practices which may actually be alien to the teacher. Often when teachers undertake an initial observation and analysis of their classrooms, they tend to take an unduly self-critical and dismissive attitude towards their current practice. This is something which the research facilitator or workshop co-ordinator must help teachers work through and resolve.

Facilitators should also be open to the issues which teachers feel are important and relevant to them, and need to be aware of the dangers of steering teachers into projects which, while they might seem more pertinent to the facilitator, are of peripheral interest to the teacher. In helping teachers shape a research project, a delicate balance needs to be maintained. One wants a project which is both manageable and relevant.

We have already noted the importance of collaborative research, and here we only need to note the desirability of stimulating projects which promote interaction and collaboration between researchers, facilitators, teacher-researchers, their colleagues and their learners.

An essential component of any research project, curriculum innovation, or classroom investigation is evaluation. Evaluation is essentially a judgmental activity and, as such, is most useful if it occurs formatively rather than summatively. In other words, it should partly take place during the course of a project rather than at the end.

Teacher-research is an investigative process which is focused on the teacher's classroom. The facilitator should take the part of a participant observer who is not only helping the teacher shape her project, but who is also genuinely interested in learning from the teacher's experience as a researcher. Additionally, as I have repeatedly stressed, research should begin from a close observation and analysis of the classroom itself. The last word should be left to Breen and his colleagues:

Our programme has developed from a focus on materials, through a focus on learning to a focus on classroom-derived information and from there to aspects of classroom management involving learners. We continue to be concerned with the introduction and implementation of innovation in language teaching. Other starting points and other teaching contexts may open the exploration of other routes and a different evolutionary process than ours. We are confident of two matters, however: first, whatever the specific initial focus of the in-service training, once a dialogue is established between trainer and trainee the focus of concern will expand from the particular to more general and underlying aspects of the management of classroom language learning.

Secondly, the trainer needs to be open to the likelihood that the programme may move in unexpected directions. Training as transmission forecloses both these possibilities. The comfort of its predictability and its convergence has to be assessed against its limited influence for change on actual practice (Breen *et al.* 1989).

7.6 Conclusion

In this chapter, we have looked at some of the factors which need to be taken into consideration in implementing research projects by classroom teachers. While not wishing to minimise the difficulties involved, I have argued the benefits of adopting a collaborative approach. I have also outlined some of the pitfalls and obstacles likely to confront individuals and institutions embarking on teacher-research, and have made some suggestions about how these might be overcome. I have also set out some ideas on how research might be carried to the wider professional community.

As this is the last chapter in the book, I have also taken the opportunity of looking at the implications of teacher-research. I have done so by adapting a number of generalisations made by Breen and his colleagues in a major in-service education exercise in Denmark. In the postscript following this chapter, I shall try to draw together the various issues and themes which have emerged during the course of this book.

7.7 Questions and tasks

1. Review the seventeen precepts for collaborative research extracted and adapted from Kemmis and McTaggart, and make a shortlist of those which seem most relevant to you, given your own situation.
2. Arrange an informal meeting with a group of colleagues who you think might be interested in a collaborative research project and work through the list, discussing each point as it relates to a possible research project by you.
3. Which of the observations by Kemmis and McTaggart are reflected in the study by Schecter? What do you think went right, and what went wrong with the Schecter study?
4. With the wisdom of hindsight, how would you have dealt with the conflict between the university- and school-based participants in Schecter's collaborative research project?
5. Is lack of time a factor likely to inhibit your own research? If so, study the list of suggestions on saving time provided by Elliott, then select and prioritise those which would be feasible to try out in your own situation.

    Keep a detailed diary for a week and note the number of hours which could have been rescued from other activities and devoted to research.
6. Which of the methods of reporting research set out in Section 7.4 seem most relevant for your own purposes?
7. If you have already carried out a research project, or are currently carrying out a project, develop a reporting and disseminating brief by working through and responding to the questions set out at the end of Section 7.4.
8. Write a mini-report (4–5 pages) following the outline suggested by Hopkins. How useful was the outline? What modifications, if any, would you make to it?
9. Summarise and then prioritise the points made in the final section of the chapter.

Postscript

In this book, I have argued that the development of skills in classroom observation, particularly if these lead into adoption of a research orientation by teachers to their classrooms, provides a powerful impetus to professional self-renewal. Such an orientation implies a particular role for the teacher. It is inconsistent with either the teacher as passive implementer of someone else's curriculum, or the notion of teaching as technology. The teacher-researcher is one who is involved in the critical appraisal of ideas and the informed application of these ideas in the classroom.

I have suggested that this approach is consistent with the notion of reflective teaching which is broader in focus than the notion of effective teaching. This latter concept shares certain basic assumptions with the 'methods' approach to language teaching. Implicit in both is the belief that somewhere there exists a set of ruling principles which, once discovered and appropriately applied, will result in learning for all. The major difference between the two is that while the methods approaches generally import principles from outside the classroom, the technology of effective teaching is grounded in the classroom, and seeks to derive principles for action from the classroom itself. Thus far, it has not been spectacularly successful in this endeavour.

Like the effective teaching movement, the teacher-research approach grounds its theory and practice firmly inside the classroom. However, the teacher-researcher is less concerned with a search for the one best way than with the exploration of a number of variables in a range of classrooms with a diversity of learner types. Such exploration may, in fact, reveal that the complex mix of elements and processes results in variable outcomes and that what works in one classroom with a particular group of learners may not be as successful in a different classroom with different learner types.

While it is not inconceivable that teachers observing and investigating their own classrooms might add to our body of basic knowledge about language learning and teaching, this is not its primary purpose or rationale for the ideas set out here. However, as we have seen at several points in this book, teachers can profitably recreate, and thus test against the reality of their own classrooms, claims from published research. The research literature is certainly a rich source of ideas on issues, methods and approaches, many of which are amenable to teacher-research, and many studies, including most of those which illustrate these pages, can stimulate the teacher to ask 'what might happen in *my* particular classrooms with *my* particular learners as a result of a particular intervention? Here I am following the lead of Cronbach (1975) who suggested that 'When we give proper weight to local conditions, any generalization is a working hypothesis, not a conclusion' (p. 125).

We might take, by way of illustration, the insight that the use of referential rather than display questions prompts longer and syntactically more complex responses from learners, or the finding that two-way information-gap tasks stimulate more modified interaction than one-way tasks. In testing notions such as these against the realities of her own classroom, the teacher-researcher needs to ask:

1. Does this intervention have the same result with all learners in all classrooms under all conditions?
2. Does the result hold up over time?
3. Does it matter/make a difference anyway?

In recent years interest has grown in the notion of the self-directed learner, that is the learner who is able to identify and exploit his/her own best ways of learning. By analogy, we can say that the teacher–researcher concept is predicated on the notion of the self-directed teacher. In other words, it is a way of helping teachers find, exploit and extend their own best ways of teaching.

Given limitations of space, I have not been able to provide an exhaustive coverage of issues and methods for teacher-research. In any event, this would be undesirable. As a result of reading this book and considering the questions and tasks at the end of each chapter, teachers should be able to formulate their own issues, methods and possible solutions. What I have attempted to do is provide sufficient illustration to show the range of possibilities.

In terms of research methods and design, I have suggested that interpretive approaches are more likely to be of value that psychometric ones, although I have also indicated that the distinction between the two research traditions is a rather crude one. Nonetheless, I am substantially in agreement with Heath (1983), who observes that:

> Often the approaches to research in education have been quantitative, global, sociodemographic, and dependent on large-scale comparisons of many different schools. Terms from business predominate: input, output, accountability, management strategies, etc. Input factors (independent variables) are said to influence, predict, or determine output factors (dependent variables). Pieces of data about social groups, such as number of siblings or time of mother-child interactions in preschool daily experiences, are correlated with the output of students expressed in terms of test scores, subsequent income, and continued schooling. The effects of formal instruction have been evaluated by correlating these input factors with educational output.
>
> From an ethnographic perspective, the irony of such research is that it ignores the social and cultural context which created the input factors for individuals and groups. Detailed descriptions of what actually happens to children as they learn to use language and form their values about its structures and functions tell us what children do to become and remain acceptable members of their own communities.

In making a call for teacher-research, I have tried not to overlook or minimise the difficulties and obstacles likely to confront those answering the call. While each situation is likely to pose its own problems and therefore demand its own unique mix of solutions, there are several commonly recurring impediments to teacher-research. I have attempted in the book to indicate what these are, and to outline possible solutions. I have also suggested that collaborative approaches to research, while they increase the risks, also increase the potential rewards.

There may be those who feel that by defining research as the observation of, intervention in and critical reflection on practice, I am imposing on the term a burden it was never meant to bear. To them I can only respond that I am in good company. There is a rapidly growing tradition stretching back to Stenhouse (1975) and beyond which defines research in terms of its potential for the emancipation of the classroom practitioner. This book has been written for teachers, and it will be justification enough if it speaks to their concerns.

Appendix A

Lesson Transcripts

This appendix contains excerpts from two different lessons. They have been included to provide material for analysis for readers who may not have their own lesson transcripts.

Extract 1 is taken from the beginning of a lesson with pre-intermediate, intermediate level learners. The teacher is introducing the students to an information-gap activity.

Extract 2 is from a lesson with a group of beginners. The learners have just completed a small-group picture-sequencing task. Each group was given five pictures showing an accident between a milk van, a bicyclist and a dog. Their task was to correctly sequence the pictures.

Extract 1

T   Of course I had lunch ... not enough ... why? why? Well, like I say, I want to give you something to read. So what you do is, you have to imagine what comes in between, that's all ... Bring, er, bring your chairs a little closer, you're too far away. Er, ha, not that close.

SS Quiss?

T   Pardon?

S   It will be quiss? It will be quiss? Quiss?

SS Quiss?

T   Ahm, sorry ... try again.

S   I ask you ...

T   Yes?

S   You give us another quiss?

T   Oh, quizz, oh! No, no, not today ... it's not going to be a quiss today ... sorry. But, um, what's today, Tuesday is it?

S   Yes.

T   I think on Thursday, if you like. Same one as before ... Only I'll think up some new questions – the other ones were too easy ... Um, OK, er I'll take some questions from, er, from newspapers over the last few weeks, right? So – means you've got to watch the news and read the newspaper and remember what's going on ... if you do, you'll win ... if not, well, that's life.

S   Will be better from tv.

    [*Laughter*]

T   From the tv? ... What, er, what programmes?

Ss News. News.

T   Did you say ...? Oh, ok, we'll have, er, it'll be the s..., it'll be the same ... there'll be different ...? Er, there'll be different ...? Different? Different? The questions will be on different ...

    what? Different?

S   Talks

T   Tasks? What?

S   Subject?

T   Different sub ...?

S   Subjects.

T   Subjects, subjects, thank you ... right, yes. The questions will be on different subjects, so, er, well, one will be about, er, well, some of the questions will be about politics, and some of them will be about, er, ... what?

S   History.

T   History. Yes, politics and history and, um, and ...?

S   Grammar.

T   Grammar's good, yes, ... but the grammar questions were too easy.

S   No

S   Yes, ha, like before.

S   You can use ... [*inaudible*]

T   Why? The hardest grammar question I could think up – the hardest one, I wasn't even sure about the answer, and you got it.

S   Yes.

T   Really! I'm going to have to go to a professor and ask him to make questions for this class. Grammar questions that Azzam can't answer. [*laughter*] Anyway, that's, um, Thursday ... yeah, Thursday. Ah, but today, er, we're going to do something different ...

S   ... yes ...

T   ... today, er, we're going to do something where we, er, listen to a conversation – er, in fact, we're not going to listen to one conversation. How many conversation're we going to listen to?

S   Three?

T   How do you know?

S   Because, er, you will need, er, three tapes and three points.

T   Three?

S   Points.

T   What?

S   Power points.

T   Power point. If I need three power points and three tape recorders, you correctly assume that I'm going to give you three conversations, and that's true. And all the conversations will be different, but they will all be on the same ...?

Ss Subject. Subject.

T   The same?

Ss Subject. Subject.

T   Right, they'll all be on the same subject. Different conversations, but the same subject. And so, I'm going to later in the lesson divide the class into three?

S   Groups.

T   Right! And each group, each group?

S   Listens.

T   Ah huh!

S   Listen to tape.

T   Listen to a tape. Each group?

S   Will listen to conversation. One conversation.

T   Right. OK. That's right. And I'm going to give you a piece of paper, and, er, I'm going to ask each group to, er, ...

S   ... write.
T   Write. Write what?
S   Question.
S   [*Inaudible*] Listen.
T   Write about?
S   Comprehension.
T   What they?
S   What they listen.
T   What they?
S   Will listen.
S   Heard.
T   Yes, OK, write about what they listened to. I want you to get some information out of the conversations. I'll tell you what to listen for and then later I'm going to bring, er, the three groups together and you're going to put all the information together to, er, solve a little problem. But that's for later. First we talk about the subject of the conversation, then I'm going to divide you into, er into?
S   Three groups.
T   Uh huh, and?
S   And you'll listen to the cassette.
T   OK, right. [*pause*] You'll listen to the cassette? [*laughter*]
S   Your.
    You?
T   You say, 'you'll listen to the cassette'. You mean?
S   We.
T   We, we, we. Tell me again.
S   I forgot.
T   You've forgotten! All right, so've I. All right. The subject, the subject of the, er, conversation, is going to be?
S   [*Inaudible*]
T   Yes?
S   [*Inaudible*]
T   It's going to be about?
S   [*Inaudible*]
T   About, uh?
S   Person.
T   Yes, a person.
S   Er ...
S   Who wants ...
S   Who ...
S   Look ...
T   Who's looking for.
S   For job.
T   For a job? [*laughter*] OK, so what, what is the subject of the conversation?
S   She's looking for a house.
T   Ok. She?
S   He.
S   She.
S   He.
T   He.
S   He.

Ss	He. He. He. He.
T	OK. He's looking for a house. All right. Er, and, er, er, does he, uh, does he want to buy the house?
S	No.
S	Rent. Rent.
S	He wants to rent.
S	He wants to rent a house.
T	OK. He wants to rent a house. Yes, he wants to rent a house. Ah, who, ah ... What kind of office, what kind of office do you go to if you want to rent a house?
S	[*Inaudible*]
T	I beg your pardon?
S	Agent office.
T	Yes. What's the name, what's the name of the agency?
S	Housing.
T	Employment agency?
S	No.
S	Housing.
S	Housing trust.
T	What? Housing trust? Yes, that's in, er, the long-term future, but, er, you can, er freeze to death, er, waiting for a house from a housing trust. He wants a house now. Where do you go to?
S	We going ask door-to-door.
T	Door-to-door?
S	Looking newspaper.
T	What?
S	Read the newspaper.
T	That's one way, yes, you can read the newspaper.
Ss	Yes, yes.
T	Yes, you can look in the newspaper.
S	... and cheaper.
S	Yes.
T	Come on. [*Inaudible*] Yes. What do you call somebody who buys and sells and lets houses?
S	Agent.
T	What kind of an agent?
S	Agent. Agency.
T	Agent. The person is an agent. The office is an agency. Right? Ah, but what kind of an agent? A secret agent?
S	[*Inaudible*]
T	A police agent?
S	Hoss.
Ss	House, house, house.
S	Huse, eh.
S	No hoss, no hoss.
S	Real state.
S	Real estate, yeah.
Ss	Oh, oh, oh.
T	OK, a real estate agent. Or sometimes we just call them an ...?
S	Estate agent.
S	Estate agent.

T   ... estate agent. OK. Now, the person who's looking for the house, the person who's looking for the house doesn't want just any house, hmm? Because, because he, ah, uh, uh, hum? Ah hum?

S   He have children.

T   Ah, yes, he has children. And, ah, also? Also?

S   A dog.

S   He has dog.

S   He has father and mother.

T   He has a father and a mother. Ah who ...?

S   Who live with him, lives with him.

S   Live, live, live with him.

T   OK. Who live with him, yes. So how many people, how many people will be in the house?

S   Six?

T   Six?

S   ... many children,

S   [*Inaudible*]

T   OK. Six?

S   Seven.

T   Er, he has, er ...

S   Two children.

T   Uh hum, two small, uh hum ... oh well, not very small, not very small, not very small. Er?

S   Six persons, six persons.

T   Just a minute. Husband, wife, two children and?

S   Six.

T   The mother.

S   Five.

T   OK. Five. And the children are, er, six and, er, eight, right? Six years old and eight years old. OK? So, er, what's the minimum number of, er?

S   Bedrooms.

S   Three bedrooms.

S   [*Inaudible*]

T   Oh ho, four?
    [*Laughter*]

Ss Four, four yes.

S   One for children.

T   Have the husband and wife separated?

Ss No. No.

S   Three.

S   Four.

T   Four?

S   One for each child.

S   One for grandmother.

T   Yes, one for the grandmother.

S   One for husband and wife.

T   Yes, one for the husband and wife. [*Inaudible*] If he was a doctor then, er, then maybe, ah, he could, er, look for a four bedroom house and have one for each child.

S   Oh!

T   But he's very poor. He's a teacher, right? [*Laughter*] And so how many bedrooms is he looking for?

S Three.
S Two. Two.
S Three.
T Three?
S Three.
T Come on, he's not that poor. [*Laughter*] OK, so, so, what's he looking for? He's looking for a . . .?
S A house.
S With three bedrooms.
S A house with three bedrooms.
T OK, he's looking for a house with three bedrooms, or, what do we say? We don't, in English we don't usually say a house with three bedrooms . . . What do we usually say?
S Three bedroom house.
T A three bedroom house, a three bedroom house, a three bedroom house. So what's he looking for?
S For three bedroom house.
T What's he looking for?
S [*Inaudible*]
   [*Laughter*]
T What's he looking for?
S House.
T What's he looking for?
S Three bedroom house.
T All right.
S Why three bed, er, three bedroom? Why we don't say three bedrooms?
T Ahh, oh . . . I don't know, um.
S Is not right.
T We don't say it. We don't say it. There's no explanation. But we often do that in English. Three bedroom house.
S Don't ask for it.
S Yes.
T Well, do ask why. Ask why, and 99 per cent of the time I know the answer. One per cent of the time, nobody knows the answer. If I don't know it, nobody knows. [*Laughter*] Ah, no, I don't know the answer, sorry.

Extract 2

T Can you put the pictures . . . number one, number two . . .? [*Demonstrates*] [*students sequence pictures*]
T Finished? Good, good, that was quick. Let me have a look.
S [*to another student*] No, this one, you know, hospital, this one first, telephone, hospital, car.
T This the same, same this? Look at picture number one.
S Number one.
T Yes. Can you see, Hing? Where are they? Where is this?
Ss Where are, where are, um, bicycle, bicycle.
T The man's on a bicycle, mmm.
S And a man behind, behind a car. Bicycle behind a car. Behind a car.
T What's the name of this? What's the name? Not in Chinese.
Ss Van. Van.

T   Van. What's in the back of the van?

S   Milk, milk.

T   Milk.

Ss   Milk. Milk.

T   A milk van.

S   Milk van.

T   What's this man? ... Driver.

S   Driver.

T   The driver.

S   The driver.

T   The milkman.

S   Millman.

T   Milkman.

Ss   Milkman.

T   Where are they?

Ss   Where are they?

T   Where are they? Inside, outside?

S   Department.

T   Department?

S   Department store.

T   Mmm. Supermarket. They're in the street. In the street. They're in the street. Outside. They're in the street. The bicycle, and the van – where are they? Where are they? What's this?

Ss   Street.

T   In the street. OK. Is this a man or a woman?

Ss   Man.

T   A man?

S   Woman.

S   Woman.

S   Man.

S   No man.

T   She's a woman there.

Ss   Woman, woman, man, woman.

S   Boy.

T   Boy? Maybe a boy. Boy?

S   Boy.

    [*inaudible*]

T   Boy, boy, boy? OK. What's, what's he riding? What's he riding?

Ss   Bicycle. Bicycle.

T   A bicycle. A bicycle.

Ss   Bicycle.

T   Look at picture number two.

Ss   Number two.

T   What's this?

S   Dog, dog.

T   A dog, yes, What's ... [*accident*] ... the dog doing?

S   Accident.

T   The dog?

S   Running.

T   Running.

Ss	Running.
T	Running. Running. Running. Where? Where's he running?
S	Where's running?
S	Dog is running.
S	Opposite.
T	No, not opposite.
Ss	No, no.
T	Good, good thinking ... Van.
S	Hit.
T	Dog. Ow. He's running?
Ss	Front. Behind.
T	In front ... in front of the van.
Ss	In front of the van.
T	Good. In front of. In front of the van. In front of the van. Yes.
S	In front of the van.
T	Good. Now, look at picture number three. What's this on the road?
Ss	The milk ... milk.
Ss	Milk. Milk?
Ss	No, no. Yes, yes.
T	White. And glass. Milk?
Ss	Milk? Yes, yes, yes.
T	And glass.
Ss	Glass.
T	Glass.
Ss	Glass.
T	Glass.
S	In? [*points to light*]
T	Mmm, that's glass. In the light – glass.
Ss	Light, light.
S	In China [*gestures*] glass. Yes. Good?
T	Job? Cut?
S	Cut.
T	Cut glass.
S	Cut glass.
T	Oh, in China your job was to cut glass for windows.
Ss	Yes, yes.
T	Oh, good.
S	No good!
T	No? [*laughter*] How are your hands?
S	China good. Here no good.
T	No good.
S	Australia, no speak.
T	Ah, no English ... (yeah) ... no job.
S	No job.
T	Don't worry. OK. So, look at picture number one, number two and number three. What happened? What's happened? The van, the milk van is driving along the road. The man is (man is) bicycling (bicycling) along (along). The dog (the dog)
Ss	Run in front.
T	Runs in front of the van (van). Now what happened?
S	Accident.

T   Accident. Accident. Good. The bicycle, the bicycle ...
Ss Bicycle ... and van
T   And van (and van) accident.
Ss Accident. Accident.
T   Accident.
Ss Accident.
T   The van.
S   Van.
T   The dog.
Ss Dog, dog ... accident, accident.
T   The driver.
S   The driver.
T   The driver.
S   Stop.
T   Stopped. Eeee! [*mimes*]
S   Stopped.
    [*laughter*]
S   Er, bicycle ...
T   The bicycle.
S   Bicycle, boom.
Ss Uh, oh.
T   Uh huh! And what happened to the milk?
Ss Milk, milk, milk [*gestures*]
T   Yeah, very good hand. The milk, the milk fell.
Ss Fell, fell.
T   Fell.
Ss Fell, fell.
T   It fell out of the truck.
S   Fell.
T   Fell out of the truck, and it sp...
S   It spill. Put ... not good ... put on ... cut.
T   Broken!
Ss Broken.
T   Broken. Broken. Do you remember in the doctor's surgery? [*previous lesson*]
Ss Yes, yes.
T   Doctor's surgery, the man? Black eye? And the broken arm.
Ss Broken arm ... broken.
S   Leg.
S   Ah, leg.
T   Leg.
Ss Broken leg, yes, yes.
T   The milk bottles were broken (broken) broken. OK.
    Look at picture number four. The man.
S   The man.
S   Telephone.
T   Man. The man. Boy. Where's he going?
Ss Telephone ... to telephone.
T   Telephone. Why?
S   Ambulance.

T Ambulance. (Ambulance) Ambulance. (Telephone ambulance)
   Telephone ambulance. (Ambulance) Ambulance. What number?
S 000
T 000 ... 000
S 000
T Ambulance please, ambulance please. Ambulance. E-E-E Ambulance.
S Ambulance.
T Er, what's this?
S Hospital car. No.
T Hospital car. Name?
S No. I don't know?
T Ambulance.
S Ambulance.
T Ambulance. Hospital car. Ambulance.
S Ambulance.
T Ambulance.
S Ambulance.
T Ambulance. (Ambulance). Is this a woman? (Woman). Yes? Yes, it's a woman.
   What's she doing?
S Car, er, car.
T What's she doing? This woman. (car, car). No, yes, Seng. That woman. Seng. That woman.
   (Woman, woman). What's she doing?
Ss Go to [*inaudible*] Help.
T Help.
S Help.
T Help (help). She's helping the boy (boy, boy, boy)
S Is help the boy in, er, in the ...
T In the ambulance, into the ambulance.
S Into ambulance (ambulance, ambulance) OK? (ambulance, ambulance, police)
T Police or maybe the ambulance driver.
S This police? Police.
T I think, maybe ambulance driver.
Ss Yes, yes.
S This one?
T I don't know. That's the milkman.
S Milkman. Milkman.
T Milkman.
S Milkman.
T He's got a rash on his face.
S Er, milkman. Yeah, this milkman.
T Mmm
S This milkman?
T Yes.
S This milkman?
T Milkman. OK? Erm, Anastasia, Seng. Anastasia, in Greece ...
S In Greece ...
T Do you have a milk van? In Greece? Milk van?
S Er, yes, yes, yes. (yes) Yes. And, er, bus milk.
T A big, big van ...

S   Yeah, very big.

T   Bus, Oh!

S   This one.

T   Every morning? In the morning?

S   Morning, afternoon.

T   Oh, two, three times a day. What about in China? Well, Hong Kong. China. Do you have a milk van?

Ss Er, China ... no, no milk.

T   No milk?

Ss Yeah, shop, er, city, city.

T   No milk?

Ss Yeah, shop, er, city, city.

T   Ah, at the shop, the shop.

Ss Er, yes, yes.

S   Hong Kong. Hong Kong.

T   Yeah, in Hong Kong, yes.

Ss In China, yes, er [*inaudible*] city.

T   In the big cities.

Ss Big city ... city, yeah.

T   Ah huh!

Ss Guandong. Peking. Shanghai, Shanghai.

S   Yes, er city, very big, big milk car.

T   Big milk van. Ah! And city, country. In the country, no?

Ss No.

T   No. Shh, shh, shh [*gestures*]

S   That's right.

T   Yes [*laughs*]

S   I'm, er, I'm ... No, is China, er city.

T   Uh huh!

S   Er, I'm house, near, near city er, I'm go to city shopping, er, how many?

T   Buy milk.

S   Buy milk, yeah. Buy milk.

T   Buy milk.

S   Buy milk, go to home, yes.

T   Mary, in Iran, in Tehran, do you have a milk van? Yes? OK. Has, has anyone ... Sorry Mai ... has anyone got a bicycle here?

S   Bicycle.

T   In Australia?

S   Bicycle? No.

T   No? Anastasia?

S   No.

T   No? Mary? Have you got a bicycle here? [*Laughs*] Seng?

S   China, yes. Son.

T   Son, your son's got a bicycle.

S   For women ...

T   For women, no.

S   No.

T   Ah! Do you understand? In Iran, women must not ride a bicycle.

S   Car, yes.

T Uh huh!

S China, many, many bicycles.

T Many, many bicycles.

Ss Yes.

T Uh huh!

S Guanchong many many bicycles. Er, street, the street, ohh. Car stop and er bicycle like [*inaudible*]. Turn right, eee.

T Turn left, turn right, bicycles.

Ss Bicycles, many, many bicycles.

T In China, did you have a bicycle?

S Yes.

T You had a bicycle. Yeah? What about you Da Sheng?

S Yes, bicycle.

T In China? Bicycle?

S My home, er, four bicycles.

T Four bicycles? Are they expensive?

S No 'pensive.

T Expensive or cheap?

S Er, cheap.

T Cheap.

S Cheap.

T Cheap. Uh huh! Chinese bicycles?

S My bicycle is to Hong Kong. My brother use [*inaudible*] buy, buy, Hong Kong, Hong Kong.

T Oh, they bought, buy your bicycle.

S Yeah.

T Ahh. OK. Anastasia, in Greece, did you have a bicycle when you were little? (No, no) When you were a little girl?

S No, no.

T No? No. What about you Hing?

S Yeah, my son.

T Your son. What about you?

S Yes.

T Yes? When you were a little girl? Mmm, same.

S Yeah.

T Yes. Bicycle?

S Bicycle [*inaudible*]

T Many Australian children have bicycles.

S Chinese, er bicycle, er ...

S Different.

T Ohh?

S Different.

T Different.

S [*Tells teacher in Cantonese*]

T I don't understand Dai Cheng, I'm sorry.

S Chinese bicycle is Australia bicycle, er different.

T Different.

S Yeah.

T But, er, two, two wheels?

S Yes, two wheels.

T Two wheels. And pedals?
S Pedals, pedals, yes.
T And handles.
S Handles different.
T Different. Ahh. Your bicycle, does it have a horn? Toot, toot, toot. Bing, bing, bing. [*laughter*] Yes?
S Yes.
T OK, all right. In, er, well, I know in China there are many, many bicycles.
S Yeah.
T Are there many accidents?
S Accidents?
S Yeah.
T In China?
Ss Yes, yes.
T Bicycle, bicycle? [*gestures*]
S Bicycle, bicycle. Bicycle, bus. Bicycle, car.
T Ahh.
S Bicycle is, um, street, street load (load) little load. Australia big load.
T Road.
S Load, yeah.
T Road.
S Load.
T Big road.
Ss China, small, small, street.
T The street is small, thanks. The street is small.
S [*Inaudible*] Too [*Inaudible*]
S [*gestures*]
T Oh, I see. The road ...
S The road.
T Du, du, du, one, two.
S Yes.
T Uh huh, and many, many bicycles. Ah huh. In Malaysia and Singapore are there many bicycles?
S Chinese many, many bicycles. Little, little.
S Er, moto, moto. Mo, mo, mo, mo.
T Oh, motor bike.
Ss Motor bike. Motor bike.
T Motor bike.
S China, yes.
T Uh huh. In Greece. What about in Greece. Many bicycles?
S Mmm. Bicycles, motor.
T Uh huh. In Australia, er, bicycle, er, we wear a helmet.
Ss Helmet. yes, yes.
T Special [*gestures*] helmet.
Ss Ohh.
S Malaysia, same, same.
T Same in Malaysia?
Ss Yes, yes.
S Moto, moto.

T   In China, a little or a lot?
S   Motor. Some motor bicycle.
T   Motor bike.
S   Yes, yes. Bicycle, no. China, bicycle no. Motor, yes.
T   Ah huh.
S   Cap, cap.
S   Cap.
S   Hat on, hat, hat.
T   Hat.
Ss Hat. Hat.
T   Ah, in Australia, motor bike, yes. Yes, yes, yes. Bicycle, yes, good (oh). Children, special
    helmet (helment) Helmet, mmm. Special helmet.
S   Erm, China, er, there are many, many [*gestures*].
T   Many, many accidents.
S   Accidents.
T   And Greece?
S   No.
T   No? In China many bicycles. Have you ever? Have you seen an accident? Have you
    seen an accident?
S   Accident.
T   In ... yes? What happened?
S   Motor, motor.
T   Motor.
S   Motor.
T   Motor car. Car.
S   Er, motor, motor car.
T   Er, one car?
S   One motor ...
T   Motor bike.
S   Motor bike.
T   Motor bike. A car and a motor bike. (Motor bike. Motor bike.) Oh! And, er, like this, like
    this? What happened? Show me with your hands.
S   One, er, one here.
T   Ah, it turned. Turned?
S   Turned, yeah, yeah.
S   Car ... bicycle.
T   Mm, car, bicycle. Ohh, the car was doing this and then ... all over. Very bad? Bad? Um, good?
S   No good.
T   Bad.
S   Bad.
T   Bad.
S   Bad.
T   Yes.
S   Many many dead. Bad.
S   My father, accident, is dead.
T   Oh, your father was killed in an accident.
S   Mmm.
S   My husband, sick, motor bike. My husband.
T   In an accident?

S   Yeah, yeah.

T   Motor bike accident.

S   Hong Kong.

T   What happened Hing? What happened? Your husband (my husband) was riding a bike (Yeah, yeah).

S   My husband [*gestures*].

T   Oh, he fell off.

S   Yeah, fell off.

T   The milk fell off the truck. Your husband fell off the motor bike.

S   Yeah. Yeah. Yeah.

T   Did he have a helmet?

S   No.

T   No? Hospital?

S   No, no hospital.

T   No? Lucky!

Ss Lucky. Lucky.

S   [*gestures*]

T   Ah, he hurt his hand.
    [*noise – inaudible talk*]
    And your father?

S   Brother.

T   Brother.

S   Young.

T   Young brother. Your father was in a car accident or a motor bike?

S   No, motor, my father.

T   Motor bike.

S   Er, car. Opposite and the driver going.

T   Ah, the driver, didn't stop. No help.

S   No, no help, and my then uncle number car.

T   Number car – the car number.

S   And just is dead.

T   Dead? When did he die?

S   Um, sixty-eight.

T   Sixty-eight.

T   Sixty-eight years old.

T   Sixty-eight years old. Ah, that's very sad.

S   In Australia.

T   It was in Australia. Gosh. I'm sorry.

S   Australia, it's me ... my, my ...

T   Oh, you were in Australia, and your father was in Greece, and it happened in Greece. I'm sorry. Mary, you were in an accident. Were you in a ...?

S   Yes, but car.

T   Car. How many cars? One car, two cars?

S   Car.

T   Mmm.

S   [*gestures*] Boom!

T   Er, car?

S   Brrm, brrm, brrm, bang!

T   What's this?

Ss	Car. Car. Car.
T	Two cars. Like this. And, you hurt your wrist? Mmm, very bad. Ohh. Here.
S	Hospital?
S	Yes.
S	Oh, I'm sorry.
T	How long were you in hospital?
S	One month.
T	One month?
Ss	One month, one, one month.
T	Mmm.
S	One month.
T	Er, a long time ago Mary? Or, how long, how long ago?
S	Yes.
T	Er, now, 1986.
S	Oh.
T	What year?
S	What year?
S	Ten. Ten.
T	Ten years ago. 1976.
S	1976, yes.
T	OK, Da Sheng, have you been in an accident?
S	No.
T	No? Good! Lucky.
S	Lucky [*laughter*].
T	Seng?
S	No.
T	No. Little?
S	No.
T	No? You must be a good driver.
S	No good driver!
T	No? May Yu?
S	No.
T	No? Heng?
S	No.
T	No? I have, I have been in one, two, three.
Ss	Three! Oh!
T	Er, number one, my father, my father was driving and he [*gestures*] blinker. Car, whisht!
Ss	Oh, oh!
T	Number two, ah, my friend, driving, and I was sitting here. Stopped [*gestures*]. Car. Car. Car. Car. Car. Five cars. Bang! Bang! Bang! Bang! Bang! Sally, 'Ah! Ah! Ah! Ah! Ah!' And what was the other one? I can't remember. No, little, very small accident. Fingers crossed. OK, that was good. Would you like to put them together for me? [*gestures at the pictures*] Put them back together?
S	My, my father, my father?
S	My mother.
S	My mother is by bicycle. By bicycle, yes, many many water.
T	She had an accident?

S   China, my mother is a teacher, my father is a teacher. Oh, she go finish by bicycle, er, go to ...
S   House?
S   No house, go to ...
S   School?
S   My mother ...
T   Mmm
S   ... go to her mother.
T   Oh, your grandmother.
S   My grandmother. Oh, yes, by bicycle, by bicycle, oh is, em, accident [*gestures*].
T   In water?
S   In water, yeah.
T   In a river!
S   River, yeah, river. Oh, yes, um, dead.
Ss   Dead! Dead! Oh! [*general consternation*]
T   Dead? Your mother?
S   My mother.
T   How long ago?
S   How long ago?
T   How many years?
S   My mother is, er, ten, ten, nine ...
T   Twenty-nine years old. How old were you?
S   [*inaudible*] Eight.
T   Eight years' old.
S   My brother eight, and my sister six. My brother...
S   Young brother.
S   Brother.
T   Young Brother.
S   Young brother, er, three.
T   Three!
S   Yes, er, my [*inaudible*] eight month old.
T   Eight months, and your mother died in the [*inaudible*]. That's very sad, very sad. And your
     father, OK?
S   Oh, father, yeah, OK. My mother, many many [*inaudible*].
T   Ah, dear, that's a terrible story. I'm sorry.
S   Yes, er, no water, no water.
T   Oh, she couldn't breathe.
S   Yes, and, er, dizzy. Oh, no doctor, long time no doctor.
T   And she died. Er, what happens, what happens, for example, in Greece if there's an accident?
     Accident. This man run to telephone the ambulance. In Greece, same?
S   Iran, yes. Iran, yes.
T   Iran. Telephone ambulance. What about the police?
S   No police.
T   What about in Hong Kong? Heng? What about in Hong Kong?
S   999.
T   999? Telephone hospital. For the ambulance.
S   China, China, yes. 999.
S   One hundred.
T   One hundred.
S   Guandong 999.

T And police? Accident, accident, telephone police? Yes?
S Police?
T In Greece, no?
S In Greece, no.
T In Australia, us ... yes.
S No, no police, no police.
T Ambulance, police.
S Ambulance, hospital, no police.
T Number one, hospital. Number two, police.
S [*Inaudible*] Number one, police. Police telephone hospital.
T For an ambulance, for an ambulance. Right, would you like to sit down, and I'll write ambulance for you. It's a new word.

Appendix B

Sample Observation Schedules

B.1 Foreign language observational system used in an intensive observational study.

From Nerenz and Knop (1982) 'A time-based approach to the study of teacher effectiveness', *Modern Language Journal*, 66.

	Student No. Start _____ Stop _____	_____	_____	_____	_____	_____	_____
GROUPING CONTENT	Transition						
	Content Skill-getting Skill-using						
	Individual Pair Small Group Large Group						
MATERIALS	Paper/Pencil Printed Matter Visual Aid Audio Visual **Target Lang** English						
STUDENT ACTIVITIES	Eng-writing Eng-oral Eng-listening Eng-covert Noneng-waiting Noneng-interim Noneng-offtask **Target Lang** **English**						
INTERACTIONS	Target Student Small Group Large Group Teacher Target Student Small Group Large Group Teacher Repetitive Communicative **Target Lang** **English**						
TEACHER ACTIVITIES	Structuring Modeling Questioning Explaining Mon-Evaluating Man-Discipline						

B.2 Teacher's responses to students' questions.

From Good and Brophy (1987) *Looking into Classrooms*, New York: Harper and Row.

USE: When a student asks the teacher a reasonable question during a discussion or question-answer period

PURPOSE: To see if teacher models commitment to learning and concern for the students' interests

Code each category that applies to the teacher's response to a reasonable student question. Do not code if student wasn't really asking a question or if he was baiting the teacher

BEHAVIOUR CATEGORIES

1. Compliments the question ("Good question")
2. Criticises the question (unjustly) as irrelevant, dumb, out of place, etc.
3. Ignores the question, or brushes it aside quickly without answering it
4. Answers the question or redirects it to the class
5. If no one can answer, teacher arranges to get the answer himself or assigns a student to do so
6. If no one can answer, teacher leaves it unanswered and moves on
7. Other (specify)

NOTES:

CODES

1 _____	26 _____
2 _____	27 _____
3 _____	28 _____
4 _____	29 _____
5 _____	30 _____
6 _____	31 _____
7 _____	32 _____
8 _____	33 _____
9 _____	34 _____
10 _____	35 _____
11 _____	36 _____
12 _____	37 _____
13 _____	38 _____
14 _____	39 _____
15 _____	40 _____
16 _____	41 _____
17 _____	42 _____
18 _____	43 _____
19 _____	44 _____
20 _____	45 _____
21 _____	46 _____
22 _____	47 _____
23 _____	48 _____
24 _____	49 _____
25 _____	50 _____

B.3

From Pak (1986) *Find Out How You Teach*, Adelaide: National Curriculum Resource Centre.

CLASSROOM INTERACTION

Teacher-student interaction

1. (a) Was your attitude

   receptive ☐

   interested in students ☐

   accepting (ideas and feelings of students) ☐

   sensitive ☐

   friendly ☐

   patient ☐

   supportive ☐

   other? ☐

   (b) Is there any part of your attitude that you would like to change? Why?

   ....

   ....

2. (a) Did you have a friendly, approachable rapport with the students? What student reactions indicated this?

   ....

   ....

   (b) Do you see any other ways you could have enhanced this warm, trusting atmosphere (e.g. providing praise and encouragement)?

   ....

   ....

3. (a) Did you provide a natural speech model (e.g. no *excessive* slowness or clarity, normal rhythm and intonation)?

   ....

   ....

(b) Is there anything you think you would like to change about the type of model you provide?

....

....

4. (a) Did you control your language to suit the level of your students?

during verbal communication   ☐

and/or

during written communication?   ☐

How did you do this?

....

....

(b) Were you able to simplify your language without unnaturalness or raised volume?
Could you give an example?

....

....

....

....

(c) Did you use your voice to the fullest, e.g. forcefulness to express stress/emotion?

....

....

5. (a) Were you aware of the physical aspects of yourself? For example

sitting or standing   ☐

pacing and other mannerisms   ☐

who you were addressing   ☐

position when speaking to class ☐

position in relation to the board ☐

closeness to students ☐

gestures ☐

facial expressions ☐

eye contact? ☐

(b) Are there any aspects that you would like to change (e.g. always address-ing the same person/talking with back to students)?

....

....

6. (a) How was the furniture arranged?

In rows ☐

"U" shaped ☐

In groups ☐

Teacher at front behind table ☐

Other ☐

(b) Who decided on this arrangement and why?

....

....

(c) Do you think any other arrangement would be more suitable for this class?
Why/why not?

....

....

(d) Could re-arranging furniture for different sections of the lesson be useful?

....

....

7. (a) Did you have to deal with any unanticipated problems or interruptions?
    What were they?
    How did you deal with them?

....

....

....

(b) Are there any other ways you could have dealt with them without interfering with the flow of the lesson?

....

....

8. (a) What was the proportion of teacher talking time to student talking time?

....

....

(b) Would you want to change this ratio in the future?

....

....

Student-student interaction

1. (a) How were the students actively involved in the lesson? Through

   role play (all participating) ☐

   prediction exercises ☐

   gathering/reporting information ☐

   discussion ☐

   other ☐

   (b) Can you suggest other ways to provide opportunities for the students to use and extend their language?

   ....

   ....

2. (a) What was the purpose of the students' communication with each other (e.g. to share their experiences of the weekend)?

   ....

   ....

   (b) Can you see that a reason is essential for meaningful communication?

   ....

   ....

3. (a) Did you allow students to

   use their own language first by eliciting responses from them before providing them with the language ☐

   and

   share opinions on correct usage? ☐

(b) Do you see how this can increase student involvement?

....

....

4. (a) What techniques did you use to check out degree of interest in discussion topics?

....

....

(b) Could you utilise such ideas as a sociogram for this purpose, e.g. mark an imaginary line in the classroom?

0% _____ 100%

    25%   50%   75%

....

- You then call out topics quickly and students go spontaneously to a point on the line reflecting their level of interest or feelings (as directed) on that subject, e.g. football/abortion/the Labor Party.

(c) Can you suggest other ways to check on interest level?

....

....

....

5. (a) How did you help to develop rapport between the students?

"Getting to know you" starters   ☐

Your model/example   ☐

Encouraging sharing of experiences   ☐

Pleasant surroundings (pictures,
flowers, radio, etc.)   ☐

Other   ☐

(b) Can you suggest other ways to establish a sensitive and supportive feeling amongst the students?

....

....

6. (a) Were the students aware of each other's difficulties errors? How do you know?

....

....

(b) Could you increase this awareness by encouraging supportive student student correction? How?

....

....

7. (a) How was the furniture arranged?

In rows ☐

"U" shaped arrangement ☐

In groups ☐

Other ☐

(b) Who decided on this arrangement and why?

....

....

(c) Do you think any other arrangement could increase student-student interaction?

....

....

(d) Could re-arranging furniture for different sections of the lesson be useful?

....

....

8. (a) How did the students work?

Individually ☐

In pairs ☐

In groups ☐

In the whole class ☐

Out of the classroom
(e.g. community tasks, self-directed
learning centre or library in pairs) ☐

(b) Which organisation produced greatest student-student interaction?

....

....

(c) Could any other organisation provide the opportunity for increased interaction?

....

....

9. (a) Did everyone in the class talk/participate
with each other or only with the teacher?
How do you know?

....

....

(b) Could you suggest ways to analyse student participation? For example, using a tape recording you might like to focus on specifics such as

- length of statements given out by students
- frequency of statements
- who made the statements
- complexity of language used
- responses made and to what.

Any other ideas?

....

....

B.4 Target language observation scheme.

From Ullman and Geva (1984) 'Approaches to observation in second-language classrooms', in C. Brumfit (ed.) *Language Issues and Education Policies*, Oxford: Pergamon.

TEACHER

	extremely low	low	fair	high	extremely high
Use of L 1	0	1	2	3	4
Use of L 2	0	1	2	3	4
teacher talk time	0	1	2	3	4
explicit lesson structure	0	1	2	3	4
task orientation	0	1	2	3	4
clarity	0	1	2	3	4
initiate problem solving	0	1	2	3	4
personalized questions and comments	0	1	2	3	4
positive reinforcement	0	1	2	3	4
negative reinforcement	0	1	2	3	4
corrections	0	1	2	3	4
pacing	0	1	2	3	4
use of audio-visual aids	0	1	2	3	4
gestures	0	1	2	3	4
humour	0	1	2	3	4
enthusiasm	0	1	2	3	4

STUDENTS

Use of L 1 on task	0	1	2	3	4
Use of L 2 on task	0	1	2	3	4
student talk time on task	0	1	2	3	4
initiate problem solving	0	1	2	3	4
comprehension	0	1	2	3	4
attention	0	1	2	3	4
participation	0	1	2	3	4
personalized questions and comments	0	1	2	3	4
positive affect	0	1	2	3	4
negative affect	0	1	2	3	4
S to S interaction on task	0	1	2	3	4

PROGRAM

linguistic appropriateness	0	1	2	3	4
content appropriateness	0	1	2	3	4
depth	0	1	2	3	4
variety	0	1	2	3	4
listening skill focus	0	1	2	3	4
speaking skill focus	0	1	2	3	4
reading skill focus	0	1	2	3	4
writing skill focus	0	1	2	3	4
formal properties	0	1	2	3	4
functional properties	0	1	2	3	4
integration with general curriculum	0	1	2	3	4

Observation Unit	WHO – TEACHER																													
	To whom				What – Type of activity Formal–Functional Focus							Content Focus							Skill Focus				Teaching Medium							
												Linguistic				Substantive															
	Large	Small	Individual	Other	drill	dialogue	frame	spelling	translation	paraphrasing	free communication	sound	word	phrase	discourse	grammar	culture	integrated subject matter	listen	speak	read	write	text	A.V.	authentic materials	draw	poem	song	game	role playing
1																														
b																														
c																														
2																														
b																														
c																														
3																														
b																														
c																														
4																														
b																														
c																														
5																														
b																														
c																														
6																														
b																														
c																														
7																														
b																														
c																														
8																														
b																														
c																														
9																														
b																														
c																														
10																														
b																														
c																														

WHO – TEACHER (cont'd)													L Use		WHO – STUDENT																	L Use	
Teaching Act															To whom					What – Type of utterance								Type of question					
drill	narrate	explain	discuss	compare	answer	meta-comments & questions	cognitive questions	low level questions	correct	reinforce	routine	discipline	L 1	L 2	large	small	peer	teacher	other	sound	word	sentence fragment	sentence	extended discourse	non verbal	no response	meta-comments & questions	cognitive Q	low Q	routine Q	L 1	L 2

B.5

From Allen *et al.* (1984) 'The communicative orientation of language teaching (COLT)', in J. Handscombe, R. Orem and B. Taylor (eds) *On TESOL '83*, Washington, DC: TESOL.

SCHOOL
TEACHER
SUBJECT

GRADE(S)
LESSON (Minutes)

DATE
OBSERVER

Col. 1 2 3 4 5 6 7 8 9 10 11 12 13 14 15 16 17 18 19 20 21 22 23 24 25 26 27 28 29 30 31 32 33 34 35 36 37 38 39 40 41 42 43 44 45 46 47 48

TIME

ACTIVITIES

PARTIC. ORGANIZATION
- Class: 1 x c, S x c, Choral
- Group: Same, Different
- Comb: Individual, Gr. Ind.
- MAN: Procedure, Discipline

CONTENT
- LANGUAGE: Form, Function, Discourse, Socioling.
- OTHER TOPICS
  - NARROW: Classroom, Stereotyp., Pers./Bio., Other
  - LIMITED: Personal, Rout./Soc., Fam./Com., School T, Other
  - BROAD: Abstract, Pers./Ref., Imagination, World T, Other
- TOPIC CONTROL: Teacher, Teacher Stud, Student

STUDENT
- MODALITY: Listening, Speaking, Reading, Writing, Other
- MATERIALS
  - Text: Minimal, Extended
  - Type: Audio, Visual, Pedagogic, Semi-Pedag., Non-Pedag.
  - Use: High Control, Semi Control, Mini Control

STUDENT VERBAL INTERACTION

INCORPORATION of S.T. UTTERANCES	Elaboration		
	Expansion		
	Comment		
	Paraphrase		
	Repetition		
	No Incorp.		
REACTION CO MES.	Explicit Code Reaction		
FORM RESTR.	Unrestricted		
	Limited		
	Restricted		
SUST. SPEECH	Sustained		
	Minimal		
	Ultraminimal		
INFORMATION GAP	Request Info	Genuine	
		Pseudo	
	Giving Info	Unpred.	
		Pred.	
	Disc.-Initiation		
TARGET LANG.	L₂		
	L₁		
	Choral		

TEACHER VERBAL INTERACTION

INCORPORATION of S. UTTERANCES	Elaboration		
	Expansion		
	Comment		
	Paraphrase		
	Repetition		
	No Incorp.		
REACTION CO MES.	Explicit Code Reaction		
SUST. SPEECH	Sustained		
	Minimal		
INFORMATION GAP	Request Info	Genuine	
		Pseudo	
	Giving Info	Unpred.	
		Predict.	
TARGET LANG.	L₂		
	L₁		
COMMUNIC. FEATURES	Off-task		
	No talk		

Appendix C

An Introduction to Statistics

Introduction

In this appendix we look at the use of statistics in classroom research. It is unlikely that extensive use will be made of statistics by teachers as they carry out research into teaching and learning in their classrooms. In fact, as I have already suggested, I believe that interpretive approaches are more likely to provide teachers with answers to the sorts of questions they are likely to ask in relation to their own teaching and their students' learning.

This is not to say that teachers will never use statistics in their research. However, my primary reason for including this appendix has been to demystify statistics, and to provide teachers who have not been trained in the subject with insights into some of its basic concepts and principles. Hopefully, this will enable them to read and interpret empirical studies which utilise statistics of various sorts. Introductory courses and texts on research methods which do not deal with statistics for ideological reasons do no service to students and readers who are thereby denied access to the knowledge which will help them to understand, interpret and even criticise studies employing statistics. Many language teachers who have come from a humanities background are intimidated by statistics and statistical thinking and are likely to avoid psychometrically motivated articles and research reports. Hopefully, this appendix and the further readings will act as a window into what is, in fact, a fascinating world.

Descriptive statistics

Most introductory books on statistics draw a basic distinction between descriptive and inferential statistics. Descriptive statistics is concerned with identifying and describing the important general characteristics of a set of data. Inferential statistics, which, as we shall see, draws heavily on descriptive statistics, is concerned with comparing two or more sets of data and testing hypotheses in relation to these sets of data. In this section, we shall look at the descriptive function of statistics. The rest of the chapter is concerned with inferential statistics.

Basically, statistics is concerned with the manipulation and analysis of sets of numbers, or data. Data can be derived in many different ways, and can represent virtually anything which can be counted or measured. Here are some of the things which have been counted in the illustrative studies we have looked at in this book.

1. The type and frequency of teachers' questions.
2. Instances of conversational modification in discourse.
3. The frequency of use of different grammatical morphemes.
4. The frequency with which different students are addressed by a teacher.

5. The number of conversational turns taken by different students.
6. The effectiveness of different methods of instruction as measured by student achievement on standardised language tests.
7. The rating given by learners to different learning preferences and modalities.
8. The length and complexity of utterances stimulated by different task types.

Let us look at some of the descriptive statistics which can be calculated for a set of data. The following figures represent the scores received by a group of 71 second-language learners on a listening test.

10, 13, 1, 8, 8, 16, 6, 7, 10, 9, 5, 14, 17, 4, 11, 3, 16, 3, 19, 19, 18, 2, 8, 7, 9, 12, 12, 2, 17, 16, 15, 6, 10, 9, 7, 5, 14, 20, 10, 4, 12, 10, 15, 13, 11, 3, 14, 17, 18, 4, 8, 5, 9, 9, 15, 6, 12, 20, 6, 10, 11, 15, 7, 10, 8, 14, 13, 12, 9, 11, 10

How can we make sense of such data? In their present form they are not particularly illuminating. We might begin our analysis by rearranging or regrouping our data so they make more sense. One obvious way of doing this would be to rank them from highest to lowest. This would provide us with the following set of figures:

1, 2, 2, 3, 3, 3, 4, 4, 4, 5, 5, 5, 6, 6, 6, 6, 7, 7, 7, 7, 8, 8, 8, 8, 8, 9, 9, 9, 9, 9, 9, 10, 10, 10, 10, 10, 10, 10, 10, 11, 11, 11, 11, 12, 12, 12, 12, 12, 13, 13, 13, 14, 14, 14, 14, 15, 15, 15, 15, 16, 16, 16, 17, 17, 17, 18, 18, 19, 19, 20, 20

From these figures, we can construct a *frequency table* (see Table C.1). Such a table shows the number of students receiving a particular score.

TABLE C1 *Frequency table of scores on listening test*

Score	Students	
	Tally	Score
1	1	1
2	11	2
3	111	3
4	111	3
5	111	3
6	1111	4
7	1111	4
8	⊦⊦⊦⊦	5
9	⊦⊦⊦⊦ 1	6
10	⊦⊦⊦⊦ 111	8
11	1111	4
12	⊦⊦⊦⊦	5
13	111	3
14	1111	4
15	1111	4
16	111	3
17	111	3
18	11	2
19	11	2
20	11	2

Two basic and yet highly important concepts in descriptive statistics are those of *central tendency* and *variability*. Measures of central tendency tell us about the extent to which a set of data group, or cluster. Variability tells us about how they are dispersed.

Three measures of central tendency are the *mean*, the *median* and the *mode*. The mean, or average, is obtained by adding our data together and then dividing this figure by the number of observations we have. Thus the mean for the above group is: $739/71 = 10.407$.

The median is that value which has the same number of observations above and below it when the observations are ranked from highest to lowest. When we have an equal number of observations, as in our example, we take the average of the two middle scores: $(10 + 10)/2 = 10$.

The mode is the value which occurs most frequently. In the case of our data, it also happens to be 10.

In contrast with measures of central tendency, which are concerned with 'typical' values, variability, as the name suggests, is concerned with the extent to which values in a set of data depart from the average or 'typical' value or values with which the data are associated. The three measures which I shall describe here are the *range*, the *mean* (or average) *deviation*, the *variance* and the *standard deviation*.

The range is simply the difference between the highest and lowest values. For our data this would give us $20 - 1 = 19$. The range is a crude measure and can be misleading. Imagine, for example, if we had administered our test to a second group of students and recorded the following scores: 1, 1, 2, 2, 2, 2, 3, 3, 3, 3, 3, 3, 3, 4, 4, 20. Here, the range is the same as for our original group. However the pattern of the scores is very different. The mean, for example, is only 5.9. It is the mean that is misleading.

A more accurate indication of the dispersion of scores is the mean deviation. This is calculated by subtracting the mean from each of the observations, making any resulting negative values positive (otherwise our figures would add up to zero) adding all the deviations together, and dividing by the number of observations. This calculation is illustrated in Table C.2 using the following data:

2, 8, 5, 3, 4, 1, 2, 3, 5, 7   sum = 40 $n = 10$ mean = 4.0

Much more sophisticated and widely used measures of variability are the *variance* and *standard deviation*. These statistics are more complicated to calculate, although the availability of statistical packages for personal computers has made their calculation relatively straightforward.

TABLE C2 *Calculating mean deviation: a worked example*

Score	Score – Mean
2	–2
8	4
5	1
3	–1
4	0
1	3
2	2
3	–1
5	1
7	3
40	18/10 = 1.8

Mean deviation = 1.8

To obtain the variance, we first calculate the deviation of each score from the mean. Then, instead of getting rid of the minus values by simply changing them to positive as we did in calculating the mean variance, we square each value. We add these together to obtain the sum of squares, and then divide by the number of observations minus 1 (subtracting 1 from the number of observations is a correction for the fact that the variability of scores for a single group of subjects tend to be somewhat less than the true degree of variability for all possible scores). The resulting figure is the variance. A worked example, using the data from Table C.2, is set out in Table C.3:

TABLE C3   *Calculating variance: a worked example*

Score	Score – Mean	Sum of squares
2	–2	4
8	4	16
5	1	1
3	–1	1
4	0	0
1	3	9
2	2	4
3	–1	1
5	1	1
7	3	9
40	18	$46/(10 - 1) = 5.111$

The standard deviation is the square root of the variance. Thus, in our example above, it would be 2.26.

The logic of statistical inference

The concepts introduced in the preceding section are important for inferential statistics and, in this section, we shall see how they are used. In particular, we shall see how important is the concept of variance.

Whenever we collect data which can be represented numerically, we are confronted with the question: how representative or 'typical' are these figures? Think back on the scores we obtained by administering our listening test. If we re-ran this test, or ran an identical version of the test with our original 71 subjects, how likely is it that we would get the same results? No doubt there would be variations due to factors extraneous to our test such as the state of health of the subjects, the test-taking conditions, and so on. How confident can we be that these variations are not also due to inconsistencies in our test or data-collection procedures? Can we be sure that they are not indicators of test unreliability?

Similar questions can be asked of the studies we have reviewed in earlier chapters. Consider, for example, the Doughty and Pica (1986) investigation of the amount of negotiation prompted by different task types. How confident can the researchers be that the different scores did not come about by chance? Is it the function of inferential statistics to provide tools and techniques for answering questions such as these.

Before proceeding, it is necessary to describe two other important concepts. These are 'population' and 'sample'. Often, when carrying out a study, it is not feasible to study or test every single person in a particular group. In such cases, it is necessary for us to select a sample from the total population. If, for example, we wished to test how well East Europeans did on our listening test, in contrast with Southeast Asians, it would clearly be impossible for us to test every single East European and every single Southeast Asian, and we would have to select *samples* from these two *populations*. The size of the sample will depend on the size of the study and the extent of our resources. Having tested a sample, we can obtain descriptive statistics such as the mean score, the variance and the standard deviation. We can then select another sample of subjects from the population and test them. Should we do so, we would obtain a different mean, variance and standard deviation. If we kept drawing on and testing samples from our population we would get many different mean scores. If we did this for a great many samples, we could plot their frequencies on a graph, which would look something like Figure C.1. The mean of the mean scores in this example will be the same as the mean we would have obtained had it been feasible to test our entire population. By calculating the standard deviation of these mean scores, we can obtain what is known as the standard error of the mean. We can use this measure to state how confident we are that the mean of a single sample is representative of the mean for the population as a whole.

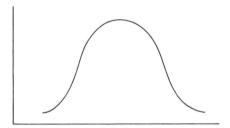

FIGURE C1 *Frequencies of mean scores for different population samples.*

In carrying out a formal experiment, the first step is to formulate an hypothesis (this is usually formulated as a negative or 'null' hypothesis). Imagine that the set of listening data we looked at earlier had been obtained from a group of second-language learners who had undertaken a course in comprehending authentic listening texts. We might have collected the data as part of a study into the efficacy of using authentic materials. In this case our research question may have been:

Do learners who are exposed to authentic materials actually develop superior listening skills to those who have traditional materials?

Our formal 'null' hypothesis would be:

There is no difference in the mean scores of subjects receiving specific instruction in comprehending authentic texts and subjects receiving traditional instruction on a test of listening comprehension.

Imagine that, having carried out our test, we obtained the following scores from a group of 'traditional' students:

11, 2, 7, 7, 14, 10, 5, 5, 16, 1, 8, 13, 4, 4, 10, 6, 5, 19, 6, 15, 3, 8, 8, 8, 6, 4, 12, 2, 7, 9, 11, 8, 13, 7, 5, 3, 17, 9, 4, 6, 6, 14, 4, 8, 7, 8, 10, 11, 5, 11, 10, 9, 8, 15, 9, 9, 6, 13, 16, 10, 7, 12, 8, 5, 6, 12, 9, 11, 8, 7, 10

In testing our hypothesis, it is not sufficient to simply test our subjects, obtain the means and compare them. In the example we have used here, we see that the group A mean is 10.407, and the group B mean is 8.479. So our experimental group has, on average, outscored our traditional group by a couple of points. However, we are not entitled, simply on the basis of this piece of evidence, to reject our null hypothesis. It may well be that the variation we have observed has simply occurred by chance. We can see from the data that there is considerable overlap in the scores, with the better students in group B doing much better than the weaker students in group A. As we have already seen, variations in the mean scores of different samples drawn from a particular population are to be expected. Our question is, what is the probability that this variation is within the normal limits expected by us in drawing samples from the mean?

In order to answer this question, we need to subject our study to a statistical test. We also need to state a significance level. For most studies in applied linguistics, the significance level is generally set at the 0.05 level of confidence. This means that if our statistical test indicates that the difference between the mean scores is significant, we can be 95 per cent confident that the difference is the result of our experimental treatment. Note, however, that there is still a 5 per cent chance that the difference has occurred by chance. If we want to be more certain than this, we can set a more stringent level. Thus, if we want to be 99 per cent sure that differences between our groups are a result of the experimental treatment, then we would set our confidence level at 0.01.

How, then, might we go about testing our hypothesis in relation to the data for the listening test? One commonly used measure for testing the difference between two means is the *t*-test. This is a useful test to know about because it can be used with small sample sizes (testing groups which have fewer than thirty subjects). We shall now look at this test and how it works.

The *t*-test for testing the significance of differences between two means

In this section we shall look at the logic behind the *t*-test and apply it to the data from our listening test. We shall see whether the mean scores for our two groups differ significantly at the 0.05 level of confidence. Should our test reveal a significant difference, there is a 95 per cent chance that the difference is a result of our experimental treatment.

What the *t*-test allows us to do is to calculate the probability that the subjects in Groups A and B have been drawn from populations with the same mean, and whether the difference we have recorded can be thereby attributed to sampling variation as discussed in the preceding section. What we want to know is, could the difference between the means (i.e. 10.408 – 8.479 = 1.929) have occurred simply as a result of sampling procedures?

In the preceding section we looked at an important concept, the standard error of the mean, which allows us to determine the probability that the mean of a single sample is representative of the mean of the population as a whole. In the present instance, however, we are interested, not in the standard error of a single mean, but the standard error of the difference between two means. This is called the *t*-distribution. The formula for calculating the *t*-distribution is as follows:

Mean for group 1 – Mean for group 2
_____

Standard error of difference between two means

The score resulting from the application of this formula is then matched against a table of critical values of *t* for significance at the 0.05 per cent level of confidence.

It is extremely tedious to compute statistics by hand, even the *t*-test, which is one of the more straightforward tests. Hand calculation can also result in error (for worked examples, see any one of a number of introductory books on statistics; Robson (1973), for example, provides an extremely clear and simple introduction). It is far easier to use one of the statistical packages now available for personal computers.

Applying the above formula to our two sets of listening data, we obtain a *t*-statistic of 2.650. In a table of critical values we find that for the size of our sample groups, at the 5 per cent significance level, this figure is significant. On statistical grounds, we can therefore reject our null hypothesis. As a result of our analysis, we might be tempted to conclude that we can be 95 per cent confident that the difference between our two means is a result of our experimental treatment.

However, at this point a note of warning should be sounded. We have seen that there is a significant difference in the mean scores of our two listening groups above and have been led to conclude that the difference between the two means is a result of the experimental treatment. Is this a valid conclusion to reach?

The simple answer is no. This is because we did not determine the listening skills of our two groups at the beginning of the experiment. It may well have been that the listening skills of subjects in group A were significantly better than the listening skills of the subjects in group B from the very beginning, and that the experimental treatment made no discernible difference whatsoever. It is for this reason that a sound experimental design would demand tests of the experimental and control groups at the beginning as well as at the end of the experiment.

This last point underlines the importance of having a sound experimental design if one is intent upon carrying out psychometric research. The statistical manipulation of data, no matter how sophisticated is, irrelevant if the basic design of one's experiment is flawed.

Analysis of variance

As we have seen, a classical experimental design contains two groups, an experimental and a control group. The two groups are tested under a particular condition, and a test of statistical inference is used to determine whether we can reasonably conclude that the two groups have been drawn from the same population.

Like the *t*-test, analysis of variance (or ANOVA as it is generally known) is used to test the significance of differences between means and, like the *t*-test, it has been widely used in applied linguistics. ANOVA is used when we wish to divide the variation observed in two or more sets of data into different parts, assign the parts to different causes, and then test to see whether the variation is greater than predicted.

A major advantage of ANOVA is that, unlike the *t*-test, it enables us to go beyond the traditional two group experimental design, such as the one we saw in the preceding section. It enables us to test more than two sets of subjects, and it enables us to look at two or more variables in relation to sets of subjects. For example, we may wish to test the effect of two different methods of learning vocabulary on two different experimental groups of learners. Group A consists of field-dependent learners, while group B consists of field-independent learners. Imagine that the two groups are taught two sets of vocabulary each according to two different methods. They are then tested and their mean scores for the vocabulary items taught according to the two different instructional methods are calculated. The means are set out in Figure C.2.

This shows the mean scores for the two groups under the two different conditions. It also shows what is called an interaction. Field-dependent learners did poorly on method 1 but well on method 2, whereas for the field-independent learners it was the reverse. Using statistical procedures similar to those employed in calculating the *t*-test, ANOVA allows us to test whether the differences between the group means are significant or not. As we can see from the example, one of its virtues is that it allows us to compare more than two groups and more than two experimental treatments.

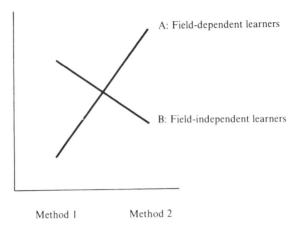

FIGURE C2 *Mean vocabulary scores for field-dependent and field-independent learners under two instructional conditions.*

Correlation

Correlation, as the term itself implies, refers to the relationship or association between sets of scores. We use correlation formulae when we want to find out whether one variable is associated or connected with another. Imagine that we have two sets of scores for a group of language learners. The first set of scores was obtained on a reading test, while the second set of scores was obtained on a listening test. Three situations might obtain in relation to the scores. In the first place, those learners who obtained high scores on the reading test might also obtain high scores on the listening test, while those with low scores on the reading test have correspondingly low scores on the listening test. In this instance, we would say the scores are positively related. If, on the other hand, a high score on one test was associated with a low score on the other test and vice versa, we would say that there was a negative correlation between the scores. Finally, we might have a situation in which there is no discernible relationship between the scores. In this instance there would be zero correlation.

If we plot sets of scores on a graph, with the vertical or y-axis representing one set of scores and the horizontal or x-axis representing the other scores, and then place a dot on the graph at the point where the scores on both tests for each subject coincide, we will obtain a visual representation of the relationship between the scores. In Figure C.3 we can see examples of positive, negative and zero correlation. In the case of graph (a) showing a positive correlation, we see that the dots slope upwards from left to right. If the dots were so aligned that they were to form a straight line, we would have an instance of perfect correlation. A correlation coefficient is the figure we obtain by applying a formula to two sets of data to test whether or not they are associated. If the variables are highly positively correlated, the figure we obtain will approach 1.0. If there is no relationship whatsoever, the figure will approach zero, and if there is a strong negative correlation, the figure will approach –1.

One commonly employed correlation test in applied linguistics research is the Pearson product-moment correlation. This has been described as follows:

> it is an index of the tendency for the scores of a group of examinees to covary (that is, to differ from their respective means in similar direction and magnitude) with the scores of the same group of examinees on another test. If, for example, the examinees who tend to make high

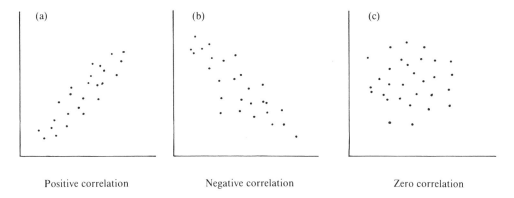

FIGURE C3 *Graphs demonstrating positive, negative and zero correlation.*

scores on a certain cloze test also tend to make high scores on a reading comprehension test, and if those who tend to make low scores on the reading test also tend to make low scores on the cloze, the two tests are positively correlated.

The square of the correlation between any two tests is an index of the variance overlap between them. Perfect correlation will result if the scores of examinees on two tests differ exactly in proportion to each other from their respective means.

One of the conceptually simplest ways to compute the product-moment correlation between two sets of test scores is as follows: first, compute the standard deviation for each test; second, for each examinee, compute the deviation from the mean on the first test and the deviation from the mean on the second test; third, multiply the deviation from the mean on test one times the deviation from the mean on test two for each examinee (whether the value of the deviation is positive or negative is important in this case because it is possible to get negative values on this operation); fourth, add up the products of deviations from step three (note that the resulting quantity is conceptually similar to the sum of squares of deviations in the computation of the variance of a single set of scores; finally, divide the quantity from step four by the standard deviation of test one times the standard deviation of test two times one less than the number of examinees. The resulting value is the correlation between the two tests (Oller 1979: 54–5).

The major mistake which is sometimes made by those employing correlation is to attribute a causal relationship between the two variables under investigation. However, significant positive or negative correlations do not necessarily mean that one variable 'causes' the relationship. The relationships may, in fact, be a result of a third or even a fourth variable (for example, one would be foolish to attribute a causal relationship between the observed decline in the birthrate in Germany after the Second World War and a corresponding decline in the stork population!).

Chi-square

Chi-square (χ) is another statistical test which is frequently used in applied linguistics research, when dealing with data in the form of frequencies rather than scores, that is, when we are analysing the number of times a particular event or events occur. Butler introduces the concept of chi-square in relation to linguistics in the following way:

In linguistics ... we are often interested in comparing the frequencies, in two or more samples or populations, of characteristics that cannot be measured in units, but are of a yes-or-no type: that is, they are nominal variables. For instance, assuming that we can decide on clear-cut criteria, we can classify finite verbs in English as present or past in form, words as being either nouns or not nouns, and so on. We cannot score a verb for its 'degree of presentness', in the way that we can score, for example, a student's performance in a language test, or even the degree of acceptability of a sentence in a given context. We can, however, count the frequency of present-tense verbs, or of nouns, or the word *and*, and in a text, and we may wish to compare this with the frequency in one or more texts (Butler 1985: 112).

In instances such as these we can use chi-square.

Data for calculating chi-square are generally set out in the form of contingency tables. These tables provide us with the frequencies of the phenomenon under investigation. Imagine that we are investigating a possible relationship between enjoyment of reading in a foreign language and language aptitude. We survey 150 learners who have been rated as either fast- or slow-track by their teachers and ask them whether they enjoy reading in their chosen foreign language. The results we obtain are set out in Table C.4.

TABLE C4   *2 × 2 contingency table for calculating chi square: actual frequencies*

		Slow-track	Fast-track	
Enjoy reading in FL	No	23	10	33
	Yes	46	65	111
		69	75	144

Using these figures, we need to determine whether fast-track readers are more likely to enjoy reading in a foreign language. We can see that the proportion of fast-track learners is greater than that of slow-track learners, but we need to conduct a statistical analysis to determine the likelihood that the difference in the relative proportions is significant. It is the purpose of the chi-square technique to provide us with this information.

If there is no association between the various cells in our 2 × 2 contingency table, we would expect the same proportions to obtain in each instance. As 33 subjects do not enjoy reading out of a total of 144, we would expect the same proportion of slow-track learners would not enjoy reading. Therefore, out of 69 slow-track learners, the expected frequency who would not enjoy reading is $69 \times 33/144 = 15.812$. Similarly, we would expect that since 111 out of 144 enjoy reading, then the proportion of slow-track readers who enjoy reading would be $69 \times 111/144 = 53.187$. Using a similar procedure for the fast-track learners we obtain the following expected frequencies:

Do not enjoy reading $75 \times 33/144$ $= 17.188$
Do enjoy reading $75 \times 111/144 = 57.81$

Table C.5 shows the expected frequencies for these data.

TABLE C5   *2 × 2 contingency table: expected frequencies*

		Slow-track	Fast-track
Enjoy reading in FL	No	15.187	17.188
	Yes	53.187	57.81

TABLE C6   *Calculating chi square: a worked example*

$$\frac{(|23-15.187|-0.5)^2}{15.187} + \frac{(|10-17.188|-0.5)^2}{17.188} + \frac{(|46-53.187|-0.5)^2}{53.187} + \frac{(|65-57.81|-0.5)^2}{57.81}$$

=	3.52	+	3.438	+	1.11	+	0.77
=	8.83						

Our table of expected frequencies shows us the proportions of learners we should expect in each category if there is no association between aptitude and enjoyment of reading in the foreign language. We use these data in computing the chi-squared statistic, which is obtained from the following formula:

$$\chi^2 = \Sigma \frac{(|\text{ observed frequency} - \text{expected frequency}| - \frac{1}{2})^2}{\text{Expected frequency}}$$

Using our example, the computation is illustrated in Table C.6.

Consulting a statistical table for chi-square, we find that at the 5 per cent level of confidence with 1 degree of freedom is 3.841. As we obtained a figure of 8.83, we can conclude that there is an association between language aptitude and enjoyment of reading in a foreign language.

Factor analysis

Factor analysis is a technique (or, more properly, a number of techniques) for studying the correlations between a number of variables simultaneously in an effort to identify a smaller number of constructs or factors. In other words, it looks at patterns of variance between variables, and determines whether or not the variables share a common variance.

Factor analysis was first developed and applied in the area of intelligence testing. Researchers have for many years been interested in finding out whether intelligence consists of a single psychological trait or ability, or several such traits, such as verbal reasoning, numerical reasoning, etc. If intelligence consists of more than one trait, we should expect to find high correlations on certain tests and not on others. For example, if we administered three tests of verbal reasoning and three tests of numerical reasoning to a group of subjects and found that the numerical tests correlated highly with each other and that the verbal tests correlated highly with each other but not with the numerical tests, then we could conclude that the concept or 'construct' of intelligence consisted of a 'verbal' factor and a 'numerical' factor. However, if one or more of the verbal tests correlated more highly with one or more of the numerical tests than with other verbal test(s), we could not conclude that these separate factors exist. If all tests correlated highly it would show that subjects who were good at verbal reasoning as measured by our tests were also good at numerical reasoning. This would add strength to the argument that a general factor of intelligence exists.

Similar reasoning has been used in relation to language. Here, the question is whether or not language proficiency consists of a single factor or several factors such as 'speaking ability', 'listening ability', 'reading ability' and 'writing ability'. Oller (1979) attempted to answer this question by administering a large number of different language tests to a group of subjects and analysing the scores for patterns of unique and common variance. The tests included reading and listening cloze tests, essay writing, oral tests of accent, grammar, vocabulary, fluency and comprehension, dictation and multiple choice tests. Oller found that a single factor explained or accounted for a substantial portion of the variance on the tests, and he concluded that a general language factor, which he called a 'pragmatic expectancy grammar', did, in fact exist. (Subsequent research has shown Oller's reasoning to be wrong, and has called his conclusions into question. It is now generally accepted that, while a general factor does exist, it is weaker than was originally postulated by Oller.)

Willing (1988) also used factor analysis in his analysis of learning-style preferences. You will recall from Chapter Three that Willing administered a learning-preferences survey containing 30 items to a large number of second-language learners and came up with four learner 'types'. These types were arrived at by examining which survey items correlated highly with which other items. As we saw in Chapter Three, the test items tended to cluster to form four groups. For example, Willing found that the following items were correlated; that is, a learner who gave a high response to one item would also tend to give a high response to the other items.

Item 3   In class, I like to learn by games.
Item 5   In class, I like to learn by pictures, films and video.
Item 14   I like to learn English by talking in pairs.
Item 26   At home, I like to learn by using cassettes.
Item 2   In class, I like to listen to and use cassettes.
Item 17   I like to go out with the class and practise English.

Having found patterns, the research then has to explain or account for these. Willing gave the label 'concrete learning style' to learners who gave high responses to the above items. These learners use very direct means of taking in and processing information. They are also people-oriented though in a spontaneous, unpremeditated way, preferring to communicate through 'games', 'excursions' or in close interaction (e.g. 'pairs'), rather than in organised, class 'conversation'.

The use of statistics in published research

Recent studies have shown that the use of quantitative methods in applied linguistics research is growing (see, for example, Henning, 1986; Teleni and Baldauf, 1988). In fact, it has been found that around 50 per cent of articles published in three leading journals (*Language Learning, Applied Linguistics* and *TESOL Quarterly*) incorporate statistics of one sort or another. If classroom practitioners are to read and interpret these articles, they need a basic understanding of statistics.

In their discussion of the trend towards the use of more statistics in applied linguistics research, Teleni and Baldauf suggest that readers need a complete understanding of how descriptive techniques are used to prepare data for further analysis and also how they are presented. Researchers in presenting their findings, need to devote less time to describing 'the minutiae of computation' and more time explaining why the particular statistical procedures used were chosen and what the results mean in terms of hypotheses. Course designers, lecturers, researchers and readers in applied linguistics need to know how to compute the various statistical tests which are used and need access to texts which provide applications and rationales for the methods used and their means of presentation.

Bibliography and Further Reading

Acheson, K. and Gall, M., (1987) *Techniques in the Clinical Supervision of Teachers*, New York: Longman.

Allwright, D. (1975) 'Problems in the study of teacher's treatment of learner error', in M. Burt and H. Dulay (eds) *On TESOL '75: New Directions in Second Language Learning, Teaching and Bilingual Education*, Washington DC: TESOL.

Allwright, D. (1978) 'Turns, topics and tasks: Patterns of participation in language learning and teaching', in D. Larsen-Freeman (ed.) *Discourse Analysis in Second Language Research*, Rowley Mass.: Newbury House.

Allwright D. (1986) 'Making sense of instruction', workshop presentation, RELC Regional Seminar, Singapore, April 1986.

Allwright, D. (1988) *Observation in the Language Classroom*, London: Longman.

Ashton-Warner, S. (1965) *Teacher*, New York: Bantam.

Bailey, K. (1988) 'Classroom research and teacher evaluation: Defining criteria for judgments', paper presented in the Colloquium on Classroom Research and Evaluation, Twenty-second Annual TESOL Convention, Chicago, March 1988.

Bailey, K. (1990) 'Teaching diaries in teacher education programs', in J. Richards and D. Nunan (eds) *Second Language Teacher Education*, Cambridge: Cambridge University Press.

Bailey, K. and Ochsner, R. (1983) 'A methodological review of the diary studies: Windmill tilting or social science?' in K. Bailey, M. H. Long and S. Peck (eds) *Second Language Acquisition Studies*, Rowley, Mass.: Newbury House.

Beasley, B. and Riordan, L. (1981) 'The classroom teacher as researcher', *English in Australia*, **55**.

Boehm, A. E. and Weinberg, R. A. (1977) *The Classroom Observer: A Guide for Developing Observational Skills*, New York: Teachers College Press.

Bowers, R. (1980) 'Verbal behaviour in the language teaching classroom', unpublished doctoral dissertation, University of Reading.

Breen, M., Candlin, C., Dam, L. and Gabrielsen, G. (1989) 'The evolution of a teacher training programme', in K. Johnson (ed.) *The Second Language Curriculum*, Cambridge: Cambridge University Press.

Brock, C. (1986) 'The effect of referential questions on ESL classroom discourse', *TESOL Quarterly*, **20**, 1.

Brown, G. and Yule, G. (1983) *Discourse Analysis*, Cambridge: Cambridge University Press.

Butler, C. (1985) *Statistics in Linguistics*, Oxford: Blackwell.

Candlin, C. (1987) 'Towards task-based language learning', in C. Candlin and D. Murphy (eds) *Language Learning Tasks*, Englewood Cliffs, NJ: Prentice Hall Inc.

Carr, W. and Kemmis S. (1985) *Becoming Critical: Knowing Through Action Research*, Victoria: Deakin University Press.

Cathcart, R. and Olsen, J. (1976) 'Teachers' and students' preferences for correction of classroom errors', in J. Fanselow and R. Crymes (eds) *On TESOL '76*, Washington DC: TESOL.

Chaudon, C. (1983) 'Foreigner talk in the classroom: An aid to learning?' in H. Seliger and M. Long (eds) *Classroom Oriented Research in Second Language Acquisition*, Rowley Mass.: Newbury House.

Chaudron, C. 1987. 'The interaction of quantitative and qualitative approaches to research: a view of the second language classroom'. *TESOL Quarterly*, **20**, 4, 709–17.

Chaudron, C. (1988) *Second Language Classrooms: Research on Teaching and Learning*, Cambridge: Cambridge University Press.

Clark, C. and Yinger, R. (1979) 'Teachers' thinking', in P. Peterson and H. J. Waldberg (eds) *Research on Teaching*, Berkeley, Calif.: McCutchen.

Clark, J. (1987) *Curriculum Renewal in School Foreign Language Learning*, Oxford: Oxford University Press.

Cohen, L. and Manion, L. (1985) *Research Methods in Education*, London: Croom Helm.

Cronbach, L. (1975) 'Beyond the two disciplines of scientific psychology', *American Psychologist*, **30**, 2.

Day, R. (1990) 'Teacher observation in second language teacher education', in J. Richards and D. Nunan (eds) *Second Language Teacher Education*, Cambridge: Cambridge University Press.

Doughty, C. and Pica, T. (1986) 'Information gap tasks: Do they facilitate second language acquisition?' *TESOL Quarterly*, **20**.

Dulay, H., Burt, M. and Krashen S. (1982) *Language Two*, New York: Oxford University Press.

Elliot, J. (1982) 'Action research into action research', *Classroom Action Research Bulletin*, **5**, Cambridge: Cambridge Institute of Education.

Erickson, F. and Wilson, J. (1982) 'Sights and sounds of life in schools', Research Series No. 125, Ann Abor, Michigan: Institute for Research in Teaching, College of Education, University of Michigan.

Flanders, N. (1970) '*Analysing Teaching Behaviour*', Reading, Mass.: Addison-Wesley.

Frohlich, M., Spada, N. and Allen, P. (1985) 'Differences in the communicative orientation of L2 classrooms', *TESOL Quarterly*, **19**.

Grotjahn, R. (1987) 'On the methodological basis of introspective methods', in C. Faerch and G. Kasper (eds) *Introspection in Second Language Research*, Clevedon, Avon: Multilingual Matters.

Hatch, E. and Farhady, H. (1982) *Research Design and Statistics for Applied Linguistics*, Rowley, Mass.: Newbury House.

Heath, S. B. (1983) *Ways With Words*, Cambridge: Cambridge University Press.

Henning, G. (1986) 'Quantitative methods in language acquisition research', *TESOL Quarterly*, **20**, 4.

Henning, G. (1987) *A Guide to Language Testing*, Rowley, Mass.: Newbury House.

Holec, H. (1979) *Autonomy and Foreign Language Learning*, Oxford: Pergamon.

Hopkins, D. (1985) *A Teacher's Guide to Classroom Research*, Milton Keynes: Open University Press.

Ireland, D. and Russell, T. (1978) 'Pattern analysis as used in the Ottowa Valley Teaching Project', *CARN Newsletter*, **21**, Cambridge: Cambridge Institute of Education.

Johnston, M. (1985) *Syntactic and Morphological Progressions in Learner English*, Canberra: Department of Immigration and Ethnic Affairs.

Kemmis, S. and McTaggart, R. (eds) (1988) *The Action Research Planner*, 3rd edn, Geelong: Deakin University Press.

Koziol, S. and Call, M. (1988) 'Constructing and using teacher self-report inventories', workshop presented at the 22nd Annual TESOL Convention, Chicago, March 1988.

Krashen, S. (1981) *Second Language Acquisition and Second Language Learning*, Hemel Hempstead: Prentice Hall International.

Krashen, S. (1982) *Principles and Practice in Second Language Acquisition*, Hemel Hempstead: Prentice Hall International.

Lange, D. (1990) 'A blueprint for the design of a teacher development program in second language education', in J. Richards and D. Nunan (eds) *Second Language Teacher Education*, Cambridge: Cambridge University Press.

Long, M. (1983a) 'Training the second language teacher as a classroom researcher', paper presented at the 34th Annual Round Table on Languages and Linguistics, Washington DC: Georgetown University.

Long, M. (1983b) 'Does second language instruction make a difference? A review of research', *TESOL Quarterly*, **17**.

Long, M. (1983c) 'Inside the "black box": Methodological issues in second language research', in H. Seliger and M. Long (eds) *Classroom Oriented Research in Second Language Acquisition*, Rowley, Mass.: Newbury House.

Long, M. and Sato, C. (1983) 'Classroom foreigner talk discourse: Forms and functions of teachers' questions', in H. Seliger and M. Long (eds) *Classroom Oriented Research in Second Language Acquisition*, Rowley Mass.: Newbury House.

Malamah-Thomas, A. (1987) *Classroom Interaction*, Oxford: Oxford University Press.

Moskowitz, G. (1968) 'The effects of training foreign language teachers in interaction analysis', *Foreign Language Annals*, **1**, 3.

Nisbet, J. and Entwhistle, N. (1970) *Educational Research Methods*, London: University of London Press.

Nunan, D. (1985) *Language Teaching Course Design: Trends and Issues*, Adelaide: National Curriculum Resource Centre.

Nunan, D. (1987) *The Teacher as Curriculum Developer*, Adelaide: National Curriculum Resource Centre.

Nunan, D. (1988) *The Learner-Centred Curriculum: A Study in Second Language Teaching*, Cambridge: Cambridge University Press.

Nunan, D. (1989a) *Designing Tasks for the Communicative Classroom*, Cambridge: Cambridge University Press.

Nunan, D. (1989b) 'Second language teacher education: Present trends and future prospects' in C. Candlin and T. Macnamara (eds) (1989) *Language, Learning and Community*, Sydney: National Centre for English Language Teaching and Research.

Oller, J. (1979) *Language Tests at School*, London: Longman.

Pica, T. and Long, M. (1986) 'The linguistic and conversational performance of experienced and inexperienced teachers', in R. Day (ed.) *Talking to Learn*, Mass.: Newbury House.

Politzer, R. L. (1970) 'Some reflections on "good" and "bad" language teaching behaviours', *Language Learning*, **20**, 1, 31–43.

Ramani, E. (1987) 'Theorizing from the classroom', *ELT Journal*, **41**, 1.

Richards, J. (1987) 'Beyond methods: Alternative approaches to instructional design in language teaching', *Prospect*, **3**, 1.

Richards, J. (forthcoming) *Effective Language Teaching: Curriculum, Methodology, Materials*, New York: Cambridge University Press.

Richterich, R. (ed.) (1983) *Case Studies in Identifying Language Needs*, Oxford: Pergamon.

Robson, C. (1973) *Experiment, Design and Statistics in Psychology*, Harmondsworth: Penguin.

Rubin, J. and Thompson, I. (1982) *How To Be a More Successful Language Learner*, New York: Heinle and Heinle.

Rutherford, W. (1987) *Second Language Grammar: Learning and Teaching*, London: Longman.

Schecter, S. (1988) 'Young writer's week: A collaborative study of a socially mediated literacy event', paper presented at the Collaborative Research Colloquium, TESOL Convention, Chicago, March 1988.

Scherer, G. and Wertheimer, M. (1964) *A Psycholinguistic Experiment in Foreign Language*

Teaching, New York: McGraw-Hill.

Schmidt, R. and Frota, S. (1985) 'Developing basic conversational ability in a second language: A case study of an adult learner of Portuguese', in R. Day (ed.) *Talking to Learn: Conversation in Second Language Acquisition*, Rowley, Mass.: Newbury House.

Shavelson, R. and Stern, P. (1981) 'Research on teachers' pedagogical thoughts, judgments, decisions and behaviour', *Review of Educational Research*, **51**, 4, 455–98.

Shaw, J. and Dowsett, G. (1986) 'The evaluation process in the adult migrant education program', Adelaide: National Curriculum Resource Center.

Sinclair, J. and Coulthard, M. (1975) *Towards an Analysis of Discourse*, London: Oxford University Press.

Spada, N. (1989) 'Observing classroom behaviours and learning outcomes in different second language programs', in J. Richards and D. Nunan (eds) (1990) *Second Language Teacher Education*, Cambridge: Cambridge University Press.

Stake, R. and Gjerde, C. (1974) 'An evaluation of TCITY, the Twin City Institute for Talented Youth 1971', in R. Kraft *et al.* (eds) *Four Evaluation Examples: Anthropological, Economic, Narrative and Portrayal*, AERA Monograph Series on Curriculum Evaluation, Chicago: Rand McNally.

Stenhouse, L. (1975) *An Introduction to Curriculum Research and Development*, London: Heinemann.

Swaffar, J., Arens, K. and Morgan, M. (1982) 'Teacher classroom practices: Redefining method as task hierarchy', *Modern Language Journal*, **66**, 24–33.

Teleni, V. and Baldauf, R. (1988) 'Statistical techniques used in three applied linguistics journals: *Language Learning, Applied Linguistics* and *TESOL Quarterly* 1980–1986: Implications for readers and researchers', unpublished manuscript.

Templin, P. (1979) *Photography as an Evaluation Technique*, Monograph No. 32, Research on Evaluation Program, Portland, Oregon, North Western Regional Educational Laboratory.

van Lier, L. (1988) *The Classroom and the Language Learner*, London: Longman.

Walker, R. (1985) *Doing Research: A Handbook for Teachers*, London: Methuen.

Willing, K. (1988) *Learning Styles in Adult Migrant Education*, Adelaide: National Curriculum Resource Center.

Woods, A., Fletcher, P. and Hughes, A. (1986) *Statistics in Language Studies*, Cambridge: Cambridge University Press.

Index